MARKETING A NEW PRODUCT:
Its Planning, Development, and Control

Robert D. Hisrich, Boston College
Michael P. Peters, Boston College

The Benjamin/Cummings Publishing Company, Inc.

Menlo Park, California ● Reading, Massachusetts
London ● Amsterdam ● Don Mills, Ontario ● Sydney

To our loving wives, Debbie and Tina, and daughters, Christa, Kary, Kelly, and Kimberly, whose patience, support, and understanding helped bring this effort to fruition.

The Benjamin/Cummings Publishing Company, Inc.
2727 Sand Hill Road
Menlo Park, California 94025

Preface

During the late 1970s, firms were faced with an unprecedented series of challenges. A combination of economic, environmental, social, political, and trade issues has surfaced that will continue well into the 1980s and beyond. These increased challenges have forced marketing executives to be even more concerned about being in the forefront of technological innovativeness. New product development took on increasing importance to maintain company and industry competitive parity.

Marketing a New Product: Its Planning, Development, and Control resulted from the need for a comprehensive textbook in the increasingly important area of marketing new products that will satisfy consumer wants and needs. This book focuses on the management of all the activities involved in this process. Its purpose is to present all the fundamentals of new product marketing.

The basic idea of the book is indicated in its title and subtitle and embraces three basic concepts, which are integrated throughout the text.

1. *Planning.* The main theme of this book centers around the question: How can new products be better planned and marketed more effectively? The existence of raw material shortages and the energy crisis make it increasingly important that more innovative products that will satisfy a particular market need be introduced. This calls for each firm to enhance its expertise in effectively planning new products and their introductory marketing program.

2. *Developing.* Given the continued proliferation of new industrial and consumer products in the late 1970s, it is necessary in order to survive that a firm establish a system whereby new products can be developed for successful commercialization. A product development process from idea to commercialization must be instituted so that new products can be launched to meet the ever changing needs of the market. To meet this need an organizational structure that operates efficiently, creatively, and effectively in the internal company environment must be established.

3. *Controlling.* Effective new product marketing requires that company management refrain from introducing new products that have inadequate market or financial analyses, defects, or poor introductory marketing plans. These and other problems can be monitored and controlled through implementation of a systematic new product development process.

The book is divided into five major parts. Part One, The Role of New Products: Its Basis and Organization, sets the stage for the discussion that follows. The product development process is introduced and reasons for the eventual success or failure of new products are discussed. Various organizational structures are presented that can provide the necessary mechanism for developing and launching new products.

Part Two, New Product Ideas: Obtainment and Evaluation, discusses the initial stages in the product development process—the idea stage, the concept stage, the development stage, and the test-marketing stage.

Part Three, The New Product: Acceptance and Demand Estimation, begins with a discussion of market segmentation, then considers the dimensions of the diffusion and adoption process. This part concludes with a discussion of forecasting techniques used in the product development process.

Part Four, The New Product's Marketing Program, introduces the marketing mix for the new product. An in-depth picture is presented of the basic elements of the new product's marketing plan—branding, packaging, pricing, distribution, and promotion.

And, finally, Part Five, The New Product: Its Control and Outside Impact, presents two critical aspects of successful new product introductions that are often overlooked—control and outside impact. The importance of control is specifically discussed by introducing methodologies for monitoring the new product. Then the social and environmental influences are related to the product development process.

Many people—business executives, professors, publishers, and students—have greatly contributed to this textbook. Most of their contributions are acknowledged in footnotes and other references throughout the book. We are especially indebted to our research assistants, Isabelle Capona, Sara Cornwall, Kristen Nielsen, and Marie Tseng, for all their work and to our secretary, Rosanne Picarello, for typing the manuscript.

Robert D. Hisrich
Michael P. Peters

Contents

PART ONE

**The Role of New Products: Its
Basis and Organization**   1

Chapter One/New Products: The Past and Future   3

    Market Myopia   5
    What Is a New Product?   6
    Classification of New Products   8
    Success and Failure of New Products   13
    The Environment: Its Effect on the
        Development Process   17
    The Product Development Process   21
    Summary   24
    Selected Readings   25

Chapter Two/Organizing for Marketing New Products   27

    Role of Top Management   27
    Large versus Small Company
        Organization   29
    Alternative Organizations for
        New Product Development   29
    Organizational Alternatives Need
        Executive Support   42
    Which Organizational Structure?   42
    Staffing Decisions   42
    From Planning to Commercialization   43
    The Research and Development/
        Marketing Interface   44
    Summary   45
    Selected Readings   45

PART TWO

New Product Ideas: Obtainment and Evaluation   47

Chapter Three/Introduction to the Product Planning and Development Process   49

The Product Planning and Development Process	49
Sources of New Product Ideas	53
Methods for Generating Product Ideas	57
Qualitative Screening Criteria	61
Types of Marketing Models	63
New Product Model Development	67
Specific New Product Models	69
Uses and Limitations of New Product Models	74
Summary	76
Selected Readings	76

Chapter Four/Evaluating New Product Ideas   78

General Evaluation Criteria	78
Early Stage-Testing of New Products	80
Research Design	90
Questionnaire Design for New Products	98
Summary	101
Selected Readings	101
Appendix to Chapter 4: Sampling Methodology for New Product Evaluation	103

Chapter Five/Test-Marketing the New Product   108

Nature of Test-Marketing	108
Determination of the Need to Market Test	111
The Test Market	116
Factors Affecting Test-Marketing	123
Problems in Test-Marketing	124
Test-Marketing Alternatives and Remedies	126
Summary	128
Selected Readings	129
Appendix to Chapter 5: Experimental Design in Test-Marketing	131

PART THREE

The New Product: Acceptance and Demand Estimation   **153**

Chapter Six/Market Segmentation for New Products   **155**

Undifferentiated Approach   155
Overview of Market Segmentation   156
Bases for New Product Segmentation   158
Summary   175
Selected Readings   175

Chapter Seven/Diffusion and Adoption of New Products   **177**

Historical Perspective of Diffusion Research   177
The Diffusion Process   178
The Adoption Process   183
Correlates of Innovativeness:
    Empirical Findings   188
Summary   193
Selected Readings   194

Chapter Eight/Forecasting New Product Sales   **195**

Factors Affecting New Product Forecasting   195
Series Indicators   196
Market Size Determination   198
Specific Forecasting Methods   204
Problems in New Product Forecasting   217
Summary   217
Selected Readings   218

PART FOUR

The New Product's Marketing Program   **219**

Chapter Nine/Planning the New Product Mix   **221**

Integrating Marketing Mix Decisions   221
Use of Financial Criteria   223
Program Evaluation Review
    Technique (PERT)   228
Establishing a New Product
    Information System   229
Summary   231
Selected Readings   231

Chapter Ten/Branding and Packaging the New Product   233

Importance of Brand Name   234
Importance to Manufacturer   234
Branding Policies and Strategies   235
Brand Name Research   238
The Packaging Decision   240
Packaging Design Considerations   241
Promotional Advantages of Packaging   244
Attributes of an Effective Package   244
Summary   244
Selected Readings   245

Chapter Eleven/Pricing the New Product   247

Company Price Objectives   247
Policy Formulation   251
Cost Considerations   253
Demand and Market Considerations   255
Consumer Considerations   261
Competitive Considerations   261
New Product Price and Other
        Marketing Decisions   264
Summary   266
Selected Readings   266

Chapter Twelve/Distributing the New Product   268

Channel Objectives   269
Channel Strategy Analysis   269
Channel Alternatives   274
Evaluation and Selection of Channel Members   275
Selection of Channel Members   277
Channel Management and Control   279
Appraising Channel Performance   280
Summary   281
Selected Readings   281

Chapter Thirteen/Promoting the New Product   283

The Promotional Budget   283
New Product Publicity   286
Using an Advertising Agency   287
Promotion and the Product Life Cycle   290
Positioning with Promotion   293
Summary   304
Selected Readings   305

PART FIVE

The New Product: Its Control and Outside Impact 307

Chapter Fourteen/Controlling the New Product 309

Nature of Control 309
The Control Process 311
Product Abandonment: A
    Control Application 315
Summary 326
Selected Readings 327

Chapter Fifteen/Social and Environmental Influences in New Product Development 328

Product Development and the
    Marketing Concept 330
Advantages of Environmental and
    Social Evaluation 332
Disadvantages of Environmental and
    Social Evaluation 333
Product Safety 333
New Products and Warranty Policy 337
Other Legal Requirements for New Products 341
Patents 341
Summary 346
Selected Readings 346

Name Index **348**
Subject Index **351**

Part One

**The Role of New Products:
Its Basis and Organization**

1

New Products:
The Past and Future

The 1970s has been a period of increasing domination of our society by large, highly diversified corporations operating in many markets. Marketing executives are faced with increased challenges and pressures within their industry to remain a step ahead of their competition through technological innovativeness. New product development has become a necessary element in the planning process to maintain the industry's competitive parity. For this reason the marketplace is annually inundated with new products that leave no segment of the economy untouched. However, some segments are more saturated than others, with new food products being at the top of the list. This industry is particularly significant because the shelf space for which these new food products compete is quite valuable. It has been estimated that some 6000 new food items are introduced each year and compete for this valuable space. As a result, supermarkets must drop items to make room for those new food items that they wish to sell. This high turnover indicates a short product life span for most food items.

Figure 1-1 shows that a product, like a consumer, has a life cycle that is quite important in developing new product-marketing strategy. The product life cycle is generally divided into four major stages: product introduction, market growth, market maturity, and sales decline. Time, which is represented on the horizontal axis, can vary from days to years, depending on the nature of the market. The product's marketing mix[1] also varies during these stages as a result of changes in (a) consumer tastes and attitudes,

---

[1] This concept will be referred to throughout the text in relation to the market mix elements, i.e., pricing, distribution, and promotion.

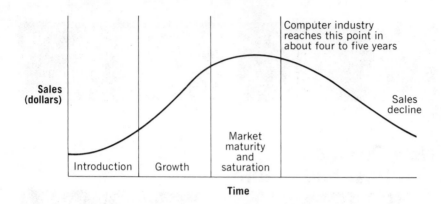

Figure 1-1. The Product Life Cycle

(b) cultural changes, (c) competition, (d) government, and (e) economic changes. The most desirable stage to the seller is the growth stage, where the greatest profits are earned. Sales of the total industry rise rapidly in this stage as more and more customers enter the market. Because of the nature of this stage in the product life cycle, manufacturers are concerned with attempting to extend the growth period by introducing a stream of new products or modifying them to bring them back through the life cycle.

Apparently, there will be little, if any, decrease in the future marketing of new products, even though we have been confronted with dramatic changes in consumer conditions. Before the recent energy crisis, the following observations appeared in the *Wall Street Journal.*[2] Eastman Kodak Company boasted that it was introducing better than one new or improved product every three working days in 1972. Hewlett-Packard Company, which introduced 70 new products in 1967, increased this number to between 85 and 100 for 1971 and 1972. Most of these occurred during an economic slowdown, which apparently did not affect new product introductions. Black and Decker doubled its number of new products in 1971 to 31, as opposed to 15 in 1970. A large toymaker introduced 107 new items in the first half of 1971 compared to slightly less than this number for all of 1970. These large companies indicated that new items were necessary to improve corporate sales in a highly competitive market.

The proliferation of new products has continued even after the shock of an energy crisis and severe inflation. Toy manufacturers

[2] *Wall Street Journal,* "No Letup: Companies Keep Turning Out New Products at a Rapid Rate" (April 13, 1972), p. 1.

are continuing their trend toward new products as a basis of maintaining market shares in highly competitive markets. One corporate executive of Chesebrough-Pond, a highly diversified company, recently stated that his firm had no intention of letting the recession slow its new product development.[3] New household products have also continued to enter the market at a rapid pace. New window cleaners, oven cleaners, floor wax removers, laundry care products, rug cleaners, insect sprays, drain cleaners, etc., have all been recently introduced with some new chemical, packaging innovation, or other modification. No slowdown appears imminent in most consumer-product markets because of the increased competition and intense pressures to develop that one outstanding new product.

Although a bit more cautious in most industries, the industrial market has also continued its heavy spending on research and development. The computer industry continues to initiate new innovations that have been responsible for reducing the average product life cycle of a computer in this market to about four or five years. Although firms such as RCA, General Electric, and Xerox have left the computer market, their business has been absorbed by others, thus increasing the competition and reinforcing the need for new product development.

MARKET MYOPIA

As a result of reaching market maturity and saturation (see Figure 1-1) many firms are forced to introduce new products. Product line modifications or extensions appear to be most likely at this stage, hopefully with no cannibalization of existing products. The danger is that many firms take a myopic view of their markets and tend to gravitate to the lowest risk line extension or modification in order to stimulate continued growth in company sales. Although relatively safe, low-risk decisions carry low potential return as well as a myopic view of the market. Decision-making of this type could also lead to a cannibalization of existing brands so that the net increase in total company sales is very small or is negative.

In 1960 Ted Levitt wrote that firms in such industries as railroads and movies failed to recognize that their business was transportation and entertainment, respectively.[4] If railroads had perceived themselves as being in the transportation business, they

---

[3] *Advertising Age*, "New Product Flow Won't Slacken: Chesebrough" (May 12, 1975), pp. 45-46.

[4] Theodore Levitt, "Marketing Myopia," *Harvard Business Review* 38 (July-August 1960), pp. 24-47.

would have foreseen opportunities to diversify as well as to provide new services to meet customers' transportation needs. The movie industry also attempted to fight off competition from television instead of providing new movies and services to meet the needs of this market. Many failures resulted from the myopic view taken by companies in these two industries.

Times and conditions change rapidly perhaps more so today than ever before. Firms must take the broadest possible view of their business and should certainly take the initiative in new product introductions to prevent their customers from moving away from them.

WHAT IS A NEW PRODUCT?

One of the dilemmas faced by marketing executives is to define a "new product." Part of the distinction appears to lie in what is new in the new product.[5] Frozen oyster stew, a new product introduced some time ago, was not a truly new product since oyster stew was not new nor was the concept of frozen foods. To the consumer, only the idea of a frozen soup was new. The first home permanent product introduced by Toni is a similar example. Of course, hair permanents had long been available at hair dressing shops throughout the world. However, as a product available for home use, the home permanent was a new concept.

In these examples the newness was in the consumer concept. Other types of products, not necessarily new in concept, have also been defined as new. Nescafe recently introduced a new and improved instant coffee in which the only change in the product was the size of its granules. Yet the initial promotional campaign made definite overtures to the word *new* in its copy.

Other old products have simply been marketed in new packages or containers but have been identified as new products by the manufacturer. In 1969 an innovatively packaged food product called Zonkers was introduced in supermarkets. This product was actually caramel corn sold in a very psychedelic package of bright colors, comic figures, and riddles. Obviously, caramel corn was not a new concept in 1969.

The discovery of the aerosol can was also an example of a change in the package or container, which added the element of newness to old, established products, such as whipped cream, deodorants, and hair sprays. Flip-top cans, plastic bottles, and

[5] For a more comprehensive discussion of this important issue, see Chester Wasson, "What Is New About a New Product?" *Journal of Marketing* (July 1960), pp. 52-56.

screw-on caps also contributed to this perceived image of newness in old products. Drain cleaners are now marketed in pressurized containers so as to emit bursts of air to clean drains and pipes. Other firms, such as detergent manufacturers, have merely changed the colors of their packages in the past and then added the word *new* to the package and to their promotional copy.

Pantyhose have undergone significant marketing strategy changes in the past few years. L'Eggs was the first product to take advantage of supermarkets, new packaging, lower prices, and new displays. Now others have followed L'Eggs with similar marketing strategy.

In the industrial market it is also evident that firms use the strategy of calling their products new when only slight changes or modifications have been made in the appearance of the product. For example, improvements in metallurgical techniques have modified the precision and strength of many raw materials that are used in industrial products, such as machinery. These improved characteristics have led firms to market their products containing the new and improved metals as new. Computer manufacturers have expanded into new target markets by modifying their hardware slightly and by adopting computer software techniques to meet the needs of new customers not previously serviced, such as firms engaged in specialized wholesaling operations.

In the process of expanding their sales volume, many companies add products to their product line that are already marketed by other companies. These types of product additions, however, are often advertised as new products. For example, a drug company that added a cold tablet to its product line and a long-time manufacturer of soap pads who entered the dishwasher detergent market both advertised these products as new. In both these cases the product was new to the manufacturer but not to the consumer in the marketplace. With the increased emphasis on diversification in our economy, this type of situation is quite common today. Firms are constantly looking for new markets to exploit to increase profits and make more effective use of their resources.

Other firms have chosen new marketing mix strategy to give old products a new image. Panty hose now sold in supermarkets in special display cases or in plastic egg-shaped containers have stimulated industry sales.

Even given the variations in newness in products, there are examples of what might be labeled truly new products. There are relatively few of these types of new products, even given the sophisticated technological improvements in our present society. Some examples of what we might consider truly new products are the electronic computer, the polio vaccine, television, the transistor, and contact lenses. All of these products were based on new technology and represented something far removed from anything else available in the marketplace.

CLASSIFICATION OF NEW PRODUCTS

New products may be classified from both the consumer's viewpoint or from the firm's viewpoint. Both points of view must be carefully analyzed since both the ability of a firm to establish and attain its product objectives and consumer perception of these objectives may very well determine the success or failure of any new product subtitle.

From a Consumer's Viewpoint

There is a broad interpretation of what may be labeled a new product from a consumer's viewpoint. Robertson[6] has attempted to identify schematically these new products based on given criteria for interpreting newness. New products are classified according to how much behavioral change or new learning is required by the consumer in order to use the product. This technique looks at newness in terms of its effect on the consumer rather than whether the product is new to a company, is packaged differently, has changed physical form, or is an improved version of an old or existing product.

The continuum proposed by Robertson and shown in Figure 1-2 contains three categories all based on the disrupting influence the use of the product has on established consumption patterns. Most new products tend to fall in the continuous end of the continuum. Examples are annual automobile changes, fashion style changes, package changes, size or color changes, etc. Products such as the electric carving knife, electric toothbrush, and electric comb tend toward the dynamically continuous portion of the continuum. The truly new products are rare and require a great deal of new learning by the consumer because these products generally perform either a previously unfulfilled function or an existing function in a new way.

The basis for identifying new products according to their effect on consumer consumption patterns is consistent with the marketing philosophy that satisfaction of consumer needs must be one of the prime justifications for the firm's existence. Thus, when defining what a new product is, one must refer to the effects such

[6]Thomas Robertson, "The Process of Innovation and the Diffusion of Innovation," *Journal of Marketing* (January 1967), pp. 14-19.

Figure 1-2. Continuum for Classifying New Products

Continuous Innovations	Dynamically Continuous Innovations	Discontinuous Innovations
Least disrupting influence on established consumption patterns	Some disrupting influence on established consumption patterns	Involves establishment of new consumption patterns and the creation of previously unknown products

a product will have on consumption or behavioral patterns. This kind of operational definition is needed for consistency in analysis of research data and projections or conclusions made from different categories of new products.

From a Firm's Viewpoint

In addition to recognizing the consumer's perception of newness, the innovative firm may also find it necessary to classify its new products on some similar dimensions of newness. One possible way of classifying the objectives of new products is shown in Figure 1-3. These dimensions, first suggested by Johnson and Jones, provide an important basis for determining the extent of the marketing strategy needed to achieve company objectives.[7]

The situation in which there is new technology and a new market will be the most complicated and most difficult for the innovative firm. Since the new product involves new technology and customers that are not now being served, the firm will need a new and carefully planned marketing strategy. Product replacements, product extensions, product improvements, reformulations, and remerchandising involve marketing strategies that are less complicated since the firm will have had experience with a similar product or with basically the same target market.

Figure 1-4 illustrates how the increase in market newness and new technology affects a firm's product line. The firm in this example has an initial product mix of one product a_1. With no technological change in the product but with improved marketing strategy, the firm may increase the size of its existing market. The improved marketing strategy may consist of an increased sales

[7]S. C. Johnson and C. Jones, "How to Organize for New Products," *Harvard Business Review* 35 (May-June 1957), p. 52.

Figure 1-3. Classifying New Products Based on Product Objectives

Product objectives	Increasing technological newness		
	No technological change	Improved technology	New technology
No market change		*Reformulation* Change in formula or physical product to optimize costs and quality	*Replacement* Replace existing product with new one based on im- proved technology
Strengthened market	*Remerchandising* Increase sales to existing customers	*Improved product* Improve product's utility to customers	*Product life extension* Add new similar products to line to serve more customers based on new technology
New market	*New use* Add new segments that can use pres- ent products	*Market extension* Add new segments modifying present products	*Diversification* Add new markets with new products developed from new technology

Increasing market newness

SOURCE: Samuel C. Johnson and Conrad Jones, "How to Organize for New Products," *Harvard Business Review*, May-June 1957, Copyright © 1957 by the President and Fellows of Harvard College; all rights reserved.

Figure 1-4. Examples of New Product Classifications

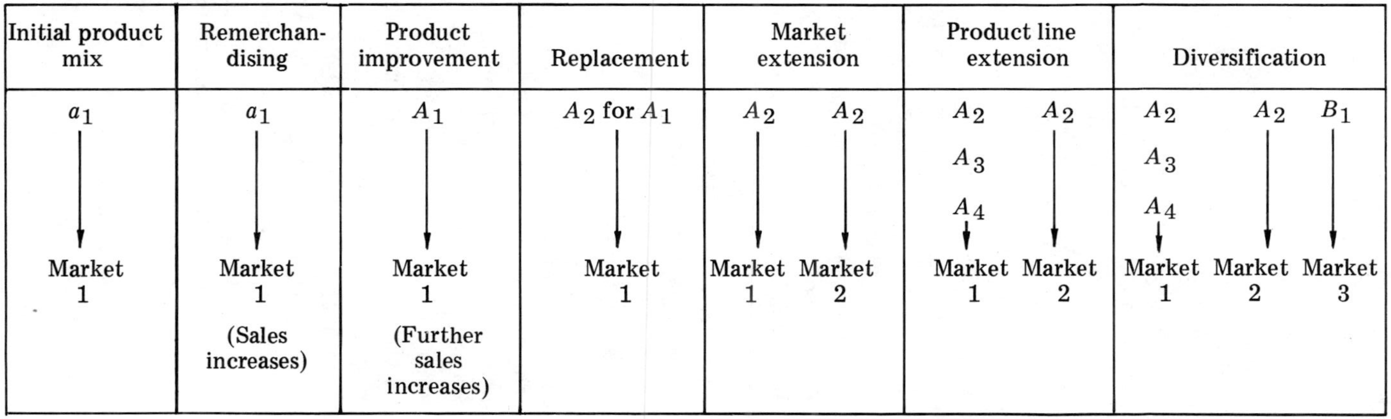

Initial product mix	Remerchandising	Product improvement	Replacement	Market extension	Product line extension	Diversification
a_1 → Market 1	a_1 → Market 1 (Sales increases)	A_1 → Market 1 (Further sales increases)	A_2 for A_1 → Market 1	A_2 → Market 1 ; A_2 → Market 2	A_2, A_3, A_4 → Market 1 ; A_2 → Market 2	A_2, A_3, A_4 → Market 1 ; A_2 → Market 2 ; B_1 → Market 3

force, increased advertising, new channels of distribution, or perhaps a lower price. This remerchandising or change in the marketing strategy results in greater sales or an expanded market.

Product improvement may consist of some improved technology in the product. For example, new developments in micro processors may now give the firm product A_1, which still satisfies the needs of the same market. It is conceivable that any product improvements could also increase the sales of the product to the same market. Thus, customers may shift from other manufacturers because of the product improvements in A_1.

Significant developments in new technology are likely to lead to the fourth situation in Figure 1-4 in which the manufacturer replaces A_1 with A_2. In this situation A_1 would no longer have any demand because of the improved technology. A good example would be the technological development in pocket calculators, which left little or no demand for slide rules.

Market extension can occur with or without new technology. The same product A_2 could be introduced to a new market without having undergone any changes. For example, hair dryers are now marketed to men and women, thus providing a new market for the same product. Industrial products introduced as consumer products or expansion to an international market would also be examples of market extension.

Product line extension generally provides the company with an opportunity to use the same communication and distribution channels to service the same market. This product line extension could conceivably take two directions: It could provide consumers with some variations in style, color, quality, or other features, which may increase sales by adding new customers in the same market; or it could increase the firm's inventory. For example, Heinz added a new barbecue sauce to its tomato catsup product so that a consumer loyal to its catsup would also purchase the new product.

Diversification in Figure 1-4 consists of the addition of a new product B_1 that is significantly different from A_2. This strategy also adds a new market of customers to those presently being serviced. This diversification strategy can be achieved by the acquisition of the firm that developed B_1 or by licensing a product invented by someone else or through internal development. In all cases, the risk to the manufacturer is highest since it is servicing new customers with possibly little or no expertise in the market.

The classification system provides some basis for estimating or planning the marketing mix decisions. It may also provide some insight as to whether the firm has to seek outside help to provide the expertise for such a new endeavor.

SUCCESS AND FAILURE OF NEW PRODUCTS

It is obvious that not all new products quickly become spectacular profit or sales successes. New products are most often removed from the marketplace at one of the earlier stages of their introduction because of low sales volume (see Figure 1-1). Yet research and development appropriated to new products in 1976 amounted to over $38 billion,[8] which provides some insight into the substantial losses suffered each year from product failure.

The estimated rate of failure varies from 10% to 90%, depending on the reporting source. For example, the National Industrial Conference Board indicated that about 30% of the new products introduced on the market are unsuccessful.[9] Buzzell and Nourse reported in their study that 22% of new food products were discontinued after test marketing and 17% were withdrawn after they had been introduced in the marketplace.[10] In a later study Lazo referred to failure rates of 80% to 90%, which included all products introduced by firms of varying size and competence.[11]

The disparity in these findings can be explained by examining the method used to define a new product, the manner in which a failure was determined, and the sample of the firms used in each study. Variations in these three aspects resulted in different conclusions regarding the percentage or the number of new product failures.

Reasons for New Product Failure

The National Industrial Conference Board study suggested the following reasons and their percentage of occurrence for new product failures:

1.	Inadequate market analysis	32%
2.	Product defects	23%

---

[8] More information and breakdown of expenditure patterns can be found in U.S. Department of Commerce, Bureau of the Census, *Statistical Abstract of the United States* (1976), p. 567.

[9] Betty Cochran and G. Thompson, "Why New Products Fail," *The National Industrial Conference Board Record* 1 (October 1964), pp. 11-18.

[10] Robert D. Buzzell and Robert E. M. Nourse, *Product Innovation in Food Processing, 1954-1964* (Boston: Division of Research, Harvard Business School, 1967).

[11] Hector Lazo, "Finding a Key to Success in New Product Failures," *Industrial Marketing* (November 1965), pp. 74-75.

3.	Higher costs than anticipated	14%
4.	Poor timing	10%
5.	Competition reaction	8%
6.	Inadequate marketing effort (includes weaknesses in sales force, distribution, and advertising)	13%
		100%[12]

A breakdown of these figures indicates that marketing problems or inadequacies are the cause for most failures (inadequate market analysis, poor timing, competition and sales force, distribution, and advertising). Buzzell and Nourse also found that a substantial percentage (approximately 80%) of the reasons given for discontinuing a product was a result of marketing misjudgments or inadequacies.[13]

New Product Failures: Some Examples

There are numerous examples of new product failures, probably the most famous of which was the Ford Edsel. The failure of the Edsel has been analyzed over and over again through the years, and we will not examine it here. More recently, Corfam, a synthetic substitute for leather manufactured by DuPont, was removed from the market after seven to eight years of commercialization. This ended a period of uneasiness for the $700 million leather industry, which had been quite shaken by the possibility of a synthetic substitute for leather. Before introducing Corfam, DuPont had spent some 13 years in the laboratory searching for the synthetic material that could be used in the manufacture of shoes. Other synthetic materials were available at that time, but they were not as versatile and effective as Corfam. However, the product did develop some problems. Failure appears to have stemmed from a flooding of the U.S. market by foreign leather shoes, which sold at lower prices than Corfam-made shoes, increased domestic competition, and an overall slump in U.S. retail shoe sales. Sales in 1970 had suffered drastically and prompted Corfam's withdrawal from the market. Millions of dollars invested in its development were thus lost when it was discontinued.

Another noted example of an unsuccessful product is Campbell's line of Red Kettle dry soups. It was introduced in 1962 with

[12] Cochran and Thompson, "Why New Products Fail," p. 14.

[13] Buzzell and Nourse, *Product Innovation in Food Processing*.

lavish advertising expenditures. In 1965, after $10 million in advertising, Campbell finally dropped this line. Competition, particularly from Lipton, had proven too difficult to overcome.

In 1971, amidst a great deal of fanfare, Brown-Forman Distillers introduced Frost 8/80, a dry, white whiskey. Research indicated that there was widespread acceptance of the product. About two years later Frost 8/80 was taken off the shelves at a loss of about $2.5 million to Brown-Forman. Apparently, the concept of a white whiskey was too drastic a change for consumers to accept, and it also caused a great deal of confusion since many whiskeys were promoted as light whiskeys and consumers assumed Frost 8/80 was a light whiskey. This confusion led to its downfall in the marketplace.

The list of familiar new product failures is, of course, quite extensive. Many other new products fail much earlier in their life cycles and thus are much less familiar to the average consumer. These products generally go unnoticed except by the manufacturer who must endure the financial loss. A good example of such a loss occurred a number of years ago when a drug company decided that the success of antacid pills and analgesics warranted the development of a combination antacid and pain killer that could be taken without water. The company's laboratories worked feverishly and finally came up with a cherry-flavored combination tablet called Analoz. The product was then tested using a consumer panel that was also given competing products to compare with Analoz. The panel overwhelmingly preferred Analoz. With the support of heavy advertising, the company then proceeded to introduce the product in a number of test markets. The product was advertised as a combination analgesic/antacid that worked without water. Impact analysis had also indicated that the advertisements were reaching a desirable number of consumers. However, sales were so low that after a number of months the company withdrew the product. Later research indicated that the fatal flaw was the feature emphasizing that the product worked without water. People who used pain killers felt that water was a necessary ingredient in order to cure the pain and thus had no confidence in taking the pill without water. This is a good example of a firm's failure to relate consumer attitudes toward pain-killing remedies and its new concept in pain-killing. Analoz failed primarily because of inadequate market analysis—a main cause of new product failure.

New Product Successes: Some Examples

Although the list of new product failures is devastating, there have been numerous successes that are worth analyzing to deter-

mine the main reasons for their success. One of the most note-
worthy recent successes has been the Ford Mustang. At the time
of its introduction, this product was a rather new concept in
the automobile industry and later proved to be a trend setter
for the other manufacturers in the industry. The car could
initially be described as having continental styling and sports car
appeal, with a package of options that could satisfy any consumer
at a wide range of prices. The name Mustang also reflected the
innovativeness in the styling and appeal of the car itself. Ford
spent a great deal of money determining the existing needs of
the consumer in this market. This thorough market analysis
certainly provided the firm with a running start in the introduction of the Mustang and reduced the risk of failure in one very
common failure area. The Mustang introduction was such a
success that sales far surpassed the volume forecasted by Ford.
In the first eight months of its existence, 248,916 new Mustangs
were registered in the United States. The demand for this car
was so great that long waiting periods for delivery became necessary, since such a backlog of orders existed.

    In 1947-1948 Polaroid Corporation startled the photographic
industry with "instant photography." This developing process,
although having been refined and improved, basically remains the
same in today's Polaroid cameras and has proven to be one of
the major innovations in the photographic industry in the last
25 years. Most photography professionals felt that the product
was just an expensive toy but were quickly embarrassed when
they saw the rate at which the original model 9 was selling.
Similarly, at Polaroid's annual stockholders' meeting in April
1972, founder and president Edwin H. Land demonstrated that
the company's new pocket camera—the SX-70—could produce
colored pictures at the rate of one every 1.2 seconds. Thus far
the company's successful new product introduction speaks for
itself in this industry.

    The coffee industry has long maintained its position as the
largest single beverage category by broad demographic appeal and
by an ability to meet many needs and serve many functions. One of
the major successful new product introductions during the mid-
1960s was Maxim coffee, developed by the Maxwell House Division
of General Foods. Although not truly new, this product did represent
a special process that provided a soluble, crystalline concentrate that
rivaled the flavor of regular ground coffee. As did Ford and
Polaroid, General Foods had very carefully designed and developed
a marketing plan based on thorough market analysis, which led to
Maxim's successful sales and profits.

    Gillette also has a history of successful new product introduc-
tions. The Gillette Dry Look hair spray brought instant success for

this product. The major concern with this product will be the possible change to shorter hair styles, which will require major modifications in the marketing efforts for the product. The Trac II, Cricket Lighters, and Earth Born shampoo are other recent examples of successful Gillette new products.

The preceding examples point out the importance of developing a sound marketing plan to avoid or reduce the probability of failure. There are many other examples of new product successes that could be mentioned. However, in most cases their success is a result of adequate marketing planning and strategy. Through the use of sound marketing strategies, a firm can fulfill its need to initiate new products. This need for new products can be best visualized in terms of the effects of consumers' preferences, competition, and social change.

THE ENVIRONMENT: ITS EFFECT ON THE DEVELOPMENT PROCESS

All marketing decisions must be carefully made in terms of the firm's ability to reach its objectives as well as in terms of environmental impact on its market plan. These environmental factors cannot be controlled and hence must be understood for marketing mix strategy decisions.

Effects of Consumer Preference

As previously indicated, many new products are only updated versions or modifications of older models, such as the annual automobile models. Critics of this type of strategy have called it "planned obsolescence." The regular update or modification, however, can be quite beneficial from the firm's standpoint, since these new models may move a firm from the maturity or decline stage in the product life cycle back to the more profitable growth stage. However, the use of this strategy by marketers generally depends on the nature of the market. For many years Volkswagen adopted the strategy of only minor improvements rather than dramatic changes in styles, colors, and other physical features.

Even though so-called "planned obsolescence" is criticized, it is important to point out that the consumers themselves are often responsible for such a strategy. Consumers in our society appear to show a strong preference for novelty and newness in what they buy. This preference necessitates and is thereby responsible for much of the new product development strategy in existence in our society.

Effects of Competition

During the late 1970s and early 1980s it is possible that competition might reach such intensity that even those firms wishing to maintain their status in a particular industry will be forced into extensive new product development. The amount of revenue devoted to technological research and development of new products varies considerably by industry. For example, pharmaceutical firms, such as Eli Lilly, spend about 10% of revenue in this area and at the same time have shown about a threefold increase in volume.[14] Of course, not all firms in an industry can spend the necessary revenue on research to develop new products. However, these firms must then be prepared to follow the industry by patterning their new products after those already available in the marketplace. Failure to remain abreast of new developments in the market could lead to financial collapse of the firm.

Thus, competition appears to be one of the major reasons for technological change. The continued evolution of new technology may not maintain its geometric rate of expansion in the near future, but it certainly can be expected to increase at least at a mathematical rate. These technological advances generally are translated into new products that are added to the cultural inventory. Although not all are feasible, many of the inventions resulting from research are certainly a major contributing factor to new product development.

Effects of Social Change

Rapid technological advances as well as war, economic instability, energy shortages, raw material shortages, changes in consumer needs, wants, and tastes, invarably induce social change. The 1970s have been confronted with all these conditions such that social change has not only become more obvious, but also more difficult for the marketer to anticipate.

The most obvious market trends prevailing in the United States that would best exemplify the effects of social change are the growing interest in natural foods, fast food franchises, diet foods, smaller automobiles, and leisure activities.

One of the major social changes that has favorably affected the introduction of the new products is the increase in personal income. As can be seen in Figure 1-5, the number of families

---

[14] For a more detailed discussion of research and development revenues by industry, see "R & D: Still a Growth Industry," *Conference Board Official Record* 7 (May 1970), pp. 38-40.

Figure 1-5. Family Income Projections: Percentage of Families

Income class	1960	1975	1985
Under $3,000	15	6	4
$3,000 to $5,000	13	7	5
$5,000 to $7,000	15	9	6
$7,000 to $10,000	25	15	11
$10,000 to $15,000	21	26	20
$15,000 to $25,000	11	27	33
Over $25,000		10	21

SOURCE: *National Industrial Conference Board* projections using U.S. Department of Commerce data.

earning less than $5000 is rapidly decreasing. These figures are expressed in 1972 dollars (constant purchasing power), thus eliminating the effects of inflation and rising prices. Much of this increase is being spent on consumer durable goods, the sales of which are increasing at a rate of about 7% to 8% per year.[15] As family income increases, marketers begin to make changes in the quality of products and the types of products most needed in this society. It is particularly important to note the types of products and services for which consumers are most likely to spend their dollars. For example, a casual observation of the leisure activity market indicates that much of consumers' additionally earned dollars are being spent there. Once thought of as luxury items, color televisions, second cars, vacation homes, and traveling have become more common purchases. Camping has

[15] More detailed information on this subject can be found in U.S. Department of Commerce, *U.S. Industrial Outlook, 1972*, p. 103.

become one of the most rapid-growing activities in the United States, so that the availability of camp sites is far below its demand. Product introductions relating to this leisure activity have been astounding in the past few years. With these changes in income and leisure time, the types and number of new products introduced will continue to expand.

During the past two years since the energy crisis first made its greatest impact on consumers, family income has been affected by two major factors: (a) increased unemployment of the head of the household and (b) increases in the number of working wives. The changing role of women—especially in cases in which women have pursued their own careers—has had its greatest impact on the new product diffusion process (see Chapter 7). Working women have less time to gather information on new products; they are more likely to remain loyal to well-known brands and are less likely to hear of new products until those products have been on the market for some time.

Given the sudden changes occurring in our society during the 1970s, the marketer must be able to adequately anticipate these changes through a carefully outlined marketing plan or face the risk of failure and financial disaster.

Effects of Demarketing

Since the late 1950s marketing has centered around "customer orientation" backed by integrated marketing aimed at generating customer satisfaction as the key to satisfying organizational goals.[16] With the effects of changes discussed in the preceding sections it is evident that the marketer has to consider other factors besides customer satisfaction. One factor of considerable importance is raw material shortages that may have immediate effects on new product development. One strategy that may result from shortages would be to deemphasize marketing so as to discourage or reduce demand for products that are in short supply.[17] The deemphasis of marketing (demarketing) would seem to naturally influence any product line expansion, modification, or diversification. It certainly may imply that firms will have to become more efficient in the marketing decisions that are made.

One possible outcome of shortages is that new products may be

---

[16]Philip Kotler, *Marketing Management: Analysis, Planning and Control,* 3rd ed. (Englewood Cliffs, N.J.: Prentice-Hall, 1976), p. 17.

[17]For more discussion on demarketing, see Philip Kotler and Sidney J. Levy, "Demarketing, Yes, Demarketing," *Harvard Business Review* (November-December 1971), pp. 74-80.

made to last longer. If resources are scarce, then a firm will
find it inconsistent to allocate scarce resources for new products
that will function for only a short period of time.

Another possible outcome is the cessation of "me-too" products, which are virtually identical to others already on the market.
It is possible that more innovative products will be introduced
rather than the me-too types. This strategy will require the firm
to enhance its expertise in effectively planning, developing, and
marketing new products.

The existence of raw material shortages and other energy
crises could have an opposite and more dramatic effect on new
product development. Instead of demarketing, many firms may
step up their development work to design new products and
services that will use different raw materials than those in short
supply or find new solutions to energy problems. The technology
developed in these areas has barely scratched the surface, and it
is likely to continue at a rapid pace as firms strive to establish
a position of leadership in these new markets that will probably
provide significant profits to the winner.

The development work in solar energy, automobile engines,
and housing has already elicited many new ideas and products.
The future life styles of the American consumer may strongly
depend on the results of the efforts of new product development in these areas.

THE PRODUCT DEVELOPMENT PROCESS

Given some of the major issues historically confronted by firms
in developing new products and given the continued proliferation
of new consumer and industrial products in the late 1970s, it is
necessary that a firm develop some mechanism—either formal or
informal—to develop new products for commercialization.

Typically, the product development process consists of the
following areas:

1. *Idea generation.* The process of generating new
   ideas may consist of brainstorming, reverse brainstorming, attribute listing, groups, or problem
   inventory analysis.

2. *Screening.* Techniques for evaluating new ideas
   may consist of checklists or open discussion
   where ideas are either eliminated or considered
   further.

3. *Business analysis.* The use of focus groups and concept testing techniques can provide further insight as to the exact nature of the idea before its prototype is made. This analysis should also provide further evaluation of ideas in order to eliminate any of those not considered favorably at this point.

4. *Development.* Prototype development of the idea must be evaluated in terms of production problems, safety requirements, costs, and other modifications necessary before entering any test market.

5. *Testing.* The setting up of test markets can provide valuable data on the nature of the market and needed marketing strategy changes or product modifications necessary to ensure a successful launch.

6. *Commercialization.* The new product is launched into the market at full-scale production with a significant commitment of the firm's resources and reputation.[18]

The product development process requires the conscious effort of top management to prevent the launch of products that have inadequate market analysis, product defects, higher development costs, poor timing, or poor marketing strategy. These problems can be controlled through a carefully organized planning process that meets the firm's objectives.

Figures 1-6 shows the product development process, the launch, and subsequent product life cycle. This figure shows that the firm does not begin to earn profits on the product until the growth stage. Up until this point, money has been spent on developing the product and launching it into the marketplace. During the introduction stage of the product life cycle, losses can usually be expected until sales have reached the break-even point.

The development process requires an organizational structure that operates efficiently and effectively in the internal company environment. Various organizational structures can be enlisted to provide the necessary mechanism for developing new products.

---

[18] In this text, the authors use five stages that describe the product development process: the idea stage, the concept stage, the product development stage, the test marketing stage, and the commercialization stage. These five stages encompass the traditional six stages.

The type of organizational structure used will depend on the size of the firm, the industry, personnel, and resources available. The various organizational structures that can implement and monitor the new product development process will be discussed in the next chapter. The most important criterion for the choice of the organizational structure is that top management provide full support and flexibility and authority so that decisions can be made quickly and efficiently to optimize time and resources.

Part 2 discusses the initial stages in the product development process, the idea stage, the concept stage, the development stage, and the test-marketing stages. Each of these stages, which represent important logical planning prior to launching a new product, provides the student and practitioner with methodology, strategy, and techniques for bringing ideas through a vigorous evaluation process in order to ensure that the product launch meets the objectives of the firm and the needs of the market.

During the test-marketing stage, the firm should begin to finalize the market segmentation for the new product. Market segmentation analysis discussed in Part 3 will provide management with critical data necessary in developing the new product's marketing program. In addition to market segmentation, the firm should analyze the diffusion-and-adoption process for its new product. The diffusion-and-adoption process will enhance the firm's understanding of consumer acceptance of its new product so that more effective marketing strategy decisions can be made before the product launch. Also discussed in Part 3 is forecasting new product sales. Forecasting techniques are necessary for the planning of the new product's marketing program. In particular, budgeting and attainment of short-term goals will be based on forecasted sales for the new product at various critical stages during the product life cycle.

Part 4 introduces the marketing mix decisions as the product is prepared for its market launch. After the test-marketing, final decisions on branding, packaging, pricing, distribution, and promotion must be made. Modifications in any of these areas should be based on careful analysis of test market data. Each market decision should be considered as part of a system, since each element is interrelated and modification on one factor, such as price, may have an important effect on another, such as distribution.

The final part discusses two critical topics that have been largely overlooked in other texts on new products. The control chapter introduces methodology for monitoring the new product over its product life cycle and in making modifications or deletion decisions where appropriate. Firms often hesitate to delete products since some sales are being made. However,

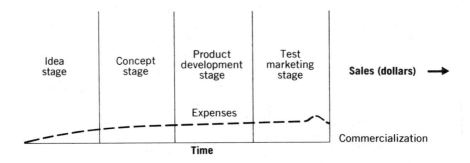

Figure 1-6. Sales and Profits during Product Development and Life Cycle

opportunities to invest resources elsewhere as well as increasing the company's efficiency make this decision a critical one for management. The final chapter relates the social and environmental influences in new product development—also an overlooked topic in new-product texts. In this chapter all legal aspects, including patents, warranties, and legislation relating to product safety and labeling, are presented. The importance of the social and environmental influences deserves special treatment since it is an ongoing consideration throughout the product development process as well as the product life cycle. Because of its importance throughout the planning process, the reader is referred to this chapter for information on any important legal decisions.

The overall focus of these five parts is to provide both the student and practitioner with an understanding and appreciation of the complexity of successfully launching a new product or service. Methodology, strategy, and techniques are presented throughout to give the reader useful tools for developing, planning, and controlling a new product or service.

SUMMARY

In the near future marketing executives will be faced with perhaps their greatest challenges and pressures. Increased competition and social, cultural, and economic changes will necessitate new product innovativeness to maintain competitive parity within each industry.

New product innovativeness varies from a modification of an old product to truly new products based on new technology repre-

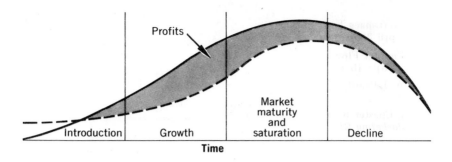

Figure 1-6—*Continued*

senting something far removed from anything else available in the marketplace. These variations in new products can be identified and classified according to how much new learning is required by the consumer in order to use the product. This process of classification is consistent with the marketing philosophy that satisfaction of consumer needs must be one of the prime justifications for the firm's existence.

There are many dramatic successes and failures of new products. Analysis of many product failures emphasizes the importance of adequate marketing analysis and decision-making to assure new product success. The success of Ford, General Foods, and Polaroid may be attributed to sound marketing planning and strategy. Thus, building a better mousetrap is not assurance of instant success.

The remainder of this book provides insight into understanding the process of new product development and management so that the most effective and successful market introduction may be achieved.

SELECTED READINGS

Abrams, George J. "Why New Products Fail." *Advertising Age* (April 22, 1974): 51-52.

Cooper, Robert G. "Why New Industrial Products Fail." *Industrial Marketing Management* (December 1975): 315-26.

Davidson, J. Hugh. "Why Most New Consumer Brands Fail." *Harvard Business Review*, vol. 54, no. 2 (March-April 1976): 117-22.

Hartley, Robert F. *Marketing Mistakes.* Columbus, Ohio: Grid, 1976.

Luck, David J. *Product Policy and Strategy.* Englewood Cliffs, N.J.: Prentice-Hall, 1972.

"More Aerospace Firms Make Products That Will Never Fly." *Industry Week* (April 28, 1975):6.

"New Product Flow Won't Slacken: Chesebrough." *Advertising Age* (May 12, 1975): 45-46.

Spitz, A. Edward. *Product Planning*, 2nd ed. New York: Petrocelli/Charter, 1977.

Wasson, Chester R. *Product Management: Product Life Cycles and Competitive Marketing Strategy.* St. Charles, Ill.: Challenge Books, 1971.

2

Organizing for
Marketing New Products

Decisions concerning the design, development, and management of new products are crucial and complex as evidenced by the failure rate discussed in Chapter 1. Because of the nature of these decisions, it is of major importance that lines of communication and cooperation within the organization are formally and firmly established. The elements of decision-making must be made into an integrated whole to allow management to function efficiently and effectively in a highly competitive environment. It is important that these complex, highly interrelated tasks for marketing new products be carefully assigned to competent personnel in the organization to assure the effective implementation of each task.

The responsibilities for the various tasks in the development and marketing of new products or services must be explicitly defined. In the assignment of these tasks, certain organizational questions will become apparent. Where will the responsibility be absorbed into the present organizational structure, such as the marketing department or the engineering department? Should new lines in the organization be established to centralize all new product decision-making? The latter approach appears to have greater overall advantages, especially because the nature of new product decisions requires an integrative (interdepartmental) approach. Regardless of the organizational structure, it is imperative that top management maintains a positive attitude toward new product activity.

ROLE OF TOP MANAGEMENT

New product planning and development is often assumed to be an undefined responsibility of either the chief executive or a few

people in top management. Whether or not it is an undefined responsibility, these executives must have the final authority in any
decisions made about new products. This is necessary because new
product planning and development is vital to a company's future
plans.

In the new product planning and development process, it is generally necessary to establish relationships with persons with new
product ideas both outside the firm and within different departments
of the company. Involvement, particularly across formal organizational lines of authority and with groups outside the organization,
necessitates top management's participation in the decision-making
process because only they have the authority to integrate recommendations from these sources with corporate goals. One problem
of the interdepartmental authority is that each department has its
own unique interests in any new product development activity. For
example, many marketing personnel are very sales and selling oriented and are therefore only concerned with new products that will
increase sales. Thus, it is possible that marketing will give no consideration to the available resources, profits, or corporate objectives.
Engineers, on the other hand, tend to be more technically oriented
and may be only concerned with the technical aspects of new
products, possibly neglecting the importance of consumers and the
satisfaction of their needs and wants. The need to include top management in the final decision-making is quite clear; its function is to
coordinate departmental interests and to improve the welfare of the
total organization. However, top-level managers would not normally
become involved in the details of decision-making because their time
is limited. A staff is usually assigned this responsibility and would
report directly to some member of top management. The staff
responsible for this function may be one person in a small company
or a committee in a large company. It is also likely that in larger
firms, product managers are given the responsibility for a specific
product or group of products.

The responsibilities of each member of the organization involved in new product decision-making should be formalized such
that effective lines of communication can be established with top
management. These individuals should be thoroughly trained to
make effective new product decisions so that individual or departmental goals are congruent with company goals.

The intention of this chapter is to discuss the various organizational structures used by firms in the marketing of a new product.
The advantages and disadvantages of different structures, the conflicts and constraints which diminish the effectiveness of new product planning are also addressed below.

LARGE VERSUS SMALL COMPANY ORGANIZATION

It appears that the smaller the firm, the greater the likelihood that the president of the firm is responsible for new product planning.[1] Even when this responsibility rests with top management, it is imperative that the planning, development, and management of the new product be carefully defined to ensure efficient and profitable introduction. One or a few top management personnel will be charged with generating new ideas, screening these ideas, determining their feasibility based on company goals as well as whether or not the product can be easily produced and tested, and finally making the decision to go or not to go with a particular idea. In the small firm the president will generally supervise all these activities and, in many cases, may carry them out personally. However, small firm managers or executives should be aware of how larger firms organize for the development and planning process. Understanding how this process works may provide them with insight that may be useful in formalizing their smaller firm's product development process.

ALTERNATIVE ORGANIZATIONS
FOR NEW PRODUCT DEVELOPMENT

Primary responsibility for new product planning can be assigned in various ways. The individual charged with these responsibilities can relate with the rest of the organization in different ways to increase compatibility within the entire organization. The alternative organizational structures for new product development generally fall into one of the following four types:

1. New product department
2. New product committee
3. New product manager
4. Venture team

The type of organization selected is largely a function of the size of the firm and its resources and objectives within the context of its product and market.

[1] Karl H. Tietjen, *Organizing the Product Planning Function* (New York: American Management Association, 1963), p. 21.

The New Product Department

Multidivisional firms may choose the new product department organization. Such departments have also been labeled new product development department, product planning department, or market development department.[2] This organizational structure separates the new product development, planning, and management tasks from the existing divisions in the organization to centralize the new product decision-making process and eliminate redundancy of these tasks across divisions. The coordination and control of new product development processes in autonomous divisions creates unique problems in corporate management. The major problems are duplication of effort and inefficient use of development funds and other company resources. These problems can be ameliorated by having a central authority direct and assist the divisions to better strive toward corporate objectives. The management of this central authority is generally given to a person who is capable of responsibility and who coordinates and controls the required tasks. This new product manager or director holds a staff function at a high level and usually reports to a vice-president or executive vice-president of the firm.[3] An example of how the new-product department might relate to other departments within the organization is shown in Figure 2-1. The manager or director of the new product department in this example reports to the executive vice-president who, in turn, reports to the president of the firm. This simplified organization chart shows the new product department positioned as a staff rather than a line function.

However, many people feel that new product development should be a line function. When considered a line function, the problems of authority become more complex because managers of other departments, such as finance, engineering, production, and marketing, technically rank higher than the new product manager. When new product development is a staff function, this problem is not as great as long as the new product department is given full support by top management. If support is not provided, the new product department has no authority over the line managers and is unable to complete the necessary tasks.

Regardless of how this function is organizationally structured, there must be clear lines of communication and authority so that new product planning and development may be performed with the least internal conflict. The continuous support of top management is a requirement for this department to succeed in implementing successful new product programs.

---

[2] *Ibid.*, p. 41; and Russell W. Peterson, "New Venture Management in a Large Company," *Harvard Business Review* (May-June 1967), p. 69.

[3] *Management of New Products* (New York: Booz, Allen and Hamilton, 1968), p. 20.

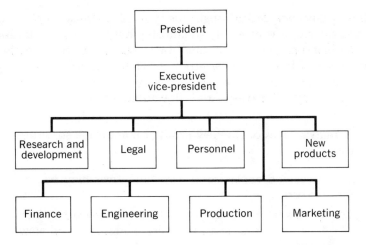

Figure 2-1. Relationship of New Product Department to Other Departments

The functions of the new product department are:

1.   Recommending new product objectives
2.   Planning exploration of new product ideas
3.   Screening new product ideas
4.   Assisting in development of new product specifications
5.   Recommending and implementing test-marketing
6.   Coordinating interdepartmental effort during the evolution process.[4]

The New Product Committee

In this organizational structure, new product development decisions are made by members of various departments or divisions within the existing organization. Thus, these individuals are involved in certain aspects of the product development as well as their regular responsibilities as managers or staff of other departments.

The new product committee may serve special functions, such as brainstorming to generate new product ideas, screening new ideas, evaluating new product proposals, coordinating and controlling the test-marketing process, or assisting in the management of the new product introduction. Because of its somewhat informal existence in the organization and because its membership may be temporary, the responsibilities and roles of the various members are not clearly

[4]*Management of New Products*, p. 21.

defined. However, even though this type of organizational structure
has weaknesses, it is probably the most widely used structure for new
product planning and development because it is informal and can be
used when needed. This new product committee structure, important particularly to smaller or more technical firms, is not necessarily
the most suitable for every firm's development process.

The advantages of the new product committee structure are:
are:

1.   Ideas and expertise of key executives may be
      pooled.
2.   Decisions made are likely to be accepted by the
      firm since the decisions were made by top manage-
      ment.
3.   The committee may be organized and used when
      needed.
4.   The members may be recruited for special
      purposes—that is, brainstorming for new product
      ideas or for the entire new product development
      process.
5.   There is no staff and line conflict since committee
      members are upper level management.

Although the advantages are clear and important, this structure has
some important weaknesses that limit its functional efficiency:

1.   Committee activity takes valuable executive time.
      Members may restrain involvement so they may
      return to their regular responsibilities.
2.   This type of committee structure lacks clear lines of
      authority and responsibility that may result in "buck
      passing."
3.   New product planning and development in many
      instances should be a full-time job and not occur
      only when there is a need.
4.   Members of the committee tend to concern them-
      selves only with their departmental objectives rather
      than with the firm's goals, resulting in a narrow
      view of the committee's purpose.
5.   Because of the structure's part-time existence, the
      members are not fully knowledgeable of the new
      product decision-making process.

It is important to recognize that a larger firm may use different executives for different functions in the new product planning and development process. One committee may exclusively serve the purpose of idea screening, whereas another may be used for business analysis, and so on. Each committee is thus a specialist in a different aspect of the development process. The major problem with this approach is that coordination becomes difficult unless one person assumes responsibility and authority over committee decisions. The product manager can fulfill this need and may be the coordinator of the new product evolution process.

The Product Manager

The product manager concept was innovated by Procter and Gamble nearly 50 years ago. The number of interpretations of the product manager's responsibilities have grown over this time as each firm institutes its own definition of responsibility and authority.[5] Regardless of the interpretations of the product manager's role, product managers today typically retain the responsibility for high-level planning and administration in decision-making for a product or group of products. They are specialists or experts in a particular product market, yet generalists in the sense that they must be concerned with all variables in the marketing mix that are relevant to their products or product lines.

At Procter and Gamble, product managers are referred to as brand managers. Each brand manager is responsible for one brand but is a part of a brand group or product line. Figure 2-2 illustrates the Procter and Gamble conception of the function of the brand manager. This structure optimizes the effectiveness of each brand manager by providing each with the resources needed to perform day-to-day marketing decisions. These resources are shown in Figure 2-3.

It is apparent from Figure 2-3 that brand managers must work closely with other managers in order to function effectively. This collaboration of effort is extremely sensitive and for some firms may not provide the desired results. This is true especially if brand managers lack the authority to effectively carry out their responsibilities. With its extremely diverse and extensive product line, Procter and Gamble has made the brand-manager concept work and has achieved great success in its product development decisions.

Figure 2-4 illustrates how a firm that uses the product-manager concept might structure its organization. As can be seen, product

---

[5] "Product Managers: Just What Do They Do?" *Printer's Ink*, special report (October 28, 1966), p. 16.

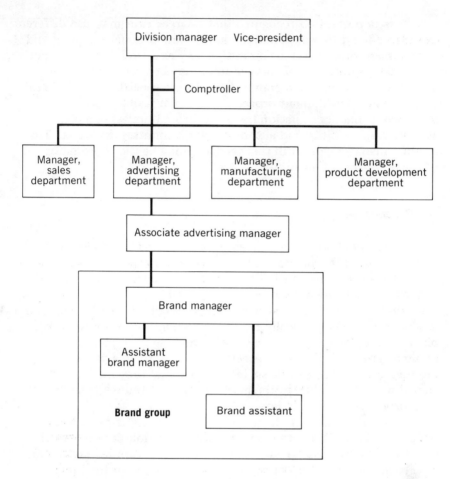

Figure 2-2. The Brand Manager Organization at Procter and Gamble. (Used with permission of Procter and Gamble Company, Cincinnati, Ohio.)

managers report to the vice-president of marketing who in turn reports to the executive vice-president. The product manager thus assumes a line function with authority over all decisions regarding his product or products.

Role of the Product Manager in Developing New Products   A significant part of product managers' duties involves marketing decisions for an existing product or products. However, product managers must also assume a role in the development of new products, particularly if the new product idea is an extension of the existing product

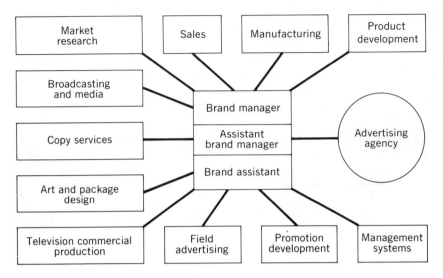

Figure 2-3. Interfacing of Product Manager at Procter and Gamble

line.[6] They may conceive of new, unique products since they are
required to have comprehensive knowledge of the buying process for
their product or products.

Product managers' roles vary in each firm. However, typically, each one's role in new product development includes all aspects of the new product evolutionary process. In an industrial,
highly technical market, product managers (who are likely to be the
creators or inventors) generally assume most, if not all, of the responsibility, especially if they have no existing product to manage.

In consumer markets, such as those of Procter and Gamble,
product managers have large staffs and extensive resources that can be
used in a coordinated development effort. Many of the new products
in the consumer market are less likely to be unique or discontinuous
than those in the highly technical product market. Thus, product
managers for consumer markets generally plan product-line extensions or modifications of existing products. They are not as likely to
be adept in all aspects of development as are their counterparts in the
highly technical market, but they will assign responsibility for specific tasks to persons whose duties normally encompass these tasks.

In the new product development process, product managers
must be in close touch with top management, particularly in the
early stages. Approval to send any new product to the development

---

[6]Philip W. Stein, "The Role of the Product Manager in New Product
Development," *The Marketing News* (October 1, 1972), p. 4.

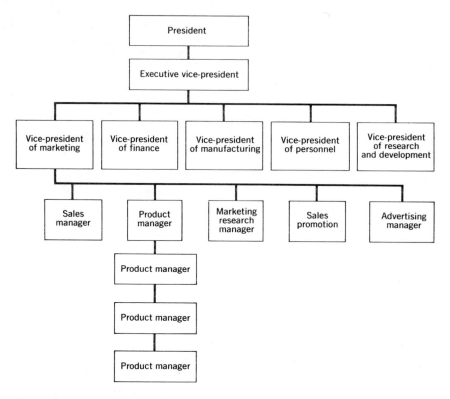

Figure 2-4. Traditional Organization and the Product Manager

route must be given by top management. Product managers must
provide top management with all the relevant data and their recommendations so that the decision to go ahead can be made expe-
diently. As new products move through the development process,
product managers must supervise the decisions and coordinate every
aspect, especially when other departments in the firm are included.
Whatever managers' participation in the various stages of new product development, they become somewhat expert in such areas as
market research and financial analysis.

Figure 2-5 outlines the typical decisions that product managers
must make or assist in making. It is evident from this illustration
that product managers have numerous duties and responsibilities. In
addition to making decisions and recommendations, they generally
will have control over significant funds that must be budgeted for the
commercialization strategy of a new product. Coordination and
supervision of all the major marketing, production, engineering, and
financial decisions regarding the new product also fall within their
auspices.[7]

[7]For a complete discussion see Gordon H. Evans, *The Product Manager's
Job* (New York: American Management Association, 1964), pp. 23-48.

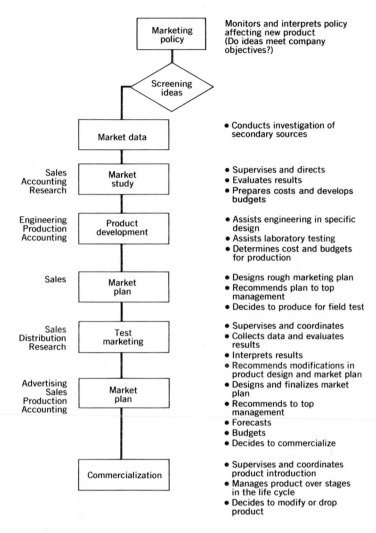

Figure 2-5. Duties of Product Manager and Contributions from Other Departments

    Product managers receive the expert advice and recommendations of other departments in the decision-making process—particularly sales, production, engineering, accounting, and advertising. All decisions must be cleared with top management before product managers are able to continue the development process.

    Figure 2-5 lists the product managers' typical responsibilities in a large firm, which markets consumer products. However, industrial product managers may not have significantly different duties in most areas with the possible exception of the marketing plan.

    In addition to duties in new product-planning and development, product managers assume the responsibility of marketing decision-making throughout the product's life cycle. Marketing mix strategy decisions to meet competitive pressures and changes in consumer needs are important responsibilities, and in many cases they will determine the success or failure of the new product. The decision to withdraw a new product from the market when it has reached the decline stage is also a job requirement of most product managers. This decision is discussed in a later chapter.

Duties of the Industrial and Consumer Product Manager   The roles of the consumer and industrial firm's product manager may vary, depending on the nature of the product, company objectives, and the industry in which the firm operates.[8] Industrial product managers usually have extensive technical background but lack marketing expertise. Thus, industrial product managers may assume only a limited role in decisions such as advertising, sales promotion, merchandising, packaging, branding, and labeling. In the consumer goods firm, product managers are more likely to have sufficient marketing background and experience to make marketing mix decisions without having to employ an outside consultant or enlisting other internal personnel.

Industrial product managers must maintain a close working relationship with research and development (R&D) because changes or new ideas are most likely to occur quickly and require immediate action to determine their feasibility. The product development process in an industrial firm is often initiated by government requests for bids or a request to design a new or improved product. Those responsibilities of industrial product managers that touch upon marketing or financial accounting will generally be assigned to others in the firm. One significant trend affecting the future role of industrial product managers is that more and more such managers are obtaining graduate business degrees that allow them to expand their responsibilities, particularly in coordinating and implementing the marketing plan.

Role Conflict and the Product Manager   One of the biggest problems confronting product managers is the amount of authority they command, which is sometimes not commensurate with their responsibilities. Since the relationships that product managers must develop in order to carry out their responsibilities are so complex, it is sometimes difficult to avoid role conflict.[9] Role conflict tends to limit effectiveness because product managers will most likely not

---

[8]*Ibid.*, p.26.

[9]B. Charles Ames, "Payoff from Product Management," *Harvard Business Review* (November-December 1968), pp. 141-52.

have the authority to supersede any department head or other manager whose cooperation is needed. For example, product managers are responsible for pricing and forecasting, yet they have no control or authority over production costs or the sales force. If product managers must know the exact manufacturing costs for their new products, they may have some difficulty in getting a firm quote from production managers. Production managers must account for all decisions to their superiors and may be reluctant to commit themselves to exact numbers in order to protect themselves. Conflicts of this sort with various units in the organization may be minimized if product managers are able to establish good working relationships and trust with their colleagues. Product managers must have broad expertise not only in marketing, accounting, production, etc., but they must also be able to communicate with others in the organization to enlist their trust in successfully implementing the market plan.[10] The frequent interaction among departments in the new product development process requires patience and diplomacy.

There are other problems inherent in the product-manager type of organization.[11] Product managers are often encumbered by trivial tasks such as correspondence with customers or with salespersons. Product managers are not only often hindered by their lack of authority, but they are also not given the necessary support staff to carry out their duties. Furthermore, the typical product manager has a short job tenure; many see the position as a stepping stone to top management.

Recent research indicates that the role of the product manager may be changing to overcome some of these weaknesses.[12] Top management has recognized the need to participate more in the decision-making process to alleviate some of the authority conflict problems that often arise in the product-manager organization. The prestige of the product manager has been enhanced by providing the position with more authority and more clearly defined responsibilities that seem to have slowed job turnover. More emphasis is also being placed on marketing experience as a job requirement rather than education alone.

Product managers are not the panacea to every firm's marketing problems. It is one of the most popular organizational approaches and appears to be growing among firms, particularly those that are in a multiproduct business where it is not practical to have physically

---

[10] For a discussion on how product managers influence action, see Gary R. Gemmill and David L. Wileman, "The Product Manager as an Influence Agent," *Journal of Marketing* (October 1969), p. 35.

[11] David J. Luck, "Interfaces of a Product Manager," *Journal of Marketing* (October 1969), p. 35.

[12] Victor P. Buell, "The Changing Role of the Product Manager in Consumer Goods Companies," *Journal of Marketing* (July 1975), pp. 3-11.

separated departments for sales, advertising, or other marketing functions. The product-manager structure allows the firm to give adequate attention to each product without separating the line divisions.

The Venture Team

This type of organization is a new approach to new product development. It seems to be better suited to the design and development of new products that do not necessarily fit into the ongoing business of the firm.

A study of 98 venture managers for industrial and consumer products at large corporations revealed that venture teams have the following characteristics:

1.   The venture team is organizationally separate from the remainder of the organization.
2.   Members are recruited from various functional areas, such as engineering, production, marketing, and finance.
3.   Existing lines of authority in the permanent organization are not necessarily valid in the venture team.
4.   The venture team manager usually reports to the chief executive officer and is given authority to make major decisions.
5.   The team is free of deadlines and remains together until the task is completed.
6.   Freedom from time pressures fosters creativity and innovativeness.[13]

Figure 2-6 illustrates the venture-team type of organization. Members of the various teams (there may be more than one team operating at any time) are chosen from the various functional areas with one person given the title of venture team manager. The venture team manager reports to the division head or some other upper level administrator.

Advantages of the Venture Team Concept   The venture team concept of organization may be compared to new product departments, new product committees, or product managers. The big-

---

[13] Richard M. Hill and James D. Hlavacek, "The Venture Team: A New Concept in Marketing Organization," *Journal of Marketing* (July 1972), p. 46.

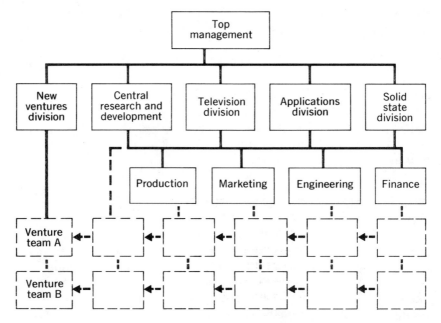

Solid lines: permanent organization

Dotted lines: venture team members

Figure 2-6. An Example of the Venture Team Organization (From Richard M. Hill and James D. Hlavacek, "The Venture Team: A New Concept in Marketing Organization," Figure 1, *Journal of Marketing* [July 1972], p. 47. Reprinted from *Journal of Marketing*, published by the American Marketing Association.)

gest question in the three types of structure is who has the authority to make the final decision. The venture team tries to overcome this difficulty by providing leadership in the venture team manager who has a direct line with top management.[14]

The new product committee approach is the most temporary of all the organizational structures. Although the venture team consists of members from many functional areas, they are assigned to the team on a permanent basis until the task is completed.

There are also disadvantages to venture team organizations. Interdepartmental conflict may often result particularly when a department head feels that one of his or her staff members is spending too much time on the venture team instead of carrying out departmental responsibilities. The unwillingness of department managers to cooperate may lead to conflict and the weakening of the venture team approach.

[14]*Ibid.*, p. 50.

ORGANIZATIONAL ALTERNATIVES NEED EXECUTIVE SUPPORT

In all of the organizational structures discussed above, one criti-cal requirement is essential to the success of all four types of organi-zations: executive support. Top managers must realize that their attitudes toward new product planning and development will be reflected in the decisions made at each stage of the development process. Negative attitudes will likely weaken new products as well as stifle innovativeness.

WHICH ORGANIZATIONAL STRUCTURE?

The adoption of any one of the organizational structures pre-sented depends largely on the size of the firm, the type of market, the company objectives, and the availability of expert personnel. The venture team organizational structure may be more suited to large corporations interested in totally new products rather than product extensions or me-too products. Smaller firms that cannot afford full-time personnel for the new product planning and devel-opment are likely to use the new product committee approach. This allows minimal commitment to new product development.

Firms with multiple product lines find the product-manager approach the most efficient structure. It provides the firm with the advantage of a centralized coordinator of various departments in-volved in the planning and development process. The new product department is better suited to those firms with a single product line and a traditional functional marketing organization.

A study by Grayson indicates that those companies that main-tain full-time new product executives produce 69% more new prod-ucts than those with part-time executives. Firms with full-time new product executives produce 60.5% more new products than firms with no new product executives.[15] These findings relate to firms that have sales of over $25 million annually. Such findings testify to the importance of full-time commitment to new product develop-ment on the part of most large firms.

STAFFING DECISIONS

Regardless of the type of organization, certain qualities are desirable in the individual who manages the product planning group. Some companies staff their planning groups with former sales repre-

[15] Robert A. Grayson, "If You Want New Products, You Better Organize to Get Them," *American Marketing Association Proceedings*, June, 1969, p. 78.

sentatives.[16] These firms feel that the salesperson is best acquainted
with the consumer and is more likely to know what their customers
want. In addition, many aspects of the product development process
require selling ideas to others within the firm. However, the salesperson is often limited in other aspects necessary for product planning. Today, most firms are staffing their product planning groups
with individuals who have had experience in some marketing capacity, such as sales, advertising, and marketing research. This
company-specific experience seemingly provides a solid understanding of corporate objectives, the product and its limitations, personnel,
and the competition. These are critical elements in the effective
management of product planning and development responsibilities.

For large, technically oriented firms, the manager of product
planning and development should have a strong technical background
in the particular market. Experience in marketing is becoming more
necessary to the technical firm's product planning leaders. For
example, in the chemical and instrumentation market, a recent study
showed that many product failures resulted from neglect of important marketing elements.[17]

FROM PLANNING TO COMMERCIALIZATION

The new product planning and development organization often
has difficulty maintaining a balance of emphasis between existing
products and products in various stages of development.[18] Why does
the preoccupation of operating personnel with products already on
the market cause difficulty in generating interest in new product
plans? Personnel in the planning and development stages do not
always participate in the product's commercialization. Once commercialization is reached, the planning personnel continue to plan
and develop new products. The problem of transferring knowledge
from planning to operations is frequently encountered but may be
resolved by allowing development personnel to move into operations.
This problem is not as great in the product manager type of organization because the product manager assumes responsibility for the
product once it achieves commercialization. With committees, new
product departments, and possibly the venture team, this transfer
of knowledge may be a more serious problem since those groups
are not likely to participate in the market introduction. This responsibility would be given to the marketing department.

[16]William J. Constandse, "How to Launch New Products," *MSU Business
Topics* (Winter 1971), p. 31.
[17]"Research Based Venture Companies—The Link Between Market and
Technology," *Research Management* (May 1974), p. 18.
[18]"Organizing the Product Planning Function," p. 66

The problems of knowledge transfer, role conflict, insufficient authority, and so on, may be minimized or eliminated completely if the firm and its employees maintain a positive attitude toward new product planning and development. A positive attitude will help to ensure the success of any of the four organizational structures presented.

THE RESEARCH AND DEVELOPMENT/MARKETING INTERFACE

Those individuals responsible for new product planning and development must interact with research and development in order to assure the technical feasibility of any new product idea, as well as to determine the actual specifications required for consumer satisfaction. This interaction often breaks down for two reasons:

1. Lack of good communication during relevant stages in the product evolution process
2. Value conflict between the research and development group and marketing personnel.[19]

The first problem occurs because research and development has the difficult responsibility of explaining new technology used in new product development to the marketing staff. New designs, materials, and procedures that must be clearly communicated to those in the new product development organization are constantly being developed. It is also imperative that research and development groups be kept informed of the long-range goals of the firm in the marketing of new products so that effort is congruent with these objectives.

Value conflict problems occur primarily because the research and development department has little appreciation for problems in branding, packaging, distribution, pricing and promotion, and it must be instilled with an awareness and understanding of how the problems faced by the marketing organization affect the success of any new product introduction.

Flexibility in managing role of research and development seems to be the key to successful cooperation. Communication and understanding of the problems faced by each member will help to minimize the conflicts of interest. Frequent meetings and careful scheduling will also aid in this interface.

[19]Warren B. Brown and Lewis N. Goslin, "R&D Conflict: Manager versus Scientist," *Business Topics* (Summer 1965), p. 75.

SUMMARY

The new product planning and development process needs special attention from the firm; thus, a separate organizational structure is needed to perform these tasks. Four organizational structures were presented:

1. New product department
2. New product committee
3. Product manager
4. Venture team

The choice of structure is a function of the size and resources of the firm, the company's objectives, types of product, the industry in which the firm operates, and the availability of expert personnel.

For smaller firms with limited resources, the new product committee is most likely to be the most efficient organizational structure. The large, multidivisional firm is better suited to the new product department organization, which provides centralization of decision-making across all divisions. The product manager approach appears to be most widely used by large, multiproduct firms. The responsibilities of planning and development of a particular product or group of products are managed by the product manager. If a large firm wishes to develop new products, it may afford the venture team type of organization.

Once the planning and development decisions have been made, the firm must ensure the transfer of knowledge to those responsible for the commercialization stage. This may be done by bringing the development personnel into operations decisions as well.

In staffing the product planning and development groups, preference is usually given to those with experience in the relevant market as well as marketing expertise. Top management must maintain a positive attitude toward new product planning and development and show a willingness to support the organization responsible for these tasks.

SELECTED READINGS

Dalrymple, Douglas J., and Parsons, Leonard J. *Marketing Management: Text and Cases.* New York: Wiley, 1976.

Grayson, Robert A. "If You Want New Products You Better Organize To Get Them." *American Marketing Association Proceedings* (June 1969): 75-9.

Haas, Raymond M. *Long-Range New Product Planning in Business.* Parsons, W. Va: McClain Printing, 1965.

Hill, James M., and Hlavacek, James D. "The Venture Team: A New Concept In Marketing Organization. *"Journal of Marketing* (July 1972): 44-50.

Lorsch, Jay W., and Lawrence, Paul R. "Organizing for Product Innovation." *Harvard Business Review* (January-February 1965): 109-22.

Management of New Products. New York: Booz, Allen and Hamilton, 1968.

Phelps, D. Maynard. *Product Management.* Chicago: American Marketing Association, 1970.

Rothberg, Robert R. *Corporate Strategy and Product Innovation.* New York: The Free Press, 1976.

Zarecor, William D. "High Technology Product Planning." *Harvard Business Review* 53 (January-February 1975): 108-15.

Part Two

**New Product Ideas:
Obtainment and Evaluation**

3

Introduction to the Product Planning and Development Process

Chapter 1 indicated that a constant flow of new products, or at least improvements in existing products, was necessary for a firm to continue to be profitable. The need for new sources of profit coupled with the high rate of failure of new products requires a continuous search for sources of new product ideas as well as new product evaluation at all stages in the development process. This chapter discusses the major stages in obtaining and evaluating new products. Then the sources for new product ideas and the various methods for generating new product ideas are examined. Finally, the role of models in new product evaluation and planning is discussed, and some specific new product models and their usefulness are examined.

THE PRODUCT PLANNING AND DEVELOPMENT PROCESS

Although the product planning and development process varies from industry to industry as well as from firm to firm within a given industry, the multitude of activities generally follows the sequential pattern indicated in Figure 3-1. The product planning and development process can be divided into five major stages: idea stage, concept stage, product development stage, test-marketing stage, and commercialization.

In the idea stage, suggestions for new products are obtained from all possible sources. In addition, all available devices for gen-

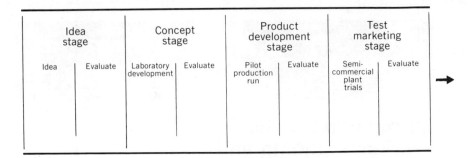

Figure 3-1. The Product Planning and Development Process

erating new product ideas should be employed.[1] These ideas should be carefully screened to determine which ones are good enough to require a more detailed investigation. It is important for the company to establish objectives and define growth areas to provide a basis for this analysis.[2]

Those ideas passing the initial screening enter the concept stage. Here the ideas are developed into more elaborate product concepts. It is important for each company to evaluate the product concept from the standpoint of the company's strengths and weaknesses as well as the needs of potential buyers. A tentative business plan consisting of product features and a marketing program is developed. A sample of potential buyers should be presented the concepts for evaluation. This can be done verbally or pictorially.

Once the concept for the new product has been approved, the concept is then developed into a physical product and tested. This occurs in the product development stage. Specifically, the technical and economic aspects of the potential new product are explored by assigning specifications for the development process to research and development. Except in the case where excessive capital expenditures are involved, laboratory-tested products should emerge that can then be produced on a pilot run basis. This pilot production run will allow for production control and product testing. These products are then evaluated by in-use consumer testing, which will determine whether the potential new product has features superior to products currently available.

[1] A complete discussion of the alternative sources of new product ideas as well as the methods for generating new product ideas follows in the remaining parts of this chapter.

[2] The planning and evaluation process in the idea, concept, and product development stages is discussed in Chapter 4; the activities in the test marketing stage are presented in Chapter 5.

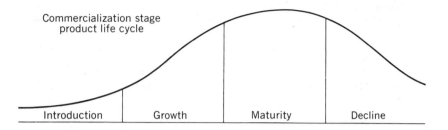

Commercialization stage
product life cycle

| Introduction | Growth | Maturity | Decline |

Figure 3-1—*Continued*

The results of the product development stage form the basis of the final marketing program for the new product. In some cases, a market test is undertaken to increase the certainty of successful commercialization. This last stage (the test marketing stage) in the evaluation process provides sales results at varying price levels to indicate the acceptance level of consumers. Although absolute certainty cannot be obtained, the market test results provide the basis for the final decision on commercialization—that is, whether or not the new product can be marketed profitably on an expanded basis.

Whether or not a market test should be undertaken as well as the extent of the evaluation in each stage of the product planning and development process depends to a great extent on the product, market, and competitive situation confronting the firm. These must be evaluated in terms of the potential long-time period between idea generation and commercialization and the costs involved. This time and cost are then weighed against the high costs of unsuccessful commercialization. Even though great technological advances in terms of new product ideas have occurred, these ideas are often not quickly transformed into the resultant new products. For example, as Table 3-1 indicates for ten products investigated, the average time from conception to new product realization was 19.2 years. This varied from six years for the video tape recorder to 32 years for the heart pacemaker. It does not appear that this time period is becoming shorter. In fact, the federal government is so concerned about the length of time before useful new products are commercially available once the idea has been generated that a great deal of federal funding has been granted in the area of technology transfer.

Yet this long time period in the product planning and development process must be carefully weighed against the costs associated in the evaluation process and the costs of commercialization.

Table 3-1. Length of Time for Product Development

Innovation	Year of first conception	Year of first realization	Duration (years)
Heart pacemaker	1928	1960	32
Hybrid corn	1908	1933	25
Hybrid small grains	1937	1956	19
Green revolution wheat	1950	1966	16
Electrophotography	1937	1959	22
Input-output economic analysis	1936	1964	28
Organophosphorus insecticides	1934	1947	13
Oral contraceptives	1951	1960	9
Magnetic ferrites	1933	1955	22
Video tape recorder	1950	1956	6
Average duration			19.2

SOURCE: Battelle Columbus Laboratories Study, Report to the
National Science Foundation (Washington, D.C., 1973).

Although eliminating about 90% of proffered ideas, the idea and
concept stages take very little time and money—about 10% of the
total time and expenditures involved in the entire product planning
and development process through commercialization. The product
development stage requires about 30% of the total expenditures
and 40% of the total time. On the other hand, the test marketing
stage takes 12% of the total money and 20% of the time. These
time-and-cost percentages must be carefully weighed against those
associated with the commercialization stage in which about 50% of
the total expenditures occur in only 23% of the total time.[3] Regardless of the time-and-cost tradeoffs made, a company still has to
actively develop sources for new product ideas so that the product
planning and development process can lead to commercialization.

[3] These time and cost estimates are presented in *Management of New
Products* (New York: Booz, Allen and Hamilton, 1968), p. 10.

SOURCES OF NEW PRODUCT IDEAS

There are many possible sources of new product ideas. The major ones are customers, competition, distribution channels, federal government, research and development, company sales force, upper level management, and employee suggestions.[4]

Customers

Companies are paying more and more attention to what should be the focal point of new products—their customers. This can take the form of monitoring ideas received on an informal basis or formally arranging for customers to have an opportunity to express their opinions. An example of the former occurred at General Foods Corporation.[5] The company receives spontaneously about 80,000 letters from consumers annually. At one point, a consistent complaint was about the size and shape of the cereal boxes. Generally, the cereal boxes were too tall to stand upright on standard kitchen shelves and also tipped over easily. These complaints led to the development of a new, more compact package.

Kimberly-Clark Corporation is an example of a firm that formally monitors customer opinions. Groups of consumers meet and discuss the relative advantages and disadvantages of the company's products. From one series of discussions, it became apparent that a group of consumers felt the tissue papers should be larger. This sparked the development and eventual introduction of "Man Size Kleenex."[6]

Competition

Companies must also establish a formal procedure for monitoring the new product activities of their competitors. This procedure should consist of two facets. Information concerning forthcoming new products can come from trade sources via the

---

[4]There are many comprehensive listings for sources of new product ideas. See, for example, Peter Hilton, *Handbook of New Product Development* (Englewood Cliffs, N.J.: Prentice-Hall, 1961) and U.S. Chamber of Commerce, *Developing and Selling New Products* (Washington, D.C.: U.S. Government Printing Office, 1955).

[5]"Helpful Consumers," *Wall Street Journal* (June 2, 1965), p.1.

[6]*Ibid.*, p.1.

company's sales force. Also, upon a competitive product's introduction, the sales performance can be monitored either by the
company's sales force or through an established, outside research
service.

Distribution Channels

Members of the distribution channels can be sources for new
product ideas. The members can suggest a completely new product due to their familiarity with the needs of the market. However,
a company can also achieve new product additions by analyzing
its distribution system. In other words, a company can add new
products in order to generate more merchandise for the stores
handling its products.

A case in point occurred in the greeting card industry. The
growth in this industry had been decreasing to such an extent that
in the 1960s Hallmark, Gibson, American Greetings, Rust Craft,
and Norcross expanded their product lines into related merchandise.[7] Hallmark introduced candles, paper plates, napkins, books,
and costume jewelry. Each of these new products could be sold
through the same outlets as were its greeting cards. Hallmark successfully expanded its entire product line by taking advantage of
the established distribution system.

Federal Government

The federal government can be helpful to a company with new
product ideas in two ways. First, the files of the Patent Office
contain numerous new product possibilities. Although these, in
themselves, may not be feasible product introductions, a patent
can frequently be a stimulus that leads to other new product ideas.
There are several government agencies and publications that can
also be helpful. For example, the *Official Gazette* published by
the U.S. Patent Office not only summarizes weekly every patent
granted but also lists any patents available for license or sale.

The Government Patents Board publishes lists of abstracts
of thousands of government-owned patents. An example is the
Government-Owned Inventories Available for License. There are
several government agencies, such as the Office of Technical
Services, that assist manufacturers in obtaining specific product
information.

---

[7]"Hallmark Tries Out the Jewelry Trade," *Business Week* (November 3,
1975), p. 29.

Secondly, consumer needs and therefore new product ideas can come from government regulations. For example, the Occupational Safety and Health Act (OSHA), passed in 1972, aims to eliminate unsafe working conditions in industry. One aspect of this act concerns the availability of a first-aid kit in a business establishment. It stipulates that every first-aid kit must contain a weatherproof package of certain items. Based on this stipulation, many new first-aid kits were developed and marketed. Each was differentiated by industry, such as construction and transportation, as well as by size of firm. New distribution companies were founded to market the new kits.

Research and Development

Many new product ideas originate in research and development departments. Studies show that this department is the source of more new product ideas than any other. In one survey, Booz, Allen and Hamilton found that 88% of new product ideas came from within the companies themselves; of this, research and development contributed 60%. Realizing the potential of basic research, many companies have large research and development budgets.

One industry where technology from research and development has increased at an accelerated rate is the telephone industry. Innovations have made the 200,000 private brand exchanges throughout the nation almost obsolete. The new exchanges, which are part computer, not only make the office telephone more versatile and efficient, but also allow cost control.[8]

When considering research and development as a source of new products, it is important to differentiate among the various types of research. In doing so, monies can be allocated to the different types of research without the corresponding expectation that new products will be immediately forthcoming. Fundamental research is done purely for the sake of knowledge. Applied research is locating, classifying, and interpreting fundamental research so that the knowledge gained from fundamental research can be used when problems arise. The last type of research is developmental research, which is done to generate new product ideas as well as adjust and find new users for present products. Since all three types of research are useful for many companies, the research and development should be evaluated by classification so that this important source for new products can be better managed.

[8]"Technology Changes the Office Telephone," *Business Week* (January 19, 1975), pp. 42-44.

Company Sales Force

With their grass roots experience and constant contact with the complaints of the consumers, the company sales force is a good source of new product ideas. This is especially the case for industrial products where the salesperson is in contact with the end user. For example, the sales manager of a small company observed the growth in the use of metallic films at Christmas. This led the company to develop metallic papers used in candy wrappings and ice cream bags.

Top Management

Top management must at least define general areas to explore for new products. These areas should be related to the strengths or weaknesses in the company's product line. A company should search for new products that are complementary to existing products of the firm. A cake mix manufacturer could add frosting mixes to the product line, or a company with highly seasonal sales can introduce products with more stable sales. For example, toy manufacturers could participate in the production of food products.

Top management can be an internal source of new product ideas by examining existing products of the firm, reviewing abandoned projects, and considering the possibilities of by-products. When examining the existing products of the firm, such factors as the design, materials, packaging, and channels of distribution should be reviewed. This review can generate new product ideas. For example, Hallmark introduced a series of new products (candles, paper plates, and costume jewelry) into its existing outlets. Similarly, in evaluating the materials used, ideas can come from either using the same raw materials, production facilities, or technical process. For example, a retail store making custom men's suits may offer custom-made ties.

Management should check the by-products of the production process for potential product ideas. This was successfully done by a small manufacturer of wooden pallets. With the increased use of wood chips in landscaping, revenue was gained by placing announcements in newspapers and local gardening magazines that the company was a source of wood chips.

Employee Suggestions

An excellent internal source for new product ideas is employee suggestions. We have already discussed the importance of salespeople and top management as idea generators. Other employees can also be a very valuable source. In fact, three-fourths of the top 500 firms have formal employee suggestion procedures.

It is important to establish specific goals for the number of suggestions desired. A company must also help an employee to develop a feasible idea. Such incentives as cash, contests, or corporate recognition and praise are important for employees to actively think about potential products. Finally, management must process all ideas from employees promptly and monitor the entire process. A corporation with a well-managed, formal employee suggestion system can gain many new product ideas.

METHODS FOR GENERATING PRODUCT IDEAS

In an effort to better use sources of new ideas, several methods have been developed to generate better ideas. These include focus groups, attribute listing, forced relationships, brainstorming, reverse brainstorming, and problem inventory analysis. Because good new product ideas come from diverse sources and often in bizarre ways, these methods are not to be taken as the end-all for idea generation. Rather, these methods should be viewed as mechanisms by which new product ideas can, in general, be more easily generated.

Focus Groups

Focus group interviews have been used in many aspects of marketing research since the 1950s. A focus group interview consists of a moderator leading a group of people through an open, indepth discussion. This is much different from a group interview in which the moderator simply asks questions to solicit responses from participants. In the focus group, the moderator focuses the discussion of the group on the new product area in a nondirective manner.

In addition to generating a new idea, the focus group is an excellent means for the initial screening of ideas and concepts. Recently, several procedures have been developed so that more quantitative analyses can be used in interpreting the focus group results. With increased use and the development of more procedures, the focus group is an increasingly valuable method for generating new product ideas.[9]

Attribute Listing

This technique consists of listing the existing attributes of a product idea or area; these attributes are then modified until a new combination of attributes emerges that will improve the product idea or area. The small company manufacturing pallets used for shipping or moving a product on a conveyor along an assembly line wanted to devise a better product. It listed the attributes that defined the existing pallets, such as wood composition, rectangular runners, and accessible on two sides by a fork lift. Then, each of these attributes was examined for any change(s) that would improve the satisfaction of the user's need. For example, the wood composition could be changed to plastic, resulting in a cheaper price; the rectangular wooden runners could be replaced by cups for easier storing, and the cups would allow the new pallet to be accessible on all four sides for ease of pick-up. Through attribute listing, this small company achieved a new pallet idea that had much improved product characteristics.

The following questions are often used in attribute listing to generate new product ideas:

Put to other uses?	New ways to use as is? Other uses if modified?
Adapt?	What else is this like? What other idea does this suggest? Does past offer parallel? What could I copy? Whom could I emulate?
Modify?	Change meaning, color, motion, sound, odor, form, shape? Other changes?
Magnify?	What to add? More time? Greater frequency? Stronger? Higher? Longer? Thicker? Extra Value? Plus ingredient? Duplicate? Multiply? Exaggerate?
Minify?	What to subtract? Smaller? Condensed?

[9] For a more indepth presentation on focus group interviews in general and quantitative applications, see "Conference Focuses on Focus Groups: Guidelines, Reports, and 'the Magic Plaque'," *Marketing News* (October 24, 1975), p. 1; Alvin J. Rosenstein, "Quantitative—Yes Quantitative—Applications for the Focus Group," *Marketing News* (May 21, 1976), p. 8; Keith K. Cox, James B. Higginbotham, and John Burton, "Application of Focus Group Interviews in Marketing," *Journal of Marketing* (January 1976), pp. 77-80.

	Miniature? Lower? Shorter? Lighter? Omit? Streamline? Split up? Understate?
Substitute?	Who else instead? What else instead? Other ingredient? Other material? Other process? Other power? Other place? Other approach? Other tone of voice?
Rearrange?	Interchange components? Other pattern? Other layout? Other sequence? Transpose cause and effect? Change pace? Change schedule?
Reverse?	Transpose positive and negative? How about opposites? Turn it backwards? Turn it upside down? Reverse roles? Change shoes? Turn tables? Turn other cheek?
Combine?	How about a blend, an alloy, an assortment, an ensemble? Combine units? Combine purposes? Combine appeals? Combine ideas?[10]

The one major drawback to attribute listing is that it focuses on the product at hand. It cannot be used in all new product situations. It may even stifle imaginative thinking to some extent. Yet, as in the case of the pallet manufacturer, it is often a useful method for developing a new product idea.

Forced Relationships

A third method for generating new product ideas is forced relationships.[11] In this technique many new ideas are first listed. Then, as the name implies, the new product ideas are considered in pairs. By considering one idea in relation to every other, new ideas are often generated. Even though this technique is not in wide use, it is a good, systematic procedure to see whether there are any new products that stem from a combination of existing products. These new products would then naturally fit into the existing product line and management expertise.

[10] Alex F. Osborn, *Applied Imagination*, 3rd ed. (New York: Charles Scribner's Sons, 1963), pp. 286-287.

[11] *Ibid.*, pp. 213-214 for an application of this technique, developed by Charles S. Whiting.

Brainstorming

This technique evolves from the principle that people can be stimulated to greater creativity by meeting with others and participating in organized group experiences. Top management of a company meet frequently in small groups of between six and ten to generate new product ideas. Many of the resultant ideas are absurd and have no basis for consideration for development, but this method often produces a large number of ideas. This is especially true when the meetings, lasting about an hour, focus on a specific area. There are four rules to be followed for most effective use of management brainstorming:

1. No criticism. Negative judgments must be withheld until later.

2. Free-wheeling is encouraged. The wilder the idea, the better; it is easier to tame down than to think up.

3. Quantity is wanted. The greater the number of ideas, the more the likelihood of useful ideas.

4. Combinations and improvements are sought. In addition to contributing ideas of their own, participants should suggest how ideas of others can be used to produce still another idea.[12]

It is also particularly important that no participant be an expert in the field or have any other trait that would stifle the group. In this regard, the group should be play rather than work oriented.

Reverse Brainstorming

This approach is a modification of the preceding technique. The objective of reverse brainstorming is to take a particular product, such as a dishwasher, and generate a list of its shortcomings. This list of negative attributes then provides the direction for discussion on new products and product improvements. The general advantages and disadvantages of this approach are similar to the management brainstorming technique. The limitation of this approach is that it is based on the problems of a product as perceived by management. There is no indication these are important problems for consumers.

[12] *Ibid.*, p. 156.

Problem Inventory Analysis

This is a recently developed method to generate new product ideas that uses consumers in a manner similar to focus groups. However, instead of asking the consumers to generate new product ideas themselves, consumers are provided with a list of problems from a general product category, such as food. The consumers are then asked what products have this particular problem. This method is often more effective than a focus group because it is much easier for consumers to relate known products to suggested problems and arrive at a new product idea than to generate a new product idea with minimal guidance. This approach is also an excellent way to test a new product idea.

An application of this approach in the food industry appears in Table 3-2. One of the most difficult aspects of this approach is developing an exhaustive list of all the problems. In food we see that such attributes as weight, taste, appearance, and cost affect a consumer's decision. Given a list of problems, participating consumers would indicate products associated with each problem.

Results from product inventory analysis must be interpreted very cautiously because certain answers given may not represent new product opportunities. For example, in a study of a food product 49% of the respondents mentioned that a package of cereal does not fit on the shelf well. Yet General Foods' introduction of a small compact cereal box was not a success. It appears that the perceived problem of package size has limited importance to consumers. Therefore, problem inventory analysis should be used primarily to identify product ideas for further investigation. These ideas should then be studied in depth to determine their importance to consumers.

QUALITATIVE SCREENING CRITERIA

The new product planning and developing process requires continual monitoring of all products in the product line as well as the social and competitive environments. Companies marketing both consumer and industrial products often rely more on executive judgement than anything else in evaluating individual product proposals and determining their marketability. Although judgement is probably the single most important element in the new product planning and evaluation process, it is better to facilitate that judgement by systematizing and quantifying as many of the decision elements as possible.

It is particularly important to rate the product continually and evaluate the market and financial criteria of each of the poten-

Table 3-2. Problem Inventory Analysis

Physiological	Sensory	Activities	Buying usage	Psychological/Social
A. Weight —fattening —empty calories	A. Taste —bitter —bland —salty	A. Meal planning —forget —get tired of it	A. Portability —eat away from home —take lunch	A. Serve to company —would not serve to guests —too much last minute preparation
B. Hunger —filling —still hungry after eating	B. Appearance —color —unappetizing —shape	B. Storage —run out —package would not fit	B. Portions —not enough in package —creates leftovers	B. Eating alone —too much effort to cook for oneself —depressing when prepared for just one
C. Thirst —does not quench —makes one thirsty	C. Consistency/Texture —tough —dry —greasy	C. Preparation —too much trouble —too many pots and pans —never turns out	C. Availability —out of season —not in supermarket	C. Self-image —made by a lazy cook —not served by a good mother
D. Health —indigestion —bad for teeth —keeps one awake —acidity		D. Cooking —burns —sticks	D. Spoilage —gets moldy —goes sour	
		E. Cleaning —makes a mess in oven —smells in refrigerator	E. Cost —expensive —takes expensive ingredients	

SOURCE: Edward M. Tauber, "Discovering New Product Opportunities with Problem Inventory Analysis," *Journal of Marketing* (January 1975), p. 69. Reprinted from *Journal of Marketing* published by the American Marketing Association.

tial new products. This rating is facilitated when a standard form is used. Table 3-3 is a form that can be generally applied in any particular company or product situation. Each of the qualitative screening criteria is rated from superior to poor and is assigned a standard (weight) depending on the importance of the criterion for successful commercialization. Each of the three major criteria is further delineated into specific characteristics relevant to the company situation. For example, specific product criteria include product uniqueness, use of existing facilities and skills, impact of changing economic conditions, and availability of raw materials. Once the forms have been filled out by selected company managers, the combined ratings can be used to give an indication of the probable market success of the proposal being evaluated.

The need to carefully screen each new product proposal quantifying the evaluation procedure to the extent possible has led to an increasing interest in establishing and using models for analyzing and predicting sales and profits for each new product proposal. Models are also used in evaluating variations of the introductory marketing plan for commercialization. Besides evaluation, the use of marketing models can contribute to the marketing orientation of the firm, thereby improving the company's new product performance.

TYPES OF MARKETING MODELS

There has been a growing interest in using models for evaluating and marketing new products. Models are representations or abstractions of real-world systems. They are usually logical representations of a problem. Since a model is an abstraction, it is not a perfect representation of the real-world phenomenon. Therefore, the model is always easier to understand and manipulate. In designing and implementing a model for new product planning and evaluation, a balance must be achieved between the completeness of the model (a measure of its validity) and its utility.

There are several ways to classify models. Perhaps one of the earliest classification schemes was developed by Donnelly and Ivancevich.[13] This classification scheme is based on the degree of abstraction of the models. As indicated in Figure 3-2, the least abstract models are physical ones—models that give the appearance of the actual system they represent. Although such models are easy to describe and to observe, they are very difficult to manipu-

[13] James H. Donnelly and John M. Ivancevich, *Analysis for Marketing Decisions* (Homewood, Ill.: Richard D. Irwin, 1970).

Table 3-3. Qualitative Screening Criteria

Criteria	Standard or weight	Superior	Excellent	Good	Fair	Poor	No opinion
Product criteria							
Product uniqueness							
Use of existing facilities and skills							
Patent position							
Servicing requirements							
Technical feasibility							
Technical know how							
Legal considerations							
Organizational support							
Seasonality							
Impact of changing economic conditions							
Availability of raw materials							

Table 3-3—*Continued*

Criteria	Standard or weight	Superior	Excellent	Good	Fair	Poor	No opinion
<u>Market criteria</u>							
Market size							
Market growth potential							
Customer need							
Effect on existing product line							
Distribution requirements							
Market life							
Competitive advantage							
<u>Financial criteria</u>							
Cost of entry							
Profit contribution							
Effect on cash flow							
Payback							
Return on investment							

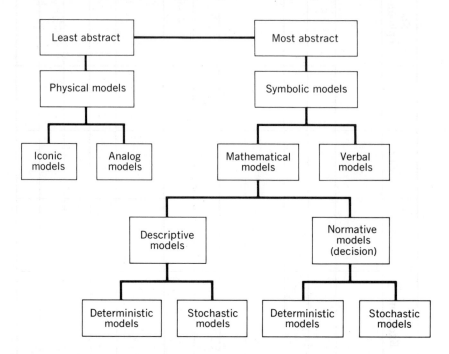

Figure 3-2. Types of Marketing Models (From James H. Donnelly and John M. Ivancevich, *Analysis for Marketing Decisions* [Homewood, Ill.: Richard D. Irwin, 1970], pp. 16, 18.)

late. For this reason, physical models are not frequently used in new product analysis and prediction. Depending on their appearance and behavior, physical models can be classified into two groups: (a) iconic, which appear like, but do not behave like, the system being represented, or (b) analog, which behave like, but do not appear like, the system being represented. As example of an iconic model for a new product would be alternative layouts for a new store. An organizational chart of a new company would be an example of an analog model.

Figure 3-2 shows that there are two types of symbolic models. These are the most abstract and are called mathematical models and verbal models. A verbal model is a written description of the system, whereas a mathematical model is a representation of a detailed system in equation form. A mathematical model often uses symbols to describe the same variables and relationships described in the verbal model. DEMON, SPECS, and SPRINTER are examples of new product mathematical models that are described later in this chapter.

Mathematical models can be further classified as either descriptive or normative. A descriptive model describes a particular phenomenon under study, such as the proposed distribution system for the new product. This model is used to provide an understanding of the process; it does not make any judgement concerning its applicability nor does it attempt to determine the best alternative. On the other hand, a descriptive model becomes a normative or decision model when it is used to evaluate several new product decision alternatives. A normative model is constructed to enable the company to select, from several alternatives, the best one for the new product under consideration.

Both descriptive and normative models can be either deterministic or stochastic in nature. When a new product model is deterministic, no chance comes into play. All of the factors surrounding the new product are considered to be exact and have determinate quantities. Although assuming that all factors are deterministic simplifies the model building process, this is usually not an accurate map of reality. Therefore, a more realistic new product model is a stochastic one. In a stochastic model conditions of uncertainty regarding the successful introduction of the new product are introduced. The uncertainty reflects data on real occurrences to the extent possible.

NEW PRODUCT MODEL DEVELOPMENT

Any manager involved in the new product development process can develop or at least aid in the development of a new product model. This can be done by helping to identify the constructs and relationships involved in the planning and marketing process. A new product manager is, of course, an important source of relevant information that can be incorporated in the model and can help establish the best parameter estimates. There are four primary steps in developing a new product model:[14]

1. Define and formulate the problem
2. Construct model
3. Test the model and develop controls
4. Implement the solution

Probably one of the most difficult tasks in developing a new product model is to define and formulate the problem in a meaningful way. This process lays the foundation for all subsequent steps. If the problem is not succinctly defined and formulated,

---

[14] This discussion is based in part on material found in Donnelly and Ivancevich, *Ibid.*, pp. 21-27.

then the model will be of little value in aiding in the planning, evaluation, or marketing of the new product. One important process in problem definition is to make the complex problem of a new product more manageable. This simplification process should be done to expedite model-building without eliminating any important variables. Three methods of simplifying the problem can be employed. The first way is to assume certainty. In some new products it may be feasible to assume that some, if not all, the variables are deterministic in nature; that is, chance does not come into play. Even if this assumption cannot be employed in the final new product model, it can be made at first to ease model development.

Simplifying relationships is another way to reduce the complexity of the problem in model building. The relationships can be assumed to be much less complex than they actually are in the new product situation being modeled. For example, linearity can be assumed (even if only on an initial basis) when the relationships among the variables are actually nonlinear.

A final way to make the problem more manageable is by isolating the operations involved in the new product planning, evaluation, and introduction processes. Each part of the problem being modeled should be isolated and broken down into its smallest components. These can be combined later in the final model if needed. In our experience with building models in the new product area, it has always been easier to combine elements than to break them down at a later date once the model has been developed.

Once the problem has been delineated, then the model must be constructed. A model is basically composed of constructs and relationships. There are three types of constructs: input, intervening, and output. Input constructs are those controllable and uncontrollable elements that are the basic components of the model. These would include such things as advertising expenditures, price of the new product, and competitive prices. Intervening constructs are those that relate the input and output constructs and often describe the state of a component. Consumer attitudes, stage in the family life cycle, and store traffic are examples of intervening constructs. Output constructs are factors such as sales, costs, demand, or profit—the results of the new product model.

Aside from constructs, relationships are the other basic part of every new product model. Basically, these specify how the constructs are related to each other. Through these relationships. the model reflects the new product marketing process.

After construction, the model must be tested before it is applied to the firm's new product operation. From this test, the effectiveness of the model can be determined on a small scale. If

any errors occur, the model can be altered before final implementation. At the same time, the necessary controls for the new product model must be established. In the dynamic environment surrounding new product planning and introduction, change is constantly occurring. Thus, tight controls are necessary to ensure that
the external environment and the variables and relationships in the
model have not dramatically changed, thereby rendering the new
product model inappropriate.

The final step in new product model development is implementation of the model in the company's operations. This is often
a more difficult task than it would seem. Some managers have
apprehensions about the usefulness of any models. This apprehen-
sion can be eased to some extent by making sure the managers
involved understand the objectives, assumptions, functions, and
limitations of the model. The advantages gained by implementing
the model and the model's solution should be particularly pointed
out.

SPECIFIC NEW PRODUCT MODELS

Several new product models have been published. Some of
these include DEMON, SPRINTER, STEAM, depth of repeat forecasting, NEWS, SPECS, PROBE, and NEWPROD. Each of these will
be discussed in terms of its composition and output.

DEMON

Decision Mapping via Optimum GO—NO Networks is a basic
new product model built on the premise that product decisions are
made in an information system in which the choice is either full-
scale product development (GO), investigate more (ON), or reject
the new product (NO).[15] The dimensions of this approach appear in
Figure 3-3. As is indicated, a GO decision means that the company
is committed to the new product and can engage in either product
or market testing before full-scale introduction. When the ON
decision is reached, more information on the new product is

[15] For a thorough presentation of DEMON see David B. Lerner, "DEMON
New Product Planning: A Case History," *Proceedings of the American
Marketing Association Conference* (June 1965), pp. 485-509; A. Charles et al.,
"DEMON: Decision Mapping via Optimum GO NO-GO Networks—A Model
for Marketing New Products," *Management Science* (July 1966), pp. 865-88;
and "DEMON: Mark II: External Equations Approach to New Product
Marketing," *System Research Report*, no. 110 (Evanston, Ill.: Northwestern
University Press, 1965).

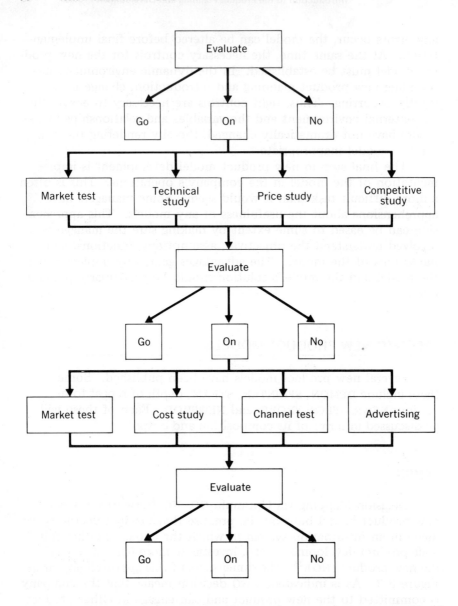

Figure 3-3. Decision Networks for New Product Evaluation in the DEMON Model
(From David B. Montgomery and Glen L. Urban, *Management
Science in Marketing*, © 1969, p. 312. Reprinted by permission of
Prentice-Hall, Inc., Englewood Cliffs, New Jersey.)

needed before a GO or NO decision can be made. When this is the case, the process is repeated. When a NO decision occurs, the new product process is discontinued.

In the DEMON model, the number of consumers trying the new product is affected by three controllable marketing variables: advertising, sales promotion, and distribution. The profits for the new product are obtained by estimating the relationship between these variables and sales over the estimated life of the product, net of costs. Uncertainties are incorporated into the model by establishing confidence limits for the best yearly sales estimates.

The DEMON model does provide good insight into the process of consumer acceptance of new products by optimizing the marketing variables of the new product situations in which the inputs can be quantified.

SPRINTER

Specifications of Profits with Interaction under Trial and Error Response was developed by Glen L. Urban.[16] The model is characterized by the classic GO—NO GO decision through the use of an information network. It is composed of three primary elements—demand, cost, and profit. The model develops an equation that describes the relationships between these elements, which maximizes the expected value of the total discounted differential of profit and uncertainty. This equation is solved through a computer simulation based on a trial-and-error technique that maximizes profits under various scenarios of price, advertising, distribution, competition, etc.

The inputs of the model via a subprogram (Marketing Reference Program) consist of various price levels, advertising expenses, distribution efforts, and life cycle. Through use of four submodels (demand, cost, differential profit, and uncertainty), the output of GO (accept the new product) or NO GO (reject the new product) is based on the probability of achieving the company's target rate of return.

Three basic versions of SPRINTER are MOD I, II, and III. SPRINTER MOD I describes the acceptance process of a new consumer product through trial, repeats, and loyalty. SPRINTER MOD II is a more detailed version that includes awareness levels

[16] The SPRINTER model is presented in Glen L. Urban, "SPRINTER: A Tool for New Product Decision Makers," *Industrial Management Review* (Spring 1967), pp. 43-54; and Glen L. Urban, "SPRINTER MOD III: A Model for the Analysis of New Frequently Purchased Consumer Products," *Operations Research* (September 1970), pp. 805-54.

and links price and advertising to the diffusion process. Sales and profits forecasts are generated for alternative strategies of the new product and its competitive products. Additional controllable variables as well as word-of-mouth communication are included in SPRINTER MOD III.

In providing a piercing view into the consumer acceptance process of new products, SPRINTER has three major advantages. First, it considers the impact of a competitive environment as well as interactions of the new product with existing products. Second, the model optimizes the marketing variables of the new product used as inputs. Finally, it allows the product manager to ask what-if questions and vary the constraints. A major disadvantage of the model is that it must have quantitative inputs that can be very expensive to collect data on.

STEAM

STEAM is a depth-of-trial-class model for new convenience products.[17] It describes the propensity of consumers to enter various product classes. This is called depth of trial class. Generally, it is a dynamic model that presumes population heterogeneity. The model uses such factors as average product use and time since last purchase. Future purchase patterns of individual households are simulated; then the results are projected to the total market. Test market data on trials and repeat purchases of households in a consumer panel serve as inputs. From this, the model produces not only the depth-of-trial-class data but simulates future sales data as well.

The STEAM model can be advantageously used for long-range forecasts of frequently purchased products. However, it does require consumer panel data on a household basis and does not take into account any promotion efforts employed after the introduction of the new product.

"Depth of Repeat" Forecasting

When making early forecasts of demand for new consumer products, a good approach is to use a depth of repeat forecasting

---

[17] See William F. Massy, "Forecasting the Demand for New Convenience Products," *Journal of Marketing Research* (November 1969), pp. 405-12; William F. Massy, "Stochastic Models for Monitoring New Product Adoptions," *Applications of the Sciences in Marketing Management*, Frank Bass, Charles King, and Edgar Pessemier, eds. (New York: Wiley, 1968), pp. 85-111; and William F. Massy, David B. Montgomery, and Donald G. Morrison, *Stochastic Models of Buying Behavior* (Cambridge, Mass.: The M.I.T. Press, 1970).

model.[18] This model, developed by Gerald J. Eskin, is similar to one of the earliest developed formal sales projection models—the Fourt-Woodlock Model.[19] Plotting the values of sales of the new product over time, the Eskin model determines which extension of the sales curve is most likely to occur. The inputs for this model are data from consumer diary panels. The model then determines whether or not the sales of the new product will grow, level out, or decay based on the initial curve.

NEWS

The New Product Early Warning System model, developed at Battan, Barton, Durstine, and Osborn, Inc., predicts the performance of a new product in a test market. The inputs for the model are such factors as amount of advertising, number of consumers exposed and number of exposures, brand awareness, product use rate, and probability of a repeat purchase. From these inputs, the model predicts a trial level for the new product, market share by purchase cycle, and short-term sales.

SPECS

The Strategic Planning, Evaluation, and Control model incorporates the Ayer New Product model for use in planning the marketing of new consumer products.[20] This model allows alternative assumptions and strategies to be evaluated prior to the actual test marketing of the new product. By putting in various levels of product, media, promotional weight, distribution, price and costs, the model forecasts probable market reaction, profit-and-loss projections, discounted cash flow, and the payback. This model is unique in that it can provide valuable information as early as the concept stage of a new product. At this stage, the inputs are, of course, subjective and are derived from norms from previously marketed new products. When data on the new product concept itself become available, then these can be used as inputs to produce more product specific results.

[18] This approach is discussed in Gerald J. Eskin, "Dynamic Forecasts of New Product Demand Using a Depth of Repeat Model," *Journal of Marketing Research* (May 1973), pp. 115-29.

[19] Louis A. Fourt and Joseph W. Woodlock, "Early Prediction of Market Success for New Grocery Products," *Journal of Marketing* (October 1960), pp. 31-38.

[20] This is described in Henry J. Claycamp and Lucien E. Liddy, "Prediction of New Product Performance: An Analytical Approach," *Journal of Marketing Research* (November 1969), pp. 414-20.

The model differs from many of the previously discussed new
product models in that its output is not a GO or NO GO decision,
but rather various forecasts for the new product. The one limitation is that the model can only be successfully implemented when
the company has had previous experience with a similar new
product.

NEWPROD

NEWPROD is a model for consumer nondurables that predicts
market share for the first year of national market introduction.[21]
It does this by simulating the number of potential buyers who are
at various stages in the adoption process. As was the case with
many of the new product models discussed, the model allows the
marketing manager to determine the sensitivity of input variables
because various combinations of key decision variables can be used.
The model incorporates key internal and external variables influencing the new product's market, such as advertising expenditures,
number of samples and coupons distributed, and awareness, trial,
and repeat purchase rates. These variables, based on actual data
from the test market and subjective estimates from the new product manager, are inputs used to predict the market share primarily
through regression analysis.

The NEWPROD model can be used to predict new product
success before any expensive test marketing is undertaken.
Another advantage is that only those variables considered critical
to the new product are used in determining market share. In
addition, such data are easily obtained, facilitating the measurement
of the effectiveness of alternative decision strategies. The only
drawback to the model, in addition to its being tested for only
consumer durable products, is that the measure of trial rate
(intention-to-buy data) may not be appropriate for discontinuous
innovations.

USES AND LIMITATIONS
OF NEW PRODUCT MODELS

One purpose of any new product model is to predict or
provide a better understanding of the new product planning and
marketing system. Relevant constructs (both internal and external)
can be delineated and the nature of the relationships between them
can be specified through the use of models. They can forecast

---

[21] See Gert Assmus, "NEWPROD: The Design and Implementation of a
New Product Model" *Journal of Marketing 39* (January 1975), pp. 16-23.

probable sales of the new product and indicate which of the decision alternatives would be best suited to the specific product/ market context.

A good new product model also serves as an information organizer. For example, any information regarding new product sales under certain competitive reactions can be summarized in an orderly fashion. This often aids in relevant discussion of various decisions regarding the new product. By providing a system for organizing information, the new product model guides the marketing research undertaken as it identifies areas in need of information (even if by default).[22]

Although a new product model can aid in new product planning, evaluation, and marketing, it may not, in all instances, impart more precision to the solution. The usefulness of the new product model is dependent upon the logic with which the model was constructed as well as the precision of the information put in. Four basic stipulations make the use of a model more effective:

1. The methodology should be explicit and easily communicated, with all assumptions clearly spelled out.

2. The methodology should be based on solid theory and testing.

3. The model should be based on hard, accurate information.

4. The model should be validated on the company's own brands, since no reliance on outside case histories is likely to be convincing. However, better and more productive methodologies should continually be sought to avoid too narrow or inbred an approach and to encourage probes into creative new areas.[23]

By making sure these four stipulations are followed, the new product manager can construct a model, which, in any event, will make the thinking and decision-making process more rigorous. Various alternative decisions can be carefully and easily evaluated to select the best one possible.

[22] For a discussion of this aspect of model building from a general viewpoint, see David A. Aaker and Charles B. Weinberg, "Interactive Marketing Models," *Journal of Marketing* (October 1975), pp. 16-23; and David B. Montgomery and Charles B. Weinberg, "Modeling Marketing Phenomena: A Managerial Perspective," *Journal of Contemporary Business* (Autumn 1973), pp. 17-43.

[23] Michael J. Naples, "First Understand Assumptions Behind Models," *Marketing News* (November 19, 1976), p. 4.

SUMMARY

The product planning and development process provides the basis for new product development. As a proposed new product idea moves through the major stages of the process—idea, concept, product development, test-marketing, and commercialization—various aspects must be constantly evaluated and monitored.

The ability of the firm to obtain and evaluate new product ideas is fundamental to its continuing success. Sources, such as consumers, distribution channels, government laws, and internal company resources, should be continuously monitored and screened for potential new products. To better use these sources, several methods for generating new product ideas could be employed. Focus groups, attribute listing, forced relationships, management brainstorming, reverse brainstorming, and problem inventory analysis are several methods useful in stimulating creativity.

The decision on whether or not a new product should be further developed or which particular marketing variable should be implemented in the product's introduction is often aided through the use of a new product model. There are various types of new product models based on their degree of abstraction. Physical models are the least abstract; symbolic ones are the most abstract. Regardless of the type, the new product model is built on a definition of the problem, construction of the model, establishment of parameters, tests of solution, and implementation.

There are many new product models, such as DEMON, SPRINTER, STEAM, depth of repeat forecasting, SPECS, PROBE, and NEWPROD. Each has certain parameters and outputs that make its usefulness dependent in part on the new product marketing conditions.

Regardless of the new product model employed, caution must be used in implementing the solution. Although a new product model is particularly useful for testing various hypotheses concerning the new product, it does not necessarily impart a precise solution. Yet, by presenting and giving an evaluation of the various alternatives, the new product model can greatly aid in the product planning and development process.

SELECTED READINGS

Assmus, Gert. "NEWPROD: The Design and Implementation of a New Product Model." *Journal of Marketing* 39 (January 1975): 16-23.

Ayal, Igal. "Simple Models for Monitoring New Product Performance." *Decision Sciences* 6 (April 1975): 221-36.

Barrett, F. D. "How to Generate New Ideas." *The Business Quarterly* 40 (Summer 1975): 33-39.

Baty, E. B. "Generating a Flow of New Product Ideas." *Machine Design* 35 (July 4, 1963): 76-79.

Bellas, C. J., and Coskun, A. "Improving New Product Planning with GERT." *California Management Review* 15 (Summer 1973): 14-21.

Breton, E. J. "Cultivating and Inducing Inventions." *Research Management* 28 (May 1975): 19-23.

Dodds, W. "Application of the Bass Model in Long Term New Product Forecasting." *Journal of Marketing Research* 10 (August 1973): 308-11.

Ellington, C. E. "Sources of New Product Ideas." *New Products/New Profits*, ed. Elizabeth Marting. Chicago: American Marketing Association, 1964.

Eskin, G. J. "Dynamic Forecasts of New Product Demand Using a Depth of Repeat Model." *Journal of Marketing Research* 10 (May 1973): 115-22.

"Generating New Product Ideas." *The Conference Board* (1972): 1-72.

Grayson, Robert A. "If You Want New Products You Better Organize to Get Them." *Marketing in a Changing World*, ed. Bernard Morin. American Marketing Association, 1969.

Harris, J. S. "How to Generate Ideas for New Products." *Business Management*, Vol. 33, no. 1 (October 1967): 83-91.

"How GM Manages Its Billion Dollar R&D Program," *Business Week* (June 28, 1976): 54.

Lanitis, T. "How to Generate New Product Ideas." *Journal of Advertising Research*, vol. 10, no. 3 (June 1970): 31-35.

Moranian, T. *The Research and Development Engineer as Manager.* New York: Holt, Rinehart and Winston, 1963.

Parssons, L. J. "Econometric Analysis of Advertising, Retail Availability and Sales of a New Brand." *Management Science* 20 (February 1974): 938-47.

Pessemier, E., and Root, H. P. "The Dimensions of New Product Planned." *Journal of Marketing* 37 (January 1973): 10-18.

Robinson, B., and Lakhani, C. "Dynamic Price Models for New Product Planning." *Management Science* 21 (June 1975): 1113-22.

Tauber, E. M. "HIT: Heuristic Ideation Technique—A Systematic Procedure for New Product Search." *Journal of Marketing* 36 (January 1972): 58-70.

Toll, Ray. "Analytical Techniques for New Product Planning." *Long-Range Planning* 1 (March 1969): 52-59.

Urban, G. L. "Perceptor: A Model for Product Positioning." *Management Science* 21 (April 1975): 858-71.

"Where Private Industry Puts Its Research Money." *Business Week* (June 28, 1976): 62.

Zwicky, Fritz. *Discovery, Invention, Research Through the Morphological Approach.* New York: Macmillan, 1966.

4

Evaluating New Product Ideas

As was indicated in the previous chapter, the product planning and development process requires a well-defined system of evaluation. At each stage of this process, critical decisions have to be made that have a great deal of uncertainty surrounding them. In order to help minimize this uncertainty, general evaluation criteria must be established. This chapter discusses these criteria and examines various screening criteria and evaluation checklists for analyzing new product proposals. The chapter concludes with a discussion of all aspects of new product research.

GENERAL EVALUATION CRITERIA

As a new product evolves, management should establish criteria, insofar as possible, by which a new product can be evaluated.[1] These criteria should be of such magnitude that products can be carefully screened at all stages of development.

Market Opportunity

There should be a new or current need for the product. This indication of adequate market demand is by far the most important

[1] For an example of a new product evaluation system, see John T. O'Meara, Jr., "Selecting Profitable Products," *Harvard Business Review* (January-February 1961), pp. 83-89; for an evaluation matrix that quantifies some qualitative considerations involved in selecting new products, see Barry M. Richman, "A Rating Scale for Product Innovation," *Business Horizons* (Summer 1962), pp. 37-44.

criterion of a proposed product. Assessing the total marketing opportunity should take into account such factors as the characteristics and attitudes of consumers or industries that may buy the product, the size of this potential market in dollars and units, the nature of the market in respect to its growth or decline, and the share of the market the product could reasonably capture.

Competition

The current competing producers, prices, and marketing policies should be evaluated, specifically in regard to their effect on the target market share of the proposed product. The new product should be able to compete successfully with products already on the market by having features that will meet or overcome current and anticipated competition. Consideration should be given to the ease with which either a present competing product could be improved or a new, strongly competitive item could be marketed.

Marketing System

It is imperative that the new product be compatible with existing management capabilities and marketing strategies. Marketing experience and expertise should be able to be fully used in this new product effort. For example, General Electric would have a far less difficult time adding a new kitchen appliance to its line than Procter and Gamble would. However, at times, the general marketing relationship may be difficult to distinguish. The new product should fit the existing marketing structure. Several factors should be considered: the degree to which the present sales force can be used, the transferability of the sales people's ability and time to the new product, the ability to sell the new product through the company's established, regular channels of distribution, and advertising and promotion required to introduce the new product.

Financial

The proposed product should fit into the company's financial structure. In this regard, the manufacturing cost per unit, sales and advertising expense per unit, the amount of capital required, and the amount of inventory required should be estimated. These estimates, combined with the price consumers would be willing to pay, will give an estimate of the length of time necessary for the product to reach the breakeven point. Finally, the long-term profit outlook for the product should be evaluated.

Production

The compatibility of the new product's production requirements with existing plant, machinery, and manpower should be determined concurrently with the financial criteria. If the new product idea cannot be integrated into existing manufacturing facilities, not only will the idea be less favorably received by management, but new plant and production costs as well as plant space must be determined if the new product is to be manufactured efficiently. Of course, all required materials should be available in sufficient quantity.

Legal

All legal requirements should be met. Before any new product idea receives further research, legal obstacles should be met and overcome. Any patentable features should be registered, the trademark protected, and all pertinent regulations adhered to.

Image

The new product should comply with, and indeed add to, the company's overall image and success. The new product idea should not be contrary to the company's established self-concept. For example, a firm normally manufacturing high-priced, high-quality, prestige merchandise should exercise great caution in adding a low-priced, low-margin item to its line.

EARLY STAGE-
TESTING OF NEW PRODUCTS

Aside from establishing criteria for each new product idea, management should be concerned with formally evaluating the idea throughout its evolution. From the marketing perspective, three pretest marketing stages can be delineated in the product's evolutionary process: the idea stage, the concept stage, and the product development stage. The relationships between these are shown in Figure 4-1. It is important in each stage to establish

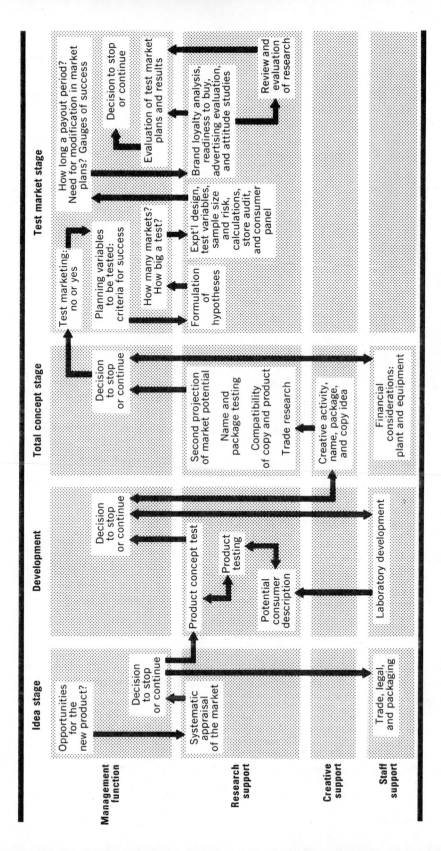

Figure 4-1. Stages in Product Development. (From Benton and Bowles Research, "Test-Marketing: New Product Must," *Printer's Ink,* vol. 279, no. 2 [April 13, 1962], p. 22.)

criteria for the decision of stop or continue the development
process. Whether or not a formal research study is conducted in
each stage depends on the firm's market and financial strengths,
the competitive environment, the newness of the product, and the
risks involved. Some products are evaluated in each of the three
pretest marketing stages; others are not. The cost of the test
market as well as the cost of failure if the product is not a success must be weighed against a long-time span before introduction
as was discussed in Chapter 3.

Idea Stage

Promising new product ideas should be identified, and imprac-
tical ones eliminated allowing maximum use of the company's
resources. One method employed in this stage is the systematic
market evaluation checklist. This is based on the premise that consumers buy ideas rather than physical products.[2] In this method each
new product idea is expressed in terms of its chief values, merits,
and benefits. Consumers are presented with these clusters of new
product values to determine which, if any, new product alternatives
should be pursued and which ones should be discarded. A company
can quickly test many new product idea alternatives with this evaluation method. Promising new product ideas can be developed more
easily without wasting resources on ideas not compatible with the
market's values.

Regardless of whether or not the market evaluation checklist
is used, it is equally important for the company to determine the
need for the new product as well as its value to the company. If
there is no need for the suggested product, then its development
should not be continued. This should also be the case if the product idea does not have any benefit or value to the firm. In order
to effectively determine the need for a new product, it is helpful
to define systemically the potential needs of the market in terms of
the kind, timing, satisfaction alternatives, benefits and risks, future
expectations, price versus product performance features and market
structure, size, and economic conditions. These factors should be
evaluated not only in terms of the characteristics of the potential new
product but also in terms of the new product's competitive strength
relative to each factor so that it can be better appraised.[3]

[2] An example of the use and importance of this process is given in
Louis Gedimen, "How to Screen New Product Ideas More Effectively,"
Printer's Ink (August 27, 1965), pp. 63-64.
[3] Checklists have been developed for appraising the need and worth
of a new product. See, for example, Schrello, Schuster Associates, Inc.,
"New Product Seminar," Long Beach, Calif., 1970.

There are two general methods for initially assessing the need for a new product on a very general basis: the SIC code method and the input/output method. One method that is very appropriate for an initial appraisal of the need for industrial products is the Standard Industrial Classification System (SIC). Standard Industrial Classifications are means by which the federal government classifies manufacturing industries. It is based on the product produced or operation performed. Each industry is assigned a two-digit, three-digit, and four-digit code. There are 82 two-digit industry groupings, such as 01 Agricultural Production–Crops, 23 Apparel and Other Textile Products, 50 Wholesale Trade–Durable Goods, 57 Furniture and Home Furnishing Stores, 62 Security, Commodity Brokers and Services, 70 Amusement and Recreation Services, and 94 Administration of Human Resources. Each two-digit grouping is further broken down into three- and four-digit groups, depending on the industry grouping being considered. For example, the three-digit groups for 72 Personal Services are: 721 Laundry, Cleaning and Garment Services; 722 Photographic Studios, Portrait; 723 Beauty Shops; 724 Barber Shops; 725 Show Repair and Hat Cleaning Shops; 726 Funeral Services and Crematories; and 729 Miscellaneous Personal Services. Where needed each three-digit group is further refined. The 721 Laundry, Cleaning and Garment Services includes such categories as 7211 Power Laundries, family and commercial; 7214 Diaper Service; 7215 Coin-Operated Laundries and Cleaning; and 7217 Carpet and Upholstery Cleaning.

To determine the primary market demand using the SIC method, it is necessary to first delineate all the possible categories that have a need for the product or service being considered. Once the groups have been selected, the appropriate base for the demand determination must be established and the published material on the industry groups obtained from the *Census of Manufacturers*. Then the primary demand can be determined from the relationship established.

Consider the primary demand estimation problem facing the KeKa Corporation, a small manufacturer of a grill cleaning compound that cleans hot working grills better than any commercial product available. The company is located in the Chicago area. Although the cleaning compound would be of interest to homemakers, the firm will look into this market at a later date because of its limited resources. The more easily accessible market is commercial restaurants. The SIC code for this market is 58 Eating and Drinking Places. This two-digit category is composed of 5812 Eating Places and 5813 Drinking Places. Since the company is not sure whether or not it has the capability of initially marketing the product on a nationwide basis, the information on this SIC code is obtained from the *Census of Business*, specifically the *Census of Retail Trade* on both a national and state basis. These figures are indicated in Table 4-1.

KeKa's management believes that due to the characteristics of the product, eating places would be the most likely prospects. As is indicated in Table 4-1 there are 253,136 eating places in the United States and 13,634 in the state of Illinois. Since the company believes that each would use approximately 1 gallon of the grill cleaner every other week these represent a potential primary demand of 6,636,536 gallons each year on a national basis and 354,484 gallons in Illinois. It appears that there is indeed a viable primary market for the grill cleaner on both a national and a state basis. From this point, KeKa's corporation can further analyze the market by evaluating the number of products presently on the market, the strength of the competition, and the market's growth rate before finally deciding on market entrance.

Another technique for evaluating the need for a particular product or product category is the input/output method. A table can be used to determine the number and size of the transactions occurring within specific sectors of the total economy. On a macro basis this table provides a summary of all exchanges between each industry grouping as well as between all industries and the final consumer. Although the total input/output structure of the U.S. economy is given on an 85-industry category basis, a sample is presented in Table 4-2.

The table reveals that household furniture sold more than four-fifths of its output to final markets and would therefore be strongly affected by any changes occurring in these markets. On the other hand, wooden containers sold almost all of its output to intermediate customers and would therefore only be indirectly affected by changes in the final markets.

The relative primary demand among industries can be derived from input/output tables by allocating the proportion of total sales of an industry to each particular industry segment. For example, of the $12,905 million of lumber and wood products except for containers, 1.5% were sold to the wooden container industry, 5.2% to the household furniture industry, and 9.2% to the paper and allied products (excluding containers) industry. This suggests that future new product efforts of the lumber and wood products group would be best oriented toward the latter industry group, as it provided the largest share of previous industry business.

Input/output tables allow at least an initial evaluation of possible primary market demand. Although these derivations are not intended to be all-inclusive indications of the market potential, they can provide a method for determining which

Table 4-1. Statistics on Eating and Drinking Places for the Total United States and the State of Illinois

1972 SIC CODE	Kind of Business	Number	Sales ($1,000)	Operated by Unincorporated Businesses — Sole Proprietorships (number)	Operated by Unincorporated Businesses — Partnerships (number)	Establishments with Payroll — Number	Establishments with Payroll — Sales ($1,000)	Establishments with Payroll — Paid Employees for Week Including March 12 (number)
58	Total United States	359,524	36,867,707	164,023	34,778	287,250	35,047,577	2,634,457
5812	Eating Places	253,136	30,385,361	108,159	23,986	208,899	29,312,731	2,317,425
5812	Restaurants and lunchrooms					112,656	16,652,826	1,353,843
5812	Social caterers					3,944	663,046	51,592
5812	Cafeterias					8,162	1,587,166	127,399
5812	Refreshment places					72,850	8,537,626	634,813
5812	Contract feeding					5,836	1,515,755	122,008
5812	Ice cream, frozen custard stands					5,451	356,312	27,770
5813	Drinking places (alcoholic beverages)	106,388	6,482,346	55,864	10,792	78,351	5,734,846	317,032
58	Total Illinois	21,388	2,254,889	10,904	2,065	16,110	2,106,897	157,412
5812	Eating places	13,634	1,790,811	6,022	1,450	11,278	1,736,663	139,036
5812	Restaurants and lunchrooms					6,105	1,006,134	82,711
5812	Cafeterias					383	75,724	6,528
5812	Refreshment places					3,798	485,001	36,458
5812	Other eating places					992	169,804	13,339
5813	Drinking places (alcoholic beverages)	7,754	464,078	4,882	615	4,832	370,234	18,376

SOURCE: *Census of Retail Trade Summary and Area Statistics* (1972).

Table 4-2. United States Input-output Table (in millions of dollars)

Industry	Lumber and wood products, except containers	Wooden containers	Household furniture	Other furniture and fixtures	Paper and allied products, except containers	Paperboard containers and boxes	Personal consumption expenditures	Net inventory change	Total federal government purchases	Total state and local government purchases	Total
Lumber and wood products, except containers	3,492	198	702	170	1,186	13	259	121	30	4	12,905
Wooden containers	33	17	2	1	1			3	24		543
Household furniture	29	4	78	55	1	1	3,861	49	56	28	5,122
Other furniture and fixtures	8		16	70	1	1	174	41	89	297	2,822
Paper and allied products, except containers	67	2	8	7	2,683	2,444	1,502	228	116	179	16,733
Paperboard containers and boxes	24	3	65	34	338	109	73	39	34	21	6,031

SOURCE: This is an abbreviated table to give an indication of the complete tables found in *Survey of Current Business* (February, 1974).

markets for the new product need further analysis. Once the markets have been selected, the appropriate market research can be undertaken to define the exact nature of the market and its value to the firm. By comparing these, the opportunities the idea affords can be appraised.

In determining the worth of the new product to the firm, various considerations must be made. Financial scheduling, such as cash outflow, cash inflow, contribution to profit, and return on investment, should be synchronized with other product ideas as well as investment alternatives. In this determination, it is especially important to be as definite as possible of the dollar amount of each of the considerations important to the new product idea. These dollar amounts should be estimated for each item regardless of accuracy so that a quantitative evaluation can be made. These figures, of course, can be revised as better information becomes available.

Concept Stage

After a new product has been determined as promising, it will then be further developed and refined through the interaction with consumers. In the concept stage, the refined product idea is tested to determine consumer acceptance without incurring the costs of making the physical product; that is, initial reactions to the concept are obtained from potential customers or members of the distribution channels, if appropriate.[4] One method used to measure consumer acceptance is conversational interviews. Selected respondents are exposed to statements that reflect the physical characteristics and attributes of the product idea. Where competing products exist, these statements can be used to compare the primary features of existing products. Favorable as well as unfavorable product features can be uncovered from analyzing the consumers' response. Favorable features can then be incorporated into the product, avoiding the difficulties if product prototypes must be changed. It should be remembered that the concept test is designed to determine only consumer interest in the basic idea of the product. It gives an indication of whether or not the product idea should be developed further. It is not a substitute for product testing. By discovering any major deficiencies in the product idea, the concept test results can direct research and development to culminate in a more marketable product.

[4] For a discussion of the importance and implementation of concept testing, see A. R. Kroeger, "Test Marketing: The Concept and How It Is Changing," *Media Scope* (December 1966), pp. 63-68.

Various aspects of the concept, such as its features, price, and promotion, must be evaluated to determine the viability of the concept. These aspects should be considered for both the concept being studied as well as for any major competing products. This way, any deficiencies or benefits can be noted. By pointing out any major deficiencies in the product concept, the test results can direct any research and development to present a more marketable product.

The idea and concept stages are properly termed pretesting stages. It is in these stages that interest in a product idea is determined and refinement of the product idea can be achieved without incurring the direct and indirect costs of actually manufacturing prototypes. The need for these techniques is determined by the nature of the new product and the time available for its testing. For example, a technically complex product that would be difficult to describe so that consumers can grasp its various features would not be as suitable for pretesting as a product idea that is less complex. Evidence in support of this strategy (see Chapter 7) indicates that the complexity of an innovation is inversely proportional to the rate of adoption.

Product Development Stage

The product development stage is the last stage of product evaluation. Test-marketing will be the next step. Product development is the determination of consumer reaction to the physical product. One method frequently used is *the consumer panel.* A panel of potential consumers is given product samples to use. Participants keep a record of when they use the product and comment on its virtues and deficiencies.

There are several weaknesses in this method. Consumers tend to react favorably to all products they test. Moreover, consumers often make erroneous comparisons between the new product and one previously used (i.e., the attributes of the previously used product are incorrectly recalled). The extent of this problem is, as yet, undetermined. These difficulties have led to the use of other testing procedures. One that is commonly used is to give a panel of potential consumers a sample of the product to test and one or more competitive products simultaneously. For example, one test product may be already on the market, whereas the other test product is new, or both products may be new with some significant variation between them. Then, one of several methods, such as multiple brand comparisons, risk analysis, level of repeat purchases, or intensity of preference analysis, is used to determine consumer preference.

When measuring consumer preference, any effect of the manufacturer's corporate or brand name must be eliminated by identifying the products in an equally obscure way. Care must be taken so that even the packages do not bias the results. For example, a test product packaged in a white container may be preferred over one in a yellow container not because the first product has outstanding attributes but merely because panel members are more accustomed to products of this type being in a white package.

In using consumer panels to test a new product in the development stage, those consumers selected should represent a segment of the market that has a buying interest in the product being tested. Then, a paired comparison or monadic test can be used.

Paired comparison tests are generally of two types: side-by-side tests or staggered tests. Each type normally uses two unidentified products—a manufacturer's potential product and a leading competitive counterpart already on the market.[5] In the side-by-side test the two products are judged simultaneously, whereas in the staggered test each product is judged separately in a short time. In using the side-by-side test, care must be taken not to overevaluate the results. Small product differences, which may be of little (if any) importance to the actual marketing of the product, may often be magnified. The staggered test, on the other hand, is more like the usual consumer use situation, because a consumer generally tries one brand after another, before selecting the preferred product. However, the results in a staggered test can be seriously affected by the sequence in which the products are tested. For example, in a staggered test comparing two grades of women's stockings, the product tested second was preferred to that tested first among the women in the panel. When the women were asked to rate the stockings on product attributes such as resiliency and durability, the stocking worn first tended to be regarded more favorably.[6]

In the monadic test, only one product is evaluated by the panel. Therefore, it is necessary when comparing two different products to employ two separate panels, one for each product. In a monadic test, various scales are used to derive rating criteria for the proposed new product. The ratings are then compared on either a combined or separate basis with ratings given

[5] The comparison with a product already being marketed makes it possible to use the test results to forecast probable sales for the new product. The use of these results in this manner, however, has some problems that are discussed in Chapter 5, "Forecasting New Product Sales."

[6] Allan Greenberg, "Paired Comparisons in Consumer Product Tests," *Journal of Marketing* (April 1958), pp. 411-14.

to a competitive product by a different consumer panel. By allowing for enumerations of various product attributes without specific comparison with any other product, the monadic test gives less restrictive results in a shorter period of time.[7]

When testing a new product in the product development stage with either the paired comparison or monadic method, care must be taken in the selection of the consumer panel. The panel should be of sufficient size, and members should have the appropriate characteristics so that the panel is representative of potential users. For example, if the innovator and early adopter (identified in Chapter 3) are not represented, the results may be misleading because their initial response to a new product is so critical. Results can also be affected by the length of product use and the methodology of the test. A test should be conducted over a sufficient period and under conditions as normal as possible to reflect true use patterns. The test should be designed to test product characteristics, to show the competitive strengths of the product. Any other variables in the marketing mix that are simultaneously tested may hide the true strengths and weaknesses of the product.

RESEARCH DESIGN

When research is conducted in the idea, concept, or product development stages, it is very important that the group of consumers to be studied is defined correctly. A subset of consumers should be selected so that the total potential market is represented. Once the group has been defined (the determination of the population), several techniques can be employed to select those who will represent this population. The technique selected for a given new product depends on cost and time limitations as well as on the importance of the decision.

Determination of Population

After it has been decided to use consumers in testing the new product, the first step is to define the population to be studied. All individuals possessing characteristics relevant to the problem must be enumerated. This is often one of the most difficult tasks in evaluating a new product because a variety of factors enter into the

---

[7]For a thorough discussion of the use and comparative results of paired comparison and monadic tests, see Jack Platten, "Where to Test and for What?" *Printer's Ink* (May 29, 1964), pp. 118-19; and Jean Caul and Shirley Raymond, "Principles of Consumer Product Testing," *Journal of Social Cosmetic Chemists* (May 1965), pp. 763-76.

decision. For example, it might be important for the population from which the sample will be selected to be differentiated according to product use; that is, when the new product is eventually marketed, its purchasers will be composed of new purchasers as well as brand switchers. The number of new purchasers that includes former users of a previously purchased brand can give a clear indication of the market share the new product may attain. In addition, by discerning the reasons for switching, buyers can be categorized according to the degree of their brand-switching tendency. This tendency can differentiate consumers who may be expected to continue to buy the new product from those who will switch brands once another alternative is available. Other factors to consider are large-volume versus low-volume consumers, the length of time needed to establish repeat purchasing, and the degree of innovativeness of the consumers purchasing the product.[8]

In light of these factors, a list of the members of the defined population should be accumulated. This list would ideally include the name, address, telephone number, and any appropriate characteristics of each consumer in the population. Sometimes this is a comparatively easy task. For example, if a company is interested in surveying automobile owners, a complete registration list can be obtained from the state department of motor vehicles or a commercial list broker such as R. L. Polk and Company.

Specialized lists for certain product categories are often available from list brokers, trade associations, government agencies, or the records of the firm. If there are no lists available, the company can compile a list from tract maps and a directory that indexes telephone subscribers by city and street. Although this list would contain only the address and telephone number of each resident in an area, the company can be sure, to a certain extent, that the population is at least segmented by economic and ethnic characteristics.

Selection of Sample

Once the population has been defined, one must decide the best way to represent this population within the company's time and cost constraints. Figure 4-2 shows that the two classes of sampling techniques must be evaluated according to the best way to collect data from that portion of the population (the sample) that will give accurate information about the entire population.

---

[8] For a brief description of some of these factors see Edgar A. Pessemier, *New Product Decisions: An Analytical Approach* (New York: McGraw-Hill, 1966), pp. 175-80.

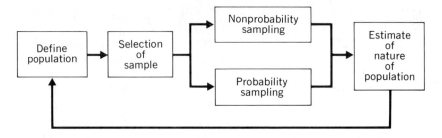

Figure 4-2. Designing a Market Test Sample

The company must obtain as much information as possible about the population with each unit of cost.

The first step is to select the sample either by a probability or nonprobability method. A nonprobability method is one in which the company uses subjective judgment to decide the size and composition of the sample. Generally, this is a simpler method than probability sampling because it relies on the judgment of a member of the company or of an outside expert or on the use of a previously used list of consumers. The accuracy of the new product test results depends on the soundness of the judgment or mailing list.

Judgment samples are often used during the exploratory phase of researching the new product, when the company is attempting to get an early indication of problems or wants to pretest a questionnaire for clarity and reliability of responses. In other words, the company is not trying to gather data that can be statistically evaluated or generalized to the entire population. Sometimes, it is possible to use a judgment sample to select consumers who are truly representative of the population. This is especially true in the case of industrial products. For example, if a company is testing a new product that could be used only in certain types of automobiles, a judgment sample could be as reliable and representative as a probability sample. Often, judgment and probability samples are combined as in the case in which a portion of the population, such as the residents of Indianapolis, may be selected using management's judgment, and a probability sample is drawn from this population. In this case, statistical testing methods may be used to generalize the sample results to the entire city, but not to the entire population. Additional cities would be needed to generalize to the entire population.

When using nonprobability sampling, it is not possible to use statistical techniques to evaluate the results. Therefore, to achieve objectivity in the sample, probability methods are used most often. In a probability sample, every consumer has a known probability of being selected; there is a variety of sampling techniques that can be used. Simple random sampling, stratified sampling, cluster sampling, multistage sampling, or systematic sampling are all examples.[9]

Simple random sampling means that each consumer has the same chance of being in the sample. In other words, if the defined population contains 20,000 consumers and 300 are randomly selected, the company would have a simple random sample. But how can the members of the 300 be selected so that each consumer in the population of 20,000 has an equal chance of being in the sample? This may seem to be a very simple process, but unless great care is taken, usually some subjective bias occurs. An easy way to avoid subjective biases in the selection of samples is to use a table of random numbers. By using any of the available standard random number tables, the sample can be obtained without any bias.[10] One must be careful in using these tables in new product research to distinguish between sampling with replacement and sampling without replacement. When sampling the population of 20,000 consumers with a sample of 300 without replacement, the probability that any single consumer will be selected is 1 in 20,000. Because one consumer is selected and removed from the total population of 20,000 (sampling without replacement), the probability of selection of the second consumer will be 1 in 19,999, and so forth. When sampling with replacement, the selected consumers are not removed. Thus, even though a consumer has already been selected, he or she still has a chance of being selected for the sample a second or even a third time. The probability of every selection remains at 1/20,000. Sample selection for new product research is generally done without replacement.

The first step in the sample survey is to project from the sample the parameters of the population. Specifically, the mean ($\overline{X}$), the standard deviation (S), and sometimes the proportion (p) of the sample must be determined. Each of these characteristics is used to project its counterpart in the population. In other words, the sample mean ($\overline{X}$) is used as an estimate of the population mean (μ); the sample standard deviation (S) is used to

[9]For a thorough presentation of the methodology of these and other sampling techniques, see Morris H. Hanse, William N. Hurwitz, and William G. Madow, *Sampling Survey Methods and Theory*, vol. I (New York: Wiley, 1966); or William G. Cochran, *Sampling Techniques* (New York: Wiley, 1963).

[10]Although there are many random number tables available, the following three are perhaps the most well known and most convenient to use: M. G. Kendall and B. B. Smith, *Tables of Random Sampling Numbers* (New York: Cambridge University Press, 1954); *Table of 105,000 Random Decimal Digits* (Washington, D.C.: Interstate Commerce Commission, Bureau of Transport Economics and Statistics, 1949); or Rand Corporation, *A Million Digits* (New York: The Free Press, 1955).

estimate the true standard deviation of the population (σ); and the sample proportion ($\hat{p}$) is used as an estimate of the population proportion (P).[11]

Any size sample can be obtained by using simple random sampling, but it might not be as efficient as other techniques in terms of the time and cost. For example, if there are certain known demographic or economic characteristics that must appear in the sample, then the *stratified sampling technique* may be superior.

In *stratified sampling*, the defined population is divided into layers called strata such that elements within each layer are as similar as possible (see Figure 4-3). For example, one company test marketing a new chili product thought it necessary to ensure that the sample contained final consumers who had been using frozen chili, canned chili, and homemade chili. Therefore, the population was divided into these three strata, and final consumers were selected from each stratum and given the new chili product to try. This example shows the population is stratified on the basis of characteristics related to the information desired. The more similar the elements within each stratum, the more efficient the sample. Stratified sampling can be used when elements in each stratum are not similar, but it will not be as efficient in terms of time and cost.

In the new chili product example, it was shown that the critical factor in stratified sampling is judgment, breaking the units of the population into strata so that the members within each stratum are as similar as possible.

Because the producer of the new product will not be able to stratify based on the characteristic being measured—that is, on how well consumers like the new product or how many they will purchase—a characteristic that is highly correlated to the characteristic to be measured is used. If many potential characteristics for stratification are available, regression analysis should be used to determine which characteristic is most closely related.[12] For example, one case involved establishing a new, statewide preventive maintenance system for Bell Telephone. The best sampling procedure was needed to determine the conditions of telephone poles in the state so that those in the worst condition could be repaired or replaced. This procedure would avoid disrupting

---

[11] The exact sampling methodology for simple random sampling, stratified sampling and cluster sampling is found in the appendix at the end of this chapter.

[12] Although the use of regression analysis in determining the best variable for stratification is beyond the scope of this book, a good, thorough explanation of regression analysis can be found in N. R. Draper and H. Smith, *Applied Regression Analysis* (New York: Wiley, 1966).

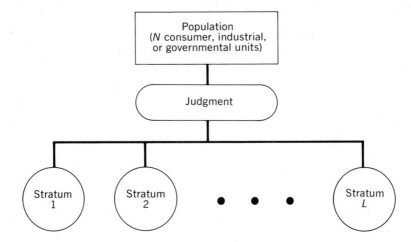

Figure 4-3. Stratified Sampling in New Product Research

service as well as more expensive repairs if the pole were to break. The only information available was the year poles were installed, their height, and their location. Which of these factors were most closely correlated to the information being sought—the condition of the poles?

Obviously, the statement that the condition of the pole is a function of its height is not reasonable at all. The condition of the pole as a function of its geographic location could be a possibility, especially if the region has wide differences in temperatures or if some poles were more apt to be involved in automobile accidents. However, the best single prediction of the condition of the pole is the year the pole was installed. The condition of the pole should be excellent when it is new, and it should deteriorate over the years. This example demonstrates the importance of judgment in stratified sampling. Without a good determination of the best stratification criteria, stratified sampling has no more value in terms of time and money than simple random sampling.

Once the strata have been delineated, a similar procedure to that used in simple random sampling is used to determine the mean, standard deviation, interval estimates, and sample size. As was the case with simple random sampling, either variable or percentage information (or both) on the new product can be the basis for the determinations.

Although the company may be primarily interested in segmenting the population by relevant characteristics, such as the type of product presently used, if such information is not available or if there is a great distance between the units, *cluster sampling* may be more efficient (see Figure 4-4). In cluster sampling, the

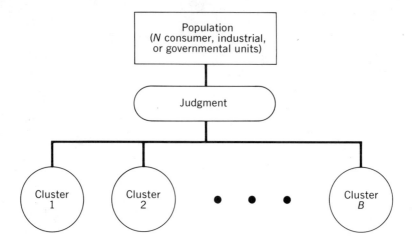

Figure 4-4. Cluster Sampling in New Product Research

population is grouped into clusters based upon physical location. For example, one company wanted to test industrial consumers' response to a newly developed valve. Because the population of the potential customers was located throughout the United States, these customers were first grouped into eight clusters, each representing a group of industrial customers. A sample was then drawn from each group. In this way, the company was assured of obtaining results from various regions of the country, each with its different climate conditions. Cluster sampling is most efficient when the consumers within each cluster are as different as possible and the means of each cluster as similar as possible.

The use of cluster sampling in new product research has several advantages. First, precise information on the nature of the consumer's attitude can be obtained without sampling the entire area; therefore, less time and travel costs would be incurred. Second, information is needed only on the primary sampling units (the clusters). Because the units within each cluster must only be identified in the first stage sampling, a substantial cost savings is achieved if it is very expensive to obtain information on the population. Finally, cluster sampling is generally faster and cheaper than simple random sampling for a given sample size.

These advantages must be balanced against several disadvantages. First, the precision of cluster sampling is much lower than that of simple random sampling for a given sample size. Although it can often be alleviated by using a larger sample at no extra cost, this problem should still be considered when choosing a sampling technique. Another major drawback of cluster sampling is that it is very difficult to determine the sample sizes required before instituting the research. Even though these disadvantages are troublesome, cluster sampling is frequently used in new product research, especially for new industrial products where the customers are geographically dispersed.

A fourth technique that can be used in new product research is *multistage sampling*. Several sampling techniques are used in stages. For example, if a company testing a new valve also wanted to stratify the companies in eight geographic clusters by firm size before selecting the sample, a multistage sampling technique would be used. This technique allows the testing company to balance the costs of obtaining the sample with the reliability desired of the information on the new product.

If the selection process itself is costly or if there is little information available concerning the population, then *systematic sampling* may be best. The mechanics of taking a systematic sample are not at all complex. If the defined population (N) consists of consumers in some order and if the desired sample size is n units, then every N/n unit in the population is chosen after the first consumer is chosen at random. For example, one company had a list of 20,000 potential customers for its newly designed projector fading unit (a device for fading slide pictures in and out). The only information known about these 20,000 customers was the name, address, and telephone number of each. A sample size of 400 was desired so the 28th customer from the first 50 customers on the list was chosen because 20,000 divided by 400 gives groups of 50; the 28th is randomly determined. This customer was the first customer in the sample, the second customer was the 78th (28 + 50 = 78), and the third was the 128th (78 + 50 = 128). In systematic sampling, the order of the elements can either have no effect, or they can increase or decrease the reliability of the sample.

Regardless of the sampling technique used to select the sample for researching the new product, care must be taken so that inaccurate information is not collected. Consumers have the tendency to give positive ratings to new products, especially if they believe that using the product enhances their status. In addition, outside distractions may affect the response as well as bias in the phrasing or sequencing of the questions. To overcome these difficulties, proper scaling and questionnaire design is imperative.[13]

[13] An example of some of these difficulties is given in Robert N. Reitter, "Product Testing in Segmented Markets," *Journal of Marketing Research* (May 1969), pp. 179-84.

QUESTIONNAIRE
DESIGN FOR NEW PRODUCTS

In designing the questionnaire for any new product research, the type of questions used depends upon the type of information sought, the method of data collection, the coding and tabulation requirements, and precautions necessary to avoid influencing the respondent. Types of questions available for use, a sample question, and some advantages and disadvantages in the use of each are presented in Table 4-3. A dichotomous question is one in which the respondent can only give one of two possible answers. Although such questions are generally easy to ask and easy to answer, they often yield biased answers. Respondents may be far more positive than they will in their purchasing behavior.

One way to avoid the arbitrary answer of dichotomous questions is to use multiple-choice questions. These questions still retain the advantages of easy to ask, answer, and tabulate. However, one must be sure that the choices presented are all-encompassing.

One type of question that is very similar to the multiple-choice question is the preference question. These questions yield information on a respondent's view of which of alternative products, packages, or prices is most preferred. Even though the preference indicated may not reflect the actual purchase choice, valuable information is obtained on what consumers like best among the options presented.

An important technique for obtaining opinions about various attributes of the new product is the rating question. Respondents are asked to indicate on a scale their feelings about various product features. Care must be taken to ensure that the distinctions on the scale are very clear and commensurate with the respondents' knowledge. This technique produces a wide range of responses on product features. If many features are used, the ratings of one attribute can be compared with those of another attribute to obtain the relative importance of each new product attribute.

If the testing firm wishes to find the order of preference of various new product alternatives, then the ranking question is used. In this technique the respondent indicates the order of preference of the alternatives given. Although this provides sound information on relative consumer opinions on products or attributes, it has been the most confusing of all types of questioning in our experience. Instructions must be provided to help consumers answer this type of question carefully and thoroughly. No more than five alternatives should be presented at one time, and the alternatives must be commensurate with respondents' knowledge. Even with these precautions, other questions should be included

Table 4-3. Questionnaire Design for New Product Research

Questioning techniques	Example	Advantages	Disadvantages
Dichotomous questions	Do you usually like to try new products? Yes No	1. Easy to answer 2. Can be used to screen before asking further questions 3. Easy to tabulate 4. Provides definite answer	1. Forces a choice 2. Provides no detailed information
Multiple choice	Which of the following four packages do you like? Package A Package B Package C Package D	1. Usually avoids forcing an arbitrary choice 2. Easy to answer 3. Easy to tabulate	1. Choices may not be all encompassing 2. Choices may not be clearly distinctive
Preference	Which of these products do you most prefer? Brand A Brand B Brand C Brand D	1. Gives information on preference 2. Easy to respond	1. Preference may not reflect purchase choice 2. Choices may present some confusion

(Continued)

Table 4-3—*Continued*

Questioning techniques	Example	Advantages	Disadvantages
Rating	On a scale from one to nine (with 1 being did not like at all and 9 being liked it very much) indicate your overall feelings about the new product by circling the number that corresponds to your feeling Did not like at all Like very much 1 2 3 4 5 6 7 8 9	1. Gives important information on relative feelings about various product attributes 2. Does not force an arbitrary choice 3. Provides a wide range of responses for comparative purposes	1. Distinctions on scale may not be clear to respondent 2. Provides scale gradations that may not be commensurate with knowledge of respondent

Ranking	Rank in order from one to five (with 1 being the best and 5 the worst) your opinion of the following products
	
	    Product A
	    Product B
	    Product C
	    Product D
	    Product E
		1. Provides valuable information on relative consumer opinions on products or attributes
		2. Provides a definite answer
		3. Yields information quickly
			1. Is probably the most confusing type of question for the consumer to answer
			2. Provides no information on how good the best product is
			3. Provides no information on relative differences between ranks of products

Open-ended questions	Why do you buy that particular product? _____	1. Does not bias respondent's response with established answers 2. Provides a wide range of information 3. Provides information of more depth	1. Interpretation of answers requires skill and may vary between interpreters 2. Difficult to tabulate

in the new product research to provide information in case respondents become confused by the ranking questions.

The last type of question useful in product research is the open-ended question. Although the responses are often difficult to tabulate and sometimes are not definitive, they do provide information without restricting respondents to an established answer. Open-ended questions are especially useful when used in conjunction with other, previously discussed questioning techniques.

SUMMARY

The ability of the firm to obtain and evaluate new product ideas is fundamental to its continuing success. In the new product process, it is very important to establish evaluation criteria that include all important aspects relevant to new product success. Guidelines in such areas as market opportunity and the marketing, financial, and production capability of the firm should be criteria with which the new product idea can be evaluated. Specific evaluation stages (the idea stage, concept stage, and product development stage) are useful in formally evaluating the product as it evolves.

In any type of sampling, one must be careful in defining the population, selecting the sample, and designing the questionnaire. Simple random, stratified, cluster, multistage, or systematic sampling can be used to select those consumers who will represent the population so that time and cost constraints can be met. Effective evaluation of the new product is needed as the idea evolves along its evolutionary process so that test marketing (the topic of the next chapter) is employed only where warranted.

SELECTED READINGS

Benge, E. J. "That New Product Idea." *Sales Management,* vol. 88, no. 7 (April 6, 1962): 95-96.

Crawford, C. Merle. "Marketing Research and the New Product Failure Rate." *Journal of Marketing* (April 1977):51-61.

————. "Strategies for New Product Development." *Business Horizons* 15 (December 1972):49-57.

————. "Unsolicited Product Ideas—Handle With Care." *Research Management* 18 (January 1975):19-24.

Dunlavey, D. C. "Protection of Inventor Outside the Patent System." 43 *California Law Review* 457, March 1968.

Forman, Howard I. "Problems Involved in the Protection, Buying and Selling of Inventories." 41 *Journal of Patent Office Society* 531, 1959.

Fox, H. W. "New Products: How to Overcome Internal Barriers." *Carroll Business Bulletin* 13 (September 1973):17-19.

Freimer, M., and Simon, L. S. "The Evaluation of Potential New Product Alternatives." *Management Science B* 13 (February 1967):279-92.

Globe, S.; Levy, G. W.; and Schwartz, C. M. "Key Factors in the Innovation Process." *Research Management* (July 1973):8-15.

Goslin, Lewis N. *The Product Planning System.* Homewood, Ill.: Richard D. Irwin, 1967.

Haas, Raymond M. *Long-Range New Product Planning in Business.* Bloomington, Ind.: Indiana University, Graduate School of Business, Bureau of Business Research, 1964.

Hamilton, H. Ronald. "Screening Business Development Opportunities," *Business Horizons* 17 (August 1974):13-24.

Holt, Knut. "Information and Needs Analysis in Idea Generation." *Research Management* 18 (May 1975):24-27.

Jackson, Thomas W., and Spurlock, Jack M. *Research and Development Management.* Homewood, Ill.: Dow Jones-Irwin, 1966.

Little, B. "New Focus on New Product Ideas." *The Business Quarterly* 39 (Summer 1974):62-69.

Lorsch, Jay W. *Product Innovation and Organization.* New York: Macmillan, 1965.

Martin, J. C., and Springate, J. R. "Protecting of Businessman's Proprietary Information." 32 *Louisiana Law Review* 497, June 1972.

Schneider, J., and Halstrom, F. N. "Program for Protecting Proprietary Information." 18 *Practicing Law* 71, October 1972.

"Screening New Product Ideas." *Marketing and the New Science of Planning,* ed. Robert L. King. *AMA Fall Conference Proceedings,* Series No. 28. American Marketing Association, August 1968, pp. 99-104.

Success and Failure in Industrial Innovation, Report on the Project Sappho by the Science Policy Research Unit of the University of Sussex Centre for the Study of Industrial Innovation, London, 1972, p. 36.

Virkkala, V. "Observations and Suggestions Concerning Creativity Training and Industrial Environment." Paper for the FEANI Seminar, "Creativity and Innovation—a Challenge of the World to the Capability of Engineers." Barcelona, October 7-10, 1974.

Zarecor, W. D. "High Technology Product Planning." *Harvard Business Review* 53 (January-February 1975):108-115.

Appendix to Chapter Four— Sampling Methodology for New Product Evaluation

Exact sampling methodology in simple random sampling depends on whether the information about the new product is a variable or a percentage. If it is a variable, the information deals with how much.[1] The data desired have a continuous measurement scale, such as how well a consumer likes a new product on a predetermined rating scale. The major items to be determined for the variables being investigated are the mean and the projectable total within a given confidence interval. On the other hand, when information about the new product is percentages, the sampling is done to determine how many. This involves determining the number, converting this figure to a percentage, then projecting it to a total percentage within a given confidence interval.

To determine how well a consumer likes the new product (variable sampling), the mean ($\overline{X}$) and standard deviation (S) of the selected sample size (n) from a population (N) must be calculated by using the following formulas:

$$\overline{X} = \frac{\sum_{i=1}^{n} X_i}{n} \tag{1}$$

where $\overline{X}$ = the sample mean (this is a point estimate of the universe mean μ)

[1] These formulas as well as those for both stratified and cluster sampling were adopted from Mathematica, Inc. and FMP, Inc., *A Course of Instruction in Statistical Sampling for D.O.C. Contract Audits* (Princeton, N.J., 1973).

X_i = each individual value

n = number in the sample

$$s = \sqrt{\frac{\sum\limits_{i=1}^{n} (X_i - \overline{X})^2}{n - 1}} \qquad (2)$$

where s = sample standard deviation

Once the sample's standard deviation has been determined, it can be used to estimate the standard deviation of the mean ($\hat{\sigma}_{\overline{X}}$) through the following formula:

$$\hat{\sigma}_{\overline{X}} = \frac{s}{\sqrt{n}} \sqrt{\frac{N - n}{N - 1}} \qquad (3)$$

where $\hat{\sigma}_{\overline{X}}$ = standard deviation of the population mean

N = the number in the population

The last part of equation 3 [$\sqrt{(N - n)/(N - 1)}$] is called the finite population correction factor. This is used to make sure no overstatement occurs, but it can be ignored if the sample size is less than or equal to 5% of the population. In other words, this term can be dropped from the equation when $n/N \leqslant 5\%$. This standard deviation of the mean is then used in conjunction with the t distribution to set a confidence interval for the population mean:

$$\overline{X} - t\, \hat{\sigma}_{\overline{X}} < \mu < \overline{X} + t\, \hat{\sigma}_{\overline{X}} \qquad (4)$$

The most important aspect of sampling for variables is the determination of the sample size needed to project the results at selected confidence and error levels. This is done through use of the following formula:

$$n = \frac{\left(\dfrac{ts}{E}\right)^2}{1 + \dfrac{\left(\dfrac{ts}{E}\right)^2}{N}} \qquad (5)$$

where t = the table value associated with a selected confidence level

     E = the error of the estimate desired by management

The final aspect of determining the degree the consumers sampled like the new product is to project this "like" to the total population. Because the sample mean $(\overline{X})$ is an estimate of the population mean (μ), the estimate of the population is obtained from the product of the size of the population (N) and the interval estimate of the sample:

$$N(\overline{X} - t \, \hat{\sigma}_{\overline{X}}) < N_\mu < N(\overline{X} + t \, \hat{\sigma}_{\overline{X}}) \tag{6}$$

    Similar methodology is used when information is needed on how many of the new product will be purchased (percentage sampling). As was the case in variable sampling, the universe proportion (p) is estimated from the sample proportion $(\hat{p})$ by first calculating the sample proportion and standard deviation and then the interval within which this proportion occurs by using the following formulas:

$$\hat{p} = \frac{x}{n} \tag{7}$$

$$\hat{\sigma}_{\hat{p}} = \sqrt{\frac{\hat{p}(1 - \hat{p})}{\sqrt{n}}} \sqrt{\frac{N - n}{N - 1}} \tag{8}$$

$$\hat{p} - t \, \sigma_{\hat{p}} < p < \hat{p} + t \, \hat{\sigma}_{\hat{p}} \tag{9}$$

     It is very important that management determine the sample size needed for the confidence level and error level desired before actually undertaking the research. The size of the sample needed is determined by substituting the respective values into the following formula:

$$n = \frac{(t/E)^2 \, \hat{p} \, (1 - \hat{p})}{1 + \dfrac{(t/E)^2 \, \hat{p} \, (1 - \hat{p})}{N}} \tag{10}$$

     In *stratified sampling* for variables the mean and standard deviation are determined so that the standard deviation of the population and the interval estimate can be established.

$$\overline{X} = \sum_{k=1}^{L} \frac{N_k}{N} \, \overline{X}_k \qquad (11)$$

where $\overline{X}_{\text{strat}}$ = the mean of the stratified sample used to estimate the population mean (μ)

$\overline{X}_k$ = the mean of each stratum (k = 1 to L with L being the number of strata)

N_k = the number of elements (people, stores, companies, or governmental units) in the population in the stratum

N = the number of elements in the total population

$$s = \sqrt{\sum_{i=1}^{n} \frac{(X_i - \overline{X})^2}{n - 1}} \qquad (12)$$

where s = the standard deviation of the stratum

X_i = each element in the stratum

$\overline{X}$ = the mean of the stratum

n = the number of elements in the sample in the stratum

The standard deviation of the mean of the overall strata must be determined so that the confidence interval estimate of the population mean (μ) can be established.

$$\hat{\sigma}_{\overline{X}_{\text{strat}}} = \sqrt{\sum_{X=1}^{L} \frac{N_k^2}{N^2} \left[\frac{s_k^2}{N_k} \left(1 - \frac{n_k}{N_k} \right) \right]} \qquad (13)$$

where $\hat{\sigma}_{\overline{X}_{\text{strat}}}$ = the standard deviation of the mean of the stratified sample

$$\overline{X} - t \, \hat{\sigma}_{\overline{X}} < \mu < \overline{X} + t \, \hat{\sigma}_{\overline{X}} \qquad (14)$$

where t = the table value associated with the specified confidence level

It is of great concern to company management to determine the sample size needed for a selected confidence and error level before the new product research begins. In the case of stratified sampling, this entails a two-step approach. First, the total sample size must be determined. Then the total sample size must be allocated to the various strata in the sample either on a proportional basis (the size of the sample in each stratum is dependent only on the population size within the stratum, regardless of variability in the stratum), or disproportional basis (the size of the sample in each stratum is dependent upon both the population size and the variability within the stratum).

$$n = \sum_{k=1}^{L} n_k \tag{15}$$

$$n_k = \frac{N_k \, \sigma_k (\Sigma N_k \, \sigma_k)}{N^2 (E/t)^2 + \Sigma (N_k \, \sigma_k^2)} \tag{16}$$

where E = the error of the estimate desired by management

$$n_k = n \frac{N_k}{N} \qquad \text{(proportional allocation)}$$

$$n_k = n \frac{N_k \, s_k}{\sum_{k=1}^{L} N_k s_k} \qquad \text{(disproportional allocation)}$$

As is indicated in equations 15 and 16, proportional allocation of the needed sample size involves a division of the sample by the number of items. Disproportional allocation involves a division of sample by number of items and stratum variability. When the population of consumers for the new product can be broken down into groups such that the elements in each group are very similar, then stratified sampling is an excellent method in terms of time and cost efficiency. Although the techniques can be used in new product research when the elements in each stratum are not very similar, it may be hard to show that stratified sampling is more efficient than alternative sampling methods.

Test-Marketing
the New Product

Test-marketing is a stage that many products go through in
their evolutionary process toward commercialization. The decision
to test a new product should, of course, never be routine. Test-
marketing is costly, time-consuming, and the information can often
be obtained more efficiently through research techniques described
in Chapter 4, if the information is needed at all.

This chapter describes the nature of test-marketing, and discusses the process by which the need for test-marketing can be
determined. The factors affecting test-marketing follow. The
chapter concludes with a discussion of the problems in test-
marketing and some alternatives to it.

NATURE OF TEST-MARKETING

Test-marketing a new product has two primary objectives:
(a) to serve as a laboratory where management can experiment with
many alternative characteristics of a new product, become aware of
any problems of the product in the marketplace, and obtain feed-
back vital to successful new product management; and (b) to forecast or predict national sales by the projection of sales results from
the test market areas. In other words, its purpose can be to test
only the physical product or the entire marketing plan (the package, promotion, price, and distribution channels).

Whether it is used during various stages of the tests discussed
in Chapter 5 or whether it is used as a single evaluative procedure,
test-marketing gives the consumer the opportunity to express product preferences in the actual market environment.

Test-marketing has a very broad scope and many interacting factors (see Figure 5-1). When the product is tested in an actual market situation, the interdependence of the variables of the marketing mix assumes a predictable pattern. Yet the decision to test and the amount of risk involved must be evaluated.

The risk inherent in test-marketing has two components: actual quantifiable costs and other losses. The actual quantifiable costs are such things as the cost of plant and machinery needed to manufacture the new product, the cost of advertising to introduce the new product, and the cost of the sales force's time. Equally important to the firm, but not always recognized, are the other costs, such as the loss by other company products of retail shelf space to the product under test, the loss of time and funds that could have been used for other company products, and most importantly, the negative impact on the company's reputation at both the consumer and distribution levels. If these risks are substantial but the investment in a test market allows them to be reduced resulting in an accurate forecast of national sales, then a market test is very desirable. Through test-marketing, a company can only minimize losses, but not maximize profits.

Four main factors should be evaluated before deciding whether or not to test the market.[1] First, the company should compare the costs and risks of product failure with the profit and probability of success. If the costs and risks of product failure are low, then national launching can proceed without a market test. Second, if the technology for the new product requires about the same investment, whether or not the new product is nationally launched or market tested, then the company has good reason to proceed directly to a national launch. However, when this is not the case and a much larger investment is required for a national launch than for a market test, then the high risk indicates that test-marketing would be the best alternative. The investment risk must be weighed against the loss of profit that could otherwise be made through national sales while the new product is being tested. Third, the time the competitors gained to develop a similar product must be assessed in terms of the possible benefits of the market test. Competition will, of course, also monitor the test while simultaneously developing their version. If the capability of competition is such that *they* could by-pass a market test, then perhaps a test should not be conducted. Finally, all other aspects of the new product must be examined. The advertising expenditures, the effort by the sales force, as well as the possible negative impact on

[1] These factors are presented in N. D. Cadbury, ' 'How, When and Where to Test Market," *Harvard Business Review* (May-June 1975), pp. 96-105.

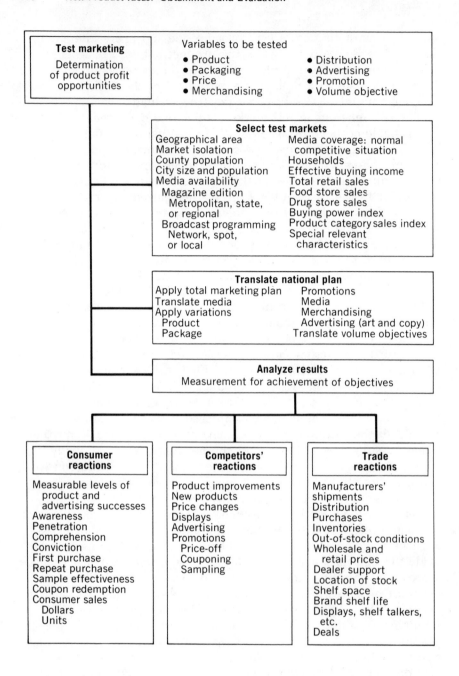

Test marketing

Determination
of product profit
opportunities

Variables to be tested
- Product
- Packaging
- Price
- Merchandising
- Distribution
- Advertising
- Promotion
- Volume objective

Select test markets

Geographical area
Market isolation
County population
City size and population
Media availability
  Magazine edition
  Metropolitan, state,
  or regional
  Broadcast programming
  Network, spot,
  or local

Media coverage: normal
  competitive situation
Households
Effective buying income
Total retail sales
Food store sales
Drug store sales
Buying power index
Product category sales index
Special relevant
  characteristics

Translate national plan

Apply total marketing plan
Translate media
Apply variations
  Product
  Package

Promotions
Media
Merchandising
Advertising (art and copy)
Translate volume objectives

Analyze results
Measurement for achievement of objectives

Consumer reactions

Measurable levels of
  product and
  advertising successes
Awareness
Penetration
Comprehension
Conviction
First purchase
Repeat purchase
Sample effectiveness
Coupon redemption
Consumer sales
  Dollars
  Units

Competitors' reactions

Product improvements
New products
Price changes
Displays
Advertising
Promotions
  Price-off
  Couponing
  Sampling

Trade reactions

Manufacturers'
  shipments
Distribution
Purchases
Inventories
Out-of-stock conditions
Wholesale and
  retail prices
Dealer support
Location of stock
Shelf space
Brand shelf life
Displays, shelf talkers,
  etc.
Deals

Figure 5-1. The Relationship and Composition of Test Marketing (From Remus Harris, "The Total Marketing System," *Marketing Insights* [January 30, 1967], p. 14. Reprinted from *Marketing Insights* published by the American Marketing Association.)

the firm's reputation if the new product fails must be carefully considered before deciding on whether or not to test it.

DETERMINATION OF THE NEED TO MARKET TEST

One method useful for evaluating whether or not test-marketing should be undertaken is the Bayesian approach.[2] Briefly, this approach uses the expected value decision rule to evaluate decisions under uncertainty. The answer to whether or not to market test depends upon several possible states of nature. The Bayesian approach assigns a probability to each state of nature that reflects the management's willingness to act. Then, the possible outcomes of the market test are reviewed in terms of how the results would revise the original probability assignments.

Let us now use the Bayesian approach for a company trying to decide whether to market test the new product or immediately launch nationally. The cost of test-marketing for this company would be $200,000. Through the research done during the concept and product development stages, management has quantified the three possible market shares for the new product (states of nature) and the present value of future profits (consequences). In addition, probabilities have been assigned to each of the three possible market shares. The management of this particular company feels that only three possible market shares are significant enough to be considered.[3] These are given in Table 5-1.

Based on the data in Table 5-1, the company would introduce the new product because the expected monetary value (EMV) of introducing the new product is significantly greater than the EMV of not introducing it. The calculations are:

$$\text{EMV}[A_i] = \Sigma(U_{ij}) \cdot P(S_j) \tag{1}$$

where $\text{EMV}[A_i]$ = expected monetary value of action A_i

U_{ij} = the outcome of that action (i.e., the present value of future profits)

---

[2] This approach can be found in most statistics or marketing research books. For a detailed discussion of the approach and an application, see Robert Schlaifer, *Probability and Statistics for Business Decisions* (New York: McGraw-Hill, 1959). A good application can also be found in Frank M. Bass, "Marketing Research Expenditures: A Decision Model," *Journal of Business* (January 1963), pp. 77-90.

[3] The market shares, as well as the possible outcomes of the market test considered later, could, of course, be considered as varying continuously from 0 to 1. Although this is indeed a more realistic case, the general procedure involved does not differ from the more simplified case presented here.

Table 5-1. Market Shares, Profits, and Probability Assignments for a
            New Product

Market shares (S_i)		Probability $P(S_j)$	Present value of future profits (U_{ij})
Capture 15% of market (S_1)		0.6	$15,000,000
Capture 6%	(S_2)	0.1	2,000,000
Capture 0%	(S_3)	0.3	−7,000,000

$P(S_j)$ = the probability of occurrence of that state
of nature

$$\text{EMV}_{\substack{\text{introducing} \\ \text{new product}}} = 0.6(\$15,000,000) + 0.1(\$2,000,000) \\ + 0.3(-\$7,000,000)$$

$$= \$7,100,000$$

$$\text{EMV}_{\substack{\text{not intro-} \\ \text{ducing new} \\ \text{product}}} = 1(\$0) \\ = \$0$$

With this information, management must decide whether or
not the additional information gained from a market test is worth
the $200,000 cost. It is often valuable to place parameters on the
decision—that is, to determine a cost for the market test beyond
which the value of the information obtained would not be worth
the costs incurred. To do this entails determining the greatest
increase in expected value that perfect information would provide—
that is, the expected profit that can be gained if management
selected the best possible course of action for the state of nature
that actually occurs. For this particular example, if the company
captured either 15% of the market or 6% of the market, the introduction of the new product would earn profits of $15,000,000 and
$2,000,000, respectively. However, if the new product were to cap-
ture none of the market, then the best course of action for the company would be to not introduce the new product and receive a payoff
of $0. If this same case occurred again and again, the company would

make a $15,000,000 profit 60% of the time, a $2,000,000 profit 10% of the time, and a $0 profit 30% of the time.[4] Therefore,

$$\text{Total Expected Profit} = 0.6(\$15,000,000)$$

$$+ 0.1(\$2,000,000) + 0.3(\$0)$$

$$= \$9,200,000$$

Subtracting the EMV of the profits occurring when introducing the new product ($7,100,000) from $9,200,000 determines the value that the cost of the market test cannot exceed. In this case this value is $9,200,000 – $7,100,000 = $2,100,000.

   In order to determine the value of the $200,000 market test, management must determine the probabilities that each of the outcomes of the market test may have on a given state of nature. To do this, management must first indicate the possible outcomes of the market test. Then the probabilities of each outcome must be assigned. The results of these management decisions are given in Table 5-2. As can be seen, management feels that three possible outcomes of the market test are relevant: selling at least 15% of the market, R_1; selling from 5% to 14% of the Market, R_2; and selling less than 5% of the market, R_3. Management has also assigned probabilities to the research outcomes given the various states of nature occurring. These probabilities are designated by:

$$P\left(\frac{R_k}{S_j}\right) \tag{2}$$

where R_k = kth survey result

   S_j = jth state of nature that actually occurs

Table 5-2 indicates that management has assigned a probability of 0.7 to $P(R_1/S_1)$; in other words, management feels that there is a 70% chance that the research results will indicate R_1, given the state of nature S_1, is the true state of nature. A probability of 0.2 is assigned to capturing 5% to 14% of the market in the test, given S_1 is the true state in $P(R_2/S_1)$. In addition, the probability assigned to capturing

---

[4] Although in theory, we are not using probabilities in terms of relative frequency, it is beneficial to think of the probabilities in this way when determining the expected profit occurring when management selects the best course of action for what actually occurs.

Table 5-2. Conditional Probabilities of Outcomes of Market Test of New Product

Outcomes of market test (R_k)	States of nature (S_j)		
	Capture 15% of market S_1	Capture 6% of market S_2	Capture 0% of market S_3
Sell at least 15% of market market in test (R_1)	.7	.2	.1
Sell 5%-14% of market in test (R_2)	.2	.7	.1
Sell less than 5% of market in test (R_3)	.1	.1	.8
Total	1.0	1.0	1.0

less than 5% of the test market, given that S_1 is the true state of $P(R_3/S_1)$, is 0.1.

Given this information, management can now determine: (a) what the EMV (profit) of introducing the new product would be given a certain result of the test market, and (b) the EMV (profit) of not introducing the new product given the same test market result. If less than 5% of the market in the market test was sold R_3, and the expected monetary value (profit) of introducing the new product was greater than the expected value (profit) of not introducing it, then the new product would be introduced. If the reverse was true, given the same market test results, the new product would, of course, not be introduced. This analysis is called posterior analysis, in which the probabilities of S_1, S_2, S_3 (being true probabilities conditional upon R_3 occurring) must be determined. These can be computed from the data in Tables 5-1 and 5-2 and the use of the following formula:

$$P\left(\frac{S_j}{R_k}\right) = \frac{P\left(\frac{R_k}{S_j}\right) \cdot P(S_j)}{P(R_k)} \tag{3}$$

This is Bayes' theorem, restated for the problem at hand. It says that the probability that state of nature j will occur is equal to the conditional probability of survey result k, given state j times the marginal probability that state j occurs, divided by the marginal probability that the survey will show result k.

The computational result for each of the three research results and each state of nature is shown in the first three columns of Table 5-3. Notice that the sum of the column values equals the previously assigned unconditional probabilities of Table 5-1. The sum of the row values (indicated in column 4 of Table 5-3) are the unconditional probabilities of $P(R_k)$. The revised probabilities in the last three columns of Table 5-3 were found by dividing each state of nature by the marginal probability of the survey result, $P(R_k)$. This is the value obtained from use of Bayes' theorem. For example, $P(S_1/R_1) = 0.42/0.47 = 0.89$; $P(S_2/R_2) = 0.07/0.22 = 0.32$; and $P(S_3/R_3) = 0.24/0.31 = 0.78$.

These revised probabilities can now be used to recalculate the EMV (profit) of each of the two courses of action. The EMV (profit) of action 1 (the decision to introduce the new brand if we sell less than 5% of the market in the test R_3) is $0.19(\$15,000,000) + 0.03(\$2,000,000) + 0.78(-\$7,000,000) = -\$2,550,000$. Under the same circumstances, the decision not to introduce the new product would, of course, result in \$0. Therefore, if the test results are R_3, the company should choose A_2 (not to introduce the new product) and make \$0. However, the opposite results occur if the test results are R_1 or R_2. For example, if the company market tests the new product and sells at least 15% of the market (R_1), then the expected profit for the decision to introduce the new brand (A_1) is $0.89(\$15,000,000) + 0.04(\$2,000,000) + 0.07(-\$7,000,000) = \$12,940,000$. Similarly, the expected profit for the decision to introduce the new brand (A_1), given the company sells between 5% and 14% of the market in the test R_2

Table 5-3. Joint Probabilities and Revision of Prior Probabilities for New Product

Survey result	State of nature (S_j)			Marginal probability of survey	Revised probabilities		
R_k	S_1	S_2	S_3	$P(R_k)$	$P(S_1/R_k)$	$P(S_2/R_k)$	$P(S_3/R_k)$
R_1	0.42	0.02	0.03	0.47	0.89	0.04	0.07
R_2	0.12	0.07	0.03	0.22	0.54	0.32	0.14
R_3	0.06	0.01	0.24	0.31	0.19	0.03	0.78
$P(S_j)$	0.60	0.10	0.30	1.00			

is 0.54($15,000,000) + 0.32($2,000,000) + 0.14(-$7,000,000) = $7,760,000. These are, of course, better than the expected profit of A_2 ($0).

From this posterior analysis, the final step to determine the unconditional EMV (profit) of the decision to market test the new product can be accomplished. The result can be compared to the EMV (profit) of acting without the information gained from a market test. This final calculation—preposterior analysis—is accomplished by summing the product of the conditional expected profits of the optimal act, times their corresponding probabilities of being correct. The probabilities are obtained from Table 5-3. The probability of R_1, resulting in the test $P(R_1)$ is 0.47, $P(R_2)$ is 0.22, and $P(R_3)$ is 0.31. The previously calculated expected profits conditional upon R_1, R_2 and R_3 are, respectively, $12,940,000, $7,760,000, and $0. Therefore, the EMV of the decision to market test is 0.47($12,940,000) + 0.22($7,760,000) + 0.31(0) = $6,081,800. This must be compared to the EMV of the decision not to test. This was previously calculated to be $7,100,000. Because the EMV of the decision not to test is greater than that for the decision to test, the market test information is considered not worth the cost; therefore, the market test would not be undertaken. However, if the EMV of the decision not to test is *less* than the EMV of the decision to test, then the test would be undertaken as long as its cost did not exceed this difference.

This Bayesian approach to determine the need for a market test by calculating the EMV under various degrees of uncertainty is a very valuable method of assessing information needs. Use of the process itself is valuable as it forces management to evaluate the market test design while considering all possible relevant results to the decision at hand. Through this method, a market test would only be conducted when the information from the test would significantly aid the decision.

THE TEST MARKET

Once the decision has been made to market test the new product, then a procedure must be formulated that will avoid distortions of the results. Care must be taken so that the conditions under which the new product is tested closely resemble those that will prevail when the product is launched. Management must know not only the sales level but also the nature of these sales and the levels of distribution. Three very important aspects of any market test procedure are sample size determination, design of the test experiment, and selection of the test market.

Selection of Test Markets

The selection of the test market is primarily determined by the product. The test markets should approach national norms in such areas as advertising, competition, distribution system, and product usage. This means a detailed, national marketing plan is prepared covering at least media selection, sales effort, and promotional budgets before the product actually enters the test market. In this way, the test market can concurrently provide evaluation of alternative marketing strategies that will subsequently be used on a national basis.

The first decision to be made is whether to test in a metropolitan or nonmetropolitan area or in a district or regional market. Once this decision is made, the exact cities or regions must be chosen. Although some unique attribute of a particular city or region may require its inclusion, a test market should generally be selected based on any criterion in Figure 5-2 that is applicable to the product to be tested.[5]

The criteria in Figure 5-2 are not all-inclusive nor should every one be considered in evaluating an area for testing every product category. The nature of the product will emphasize some factors over others, as well as exclude some factors altogether. For example, in the case of a company test-marketing a product that it will eventually sell through its own company-owned stores, the questions concerning distribution may have little meaning. The checklist is merely a means of selecting an area(s) that can be controlled as much as possible so that an approximation of the national market is accomplished, thus providing a basis for prediction.

Sample Size Determination

In test-marketing the new product, it is very important to make sure that the number of stores used is adequate to represent the "universe." The methodology in sample size determination for store audits is different from that used in consumer studies in evaluating the new product in both the idea and concept states (discussed in Chapter 4). Because the retail stores used in the test

[5] A comprehensive discussion of the advantages and disadvantages of testing on a city or regional basis, as well as enumeration of part of the criteria of Figure 5-2 appear in "The Nation's Top Test Markets," *Sales Management* (January 5, 1962), pp. 53-72.

Figure 5-2. Checklist for Selection of a Test Market

City or region _____

Criteria	Relative advantage			
	Good	Average	Poor	Does not apply
General				
Representative as to population size				
Diversification in age, religion, and number and types of families				
Typical as to per capita income				
Representation of industry and employment				
Degree of isolation from other areas				
Product oriented				
Stability of overall year-round sales				
Amount of product category sales				
Typicality in terms of sales potential for the tested product category				
Marketing mix				
Typicality of wholesale outlets				
Typicality of number and type of retail outlets				
Representative as to advertising media				
Degree of cooperation of available advertising media				
Control				
Degree of trade cooperation				
Degree of company control over entire test market operation				

market have different properties, a proportionate sampling methodology is employed. The fundamental formula for sample size is:

$$n = \frac{\left(\dfrac{ts}{d}\right)^2}{1+1/N \ \left(\dfrac{ts}{d}\right)^2} \tag{4}$$

where n = number of stores in sample

t = the value determined by the confidence coefficient
selected (i.e., t = 1.00 for 68% confidence coefficient,
t = 1.65 for 90% confidence coefficient, and t = 1.96
for 95% confidence coefficient)

d = the limit of error found by multiplying the stated
error preference by the mean sales of a similar product

s = the standard deviation of the universe obtained from
previous knowledge of the universe or from an
outside independent audit supplier

N = number of stores in the population

Using the above formula, let us determine the sample size
needed for a new product for Kelly's Toys and Games, Inc. The
company has been continuously evaluating its newest product—a
new game called *Impeachment*. This game is a political, adult game
that benefits customers through a recreational and instructional
medium. It allows consumers to put themselves in the position of
the president in a unique situation; it has both a contemporary and
a historical basis. The historical basis is in the form of a booklet
on past impeachment proceedings and the legislative, judicial, and
executive processes imbedded in the very nature of the act. The
contemporary aspect of the game is that it allows each participant
an (probable) equal chance of winning the game through use of
spaces on the board and the two sets of cards. Only the player's
skill in determining the right time for key decisions would give
that player an edge in the game.

The company has already tested this product in both the idea
stage and concept stage and feels that a test market is needed

---

[6] This formula, as well as all proofs and derivations underlying it, can be
found in William G. Cohran, *Sampling Techniques,* 2nd ed. (New York: Willey,
1963), pp. 74-76.

before limited company resources can be committed to a nationwide introduction campaign. Now the company needs to know
how many stores should be included in the test market. In its
marketing of an adult game two years ago, the company found
that the universe had a standard deviation of 2.24 with mean
product sales of 4.3. The number of stores in the market that
would carry the product was 204. The management at Kelly's
wants the number of stores to be selected at the 95% confidence
level and the 10% error level. How many stores should be included
in the test market?

From the above information, the number of stores needed can
be calculated as follows:

$$n = \frac{\dfrac{(1.96)^2(2.24)^2}{(0.43)^2}}{1 + 1/204 \left(\dfrac{(1.96)^2(2.24)^2}{(0.43)^2} \right)} = 68 \qquad (5)$$

where

N = universe size = 204

t = confidence level = 1.96 at 95% confidence level

s = standard deviation = 2.24

d = error limit = 0.10(4.3) = 0.43

In order to be 95% confident that the number of stores is
representative within a ±10% error of the mean sales for the new
product, 68 stores are needed.

If everything else remains the same in the above problem
except that the acceptable error level would be changed to ±15%,
then the number of stores needed would be reduced to 36:

$$n = \frac{\dfrac{(1.96)^2(2.24)^2}{(0.65)^2}}{1 + 1/204 \left(\dfrac{(1.96)^2(2.24)^2}{(0.65)^2} \right)} \qquad (6)$$

On the other hand, if only the confidence level would be
changed—that is, reduced from 95% to 90% while keeping every-

thing else constant—the number of stores needed would be reduced to 54:

$$n = \frac{\dfrac{(1.64)^2(2.24)^2}{(0.65)^2}}{1 + 1/204\left(\dfrac{(1.64)^2(2.24)^2}{(0.65)^2}\right)} = 54 \qquad (7)$$

The final factor that influences sample size is the standard deviation. Let us assume that the confidence level, error level, and the size of the universe remained at 95%, 10% and 204, respectively; but the mean product sales increased to 5.7 and the standard deviation decreased to 2.06. The sample size needed reduces to:

$$n = \frac{\dfrac{(1.96)^2(2.06)^2}{(0.57)^2}}{1 + 1/204\left(\dfrac{(1.96)^2(2.06)^2}{(0.57)^2}\right)} = 34 \text{ stores} \qquad (8)$$

As these examples show, the number of stores needed in a selected test market depends upon the average product sales, the standard deviation, the confidence level, the error level, and, to a slight extent, the number of stores in the universe. Yet, regardless of the levels occurring in the marketplace or the managerial decision regarding confidence level and error level desired, the correct sample size can be determined.

Design of Test Experiment

Once the company has selected the city it will use in the market test, it is important to decide the appropriate testing procedure or experimental design. The classic experimental model is indicated in Figure 5-3.

The number of stores needed are randomly assigned to either the experimental group or the control group of stores as long as the two groups are similar in terms of the product being tested. Measures of product sales are taken before the experimental variable (i.e., the new product) is introduced and then after it is removed. If the difference in sales between A and B is significantly greater than the difference in sales between C and D, the experimental variable is a success.

Figure 5-3. Experimental Model for Test-Marketing New Products

Source of variation	Time of measurement	
	Before	After
Experimental group of stores	A	B
Control group of stores	C	D

When designing a test experiment for a new product or some aspect of a new product, each of the possible formal experimental designs must be examined with respect to their propriety to the problem at hand. The four most frequently used experimental designs are: completely randomized, randomized block, Latin square, and factorial.[7] Every person involved in test-marketing new products should understand the procedure and limitations of each design as well as the situation(s) in which each is most useful.

Table 5-4 shows that the experimental designs proceed from completely randomized to factorial design in terms of the number of variables tested and difficulty of computation. Completely randomized design is used when only one variable, such as different new packages, needs to be tested. Randomized block design provides information on two test variables, such as price and package of the new product. Latin square design is used to test three variables, such as package, price, and point-of-purchase display.

All these designs are called single-factor experiments and do not evaluate the *interaction* or joint effect the new product variables may have together. For example, picture a point-of-purchase display for a new cake mix that has a big picture of the cake on it. In addition, there is a coupon attached by which the consumer can mail three box tops to the company and receive a 50¢ refund. Would the effect on sales be the same with a price of 69¢ per box of cake mix versus a price of 49¢? Of course not. In this case, the point-of-purchase display, by itself, would affect sales. The price would affect sales. In addition, the joint impact or interaction between the point-of-purchase display and price would affect sales. Whenever one wants to measure the interaction between the variables, then factorial design must be employed. Table 5-4 indicates a two-variable factorial design and therefore one interaction. This can be expanded to a variable factorial design.

---

[7]The theoretical base as well as the depth of presentation of these experimental designs can be found in many books dealing with data analysis. See, for example, Keith K. Cox and Ben M. Enis, *Experimentation for Marketing Decisions* (Scranton, Pa.: International Textbook Co., 1969); and Charles R. Hicks, *Fundamental Concepts in the Design of Experiments* (New York: Holt, Rinehart and Winston, 1964).

Table 5-4. Types of Experimental Designs Used in Test-Marketing

Type of experimental design	General model	Variables tested
Completely randomized	$x_{ij} = u + T_j + E_{ij}$	One
Randomized block	$x_{ij} = u + B_i + T_j + E_{ij}$	Two
Latin square	$x_{ij} = u + B_i + T_j + \lambda_k + E_{ijk}$	Three
Factorial	$x_{ijk} = u + A_i + B_j + AB_{ij} + E_{k(ij)}$	Two and interaction

Of course, every time an additional variable is added, more inter-actions occur. For example, with three variables, there are four interactions, with four variables, ten interactions, etc. As you can see, factorial design can become very unwieldy in terms of deter-mining significant interaction effects of the variables. Each of these four experimental designs is examined in detail in the appendix at the end of this chapter.

FACTORS AFFECTING TEST-MARKETING

When implementing and evaluating the results of test-marketing a new product, consideration must be given to a wide variety of factors that could affect the test. One essential factor is the gen-eral level of business and economic activity. These affect such con-sumer attitudes as readiness to buy and interest in capital expendi-tures and therefore can alter the evaluation of the new product. For example, if business activity is low and if a firm is evaluating the market response to a new major capital item, the evaluation of this new product might be poorer than it would be in a period of better business conditions. Similarly, the uncertainties of inflation and unemployment might bias consumers in their evaluation of a new, major durable good.

Another important factor is the existing market structure. This means the number and types of competitive products, the degree of competition, and the effectiveness of competitive market-ing strategies. These forces interact to varying extents, influencing the results of a test. Similarly, the prevailing consumer preferences and available marketing channels will contribute to the complex interacting market structure.

Competition may attempt to influence the results of a market test by offering special prices, premiums, or increasing promotional efforts during the test period. Whether or not this interference is

committed knowingly or unknowingly, the effects must be miti-
gated in order to have a reliable new product evaluation. For
example, a company recently test-marketing a new consumer product in two cities disregarded the results in one city because of an
extensive promotional campaign launched for a competing product.

Finally, the originality and appeal of the presentation, as well
as other marketing variables, such as the package and price, can
affect the market test's results. Care must be taken to test only
those new product variables desired, making sure that no other
elements interfere with the results.

PROBLEMS IN TEST-MARKETING

Several problems arise when conducting a market test of a
new product.[8] A major one is the inaccuracy of the results. Many
new products that achieved favorable test-marketing results are not
commercial successes. Even though test-marketing is used extensively, the results are often neither useful nor accurate, expecially
as a predictive device. One study on the predictive value of test-
marketing indicated large margins of error.[9] Care must be taken to
ensure greater congruence between the results of a market test and
the national market.

The unreliability of market test results is not the only problem. The cost of this technique is also a problem. Test-marketing
a new product not only requires large investments in the procedure
itself, but also in the remuneration and expenses of members of
the company, any outside agency, and/or distribution channels.
For example, in the case of company employees, time is used in
designing, monitoring, and evaluating the new product's test. Time
is diverted from other products or programs for the new product.
High per unit costs are inherent in the production of a modest number of units for use in the market test for the new product.

A major cause of inaccurate projections and the related costs
is the shortcomings in the basic design of the test-marketing program. Not only must the design be sound, but personnel must
follow the developed plans. Common mistakes committed by
companies are having testing done by unqualified personnel and
not establishing criteria for adequate evaluation of the results.[10]

[8] For a discussion of some problems, see Carl H. Hendrickson, "Some
Pitfalls of Sales Test," *Sales Management* (November 10, 1950), pp. 124-29.

[9] Jack Gold, "Testing Test Market Predictions," *Journal of Marketing
Research* (August 1964), pp. 8-11.

[10] For a discussion of this problem in test marketing, see Harry C.
Groome, "Taking the Risk Out of Test Marketing," *Sales Management* (April
17, 1964), p. 33; and A. R. Kroeger, "Test Marketing: The Concept and How
It Is Changing," *Media Scope* (January 1967), pp. 51-54.

The number and complexity of problems that arise in the collection and evaluation of data are so important that these two topics merit individual attention. Sales measurement is a frequently encountered problem in a lengthy, full-scale market test. For example, a firm attempting to measure the acceptability of a new consumer product may have to use a wholesaler who then distributes to the retailers. Initially, "sales" will reflect an inventory build-up by the wholesaler and retailer. Many weeks may elapse after actual retail sales to the final consumer before the distributor's reorders reach the producer. With various inventory decision rules being practiced, it may be difficult, if not impossible, to relate reorders to purchases by final users. Even when retail sales are audited in the test market, inventory misallocation problems are frequent.[11] Another evaluation problem is in determining whether the new product success is a result of its testing plan, mere coincidence, or the strength of the firm. For example, when a new product is introduced by a large corporation with a good distribution system, large sales force, substantial advertising investment, and good image, the reality of the success of the tested new product is unclear because the results may be clouded by the success of the firm.[12] Finally, there is the almost insurmountable measurement problem of evaluating the exact nature of the purchasers of the new product. Were they first or repeat purchasers? Were they formerly loyal purchasers of a competitive product who switched, or were they habitual product switchers? Did the purchasers buy the new product to test it, or did they see some merit in the product? Accurate measurement of who purchased the new product and the reasons for purchasing that product is invaluable to the producer of the new product.

An all-encompassing problem in test-marketing is time. Time spent in test-marketing a new product is not only costly for the firm, but it often gives competition an advantage as well. Competition may gain as much from this stage in new product planning as the initiating company; in addition, competitors may be gaining enough time to respond in a manner that will seriously reduce the new product's full-life profitability. As noted in Chapter 1, product life cycles are becoming shorter and shorter. Few, if any, companies are so far advanced in technology that a long lead time of a new discovery can be expected. For example, Sunbeam's electric skillet was copied so widely that the market was saturated within a few years. Although Lestoil (a liquid household cleaner)

---

[11] An example of this problem in obtaining reliable information is given in Edwin M. Berby, Victor L. Cole, and Jack Gold, "Testing Test Marketing Predictions," *Journal of Marketing Research* (May 1965), pp. 196-200.

[12] For a discussion of this difficulty, see E. B. Weiss, "The Trials and Tribulations of Test Marketing," *Advertising Age* (January 16, 1961), p. 84.

had a tremendous sales record of $25 million, the advent of such products as Handy Andy by Lever Brothers, Mr. Clean by Procter and Gamble, and Liquid Ajax by Colgate caused Lestoil's sales to quickly drop to $16 million. These are only a few examples in which time spent for test-marketing meant reduced total profits for a new product because the exclusivity had been reduced.

The time problem in test-marketing is indeed a paradox. If the market test period is too short, national distribution strategy may be based on inaccurate, incomplete, or inconclusive data. If a new product is tested for too long a time, competition may be able to respond with a substitute product.

Competition can be a problem in test-marketing a new product by distorting test results with heavy, abnormal promotional expenditures in the test area or by actually purchasing large quantities of the product. If strong competitive activities are implemented in a test market, new product results can be of little value. The period and the degree to which competition is able to evaluate the new product are important considerations in the decision to market test a new product.[13]

TEST-MARKETING ALTERNATIVES AND REMEDIES

One solution to some test-marketing problems is to use data from consumer panels to measure a test product's staying power. Markov chain analysis can give the test marketers insight into the dynamics of competition and the forces influencing consumer brand-switching. This method can be used to determine a new product's share of the market for the total product category at a future time by tracing its market share through preceding, successive periods of time. The product's share through the successive stages is a function of transitional probabilities; that is, the sum of the probabilities of switching from one brand to another is the square of the number of brands in the product category. For example, a company wants to determine the probability that a customer would purchase its new product at a particular future time. The customer was in one of three states when making the last purchase of the product: bought the new product, bought the leading competing brand, or bought a nonleading but competing product. From consumer panel data showing each customer's purchases over an extended period of time, the company can estimate the conditional probabilities that a customer will switch

---

[13] For examples of competitive action distorting test market results, see "Espionage and Sabotage: How They Disrupt Testing," *Printer's Ink* (August 27, 1965), pp. 90-95.

from one brand to another when given the outcome of a previous trial.[14]

Another alternative to test-marketing is to implement research that is between concept-testing and full test-marketing. A model test market can be employed. In a model test market, the total marketplace is modeled, but both the time and costs of a full market test are reduced. This step is particularly useful for new products not having conclusive concept test results, new products of small companies who cannot afford a full-scale market test, and new products requiring considerable capital investment to market test. Cadbury Limited has a very unusual model market test. A representative panel of housewives is mailed a sales catalogue describing all the products being tested, the leading brands in the product category, and any promotional efforts occurring. This material is accompanied by an order form. The housewives then receive a weekly visit at home from a salesperson with a mobile shop, and the women make their weekly selections.[15] An alternative to this model of a market test would be to set up a company store and have the representative panel of housewives shop there.

Another development to aid and refine test-marketing new products is to simulate market reality with a computer. Limited application of computer simulation techniques to test-marketing problems has, in part, been due to the problems in the quantification of consumer behavior, as well as to extensive costs. In addition, if any important variables are omitted or if the underlying assumptions are inaccurate, the results will not be valid. One such simulation model is DEMON.[16] The purpose of this system is to ensure a viable national new product introduction by assuming the best possible marketing plan in the least amount of time and efficiently balanced in relation to maximum profit, risk, and payback period. DEMON has the advantages of reducing risk and consequently the rate of new product failure, reducing the time required for new product introduction, reducing or possibly eliminating test-marketing, lowering the costs of new product introductions,

---

[14] For an elementary description of the Markov process, see S. Dutka and L. Frankel, *Markov Chain Analysis: A New Tool for Marketing* (New York: Audits and Surveys, 1966); for a more extensive discussion, see Ronald E. Frank, "Brand Choice as a Probability Process," *Journal of Business* (January 1962), pp. 43-45; Alfred A. Kuehn, "Consumer Brand Choice as a Learning Process," *Journal of Advertising Research* (December 1962), pp. 10-17; and A.S.C. Ehrenberg, "An Appraisal of Markov Brand Switching Models," *Journal of Marketing Research* (November 1964), pp. 347-62.

[15] This is described in N. D. Cadbury, "When, Where, and How to Test Market," *Harvard Business Review* (May-June 1976), p. 100.

[16] David B. Learner, "DEMON New Product Planning: A Case History," *Proceedings of the American Marketing Association Conference* (June 1965), pp. 489-509.

and ensuring maximum profits on a new product. This network system has the capacity to model the whole world simultaneously by altering, integrating, and weighting all variables against a set profit and goal and possible sales, thereby obtaining results that could only be obtained after extensive test-marketing. DEMON is only one of several simulation models used in new product decisions.[17]

Another method to solve some of the problems in conventional test-marketing is a mixture of test-marketing and national introduction. In this "roll-out method," a company selects a test area for distribution, such as a sales territory, and markets the new product using the same marketing mix variables as will be used for national distribution. When sales are substantial enough in the selected market, the company "rolls out" to the next sales territory and eventually to national distribution. This method, of course, requires extensive pretest market activity in the idea, concept, and product development stages previously discussed.

SUMMARY

Test-marketing new products is increasing in use even though it requires large expenditures. Although there are many factors and problems to be considered, test-marketing a new product helps ensure success in national distribution.

One critical aspect of test-marketing is selecting the appropriate market in which the new product will be tested. General, product-oriented marketing mix and control criteria are also important in varying degrees to market test selection. Test results should reflect these factors and be projectable onto the national market. Similarly, both the sample size determination and the design of the test experiment will greatly influence whether or not an indication of the probability of new product success is obtained.

There is a basic design for every market test situation. The formulas and examples of the major types of experimental design used in test-marketing demonstrate this. However, even with a sound experimental design, various factors can cause problems in test-marketing. Factors, such as the existing market structure, competition, and presentation appeal, can cause distortions of the

---

[17]Two other approaches are given in Marshall Freimer and Leonard S. Simon, "The Evaluation of New Product Alternatives," *Management Science* (February 1967), pp. B279-92; and Henry J. Claycamp and Lucien E. Liddy, "Prediction of New Product Performance: An Analytical Approach," *Journal of Marketing Research* (November 1969), pp. 414-20. Various aspects of these and other models were discussed in Chapter 3.

results so that they cannot be reliably used to forecast the national sales of the new product. Sales forecasting is the topic of the next chapter.

SELECTED READINGS

"Advertisers Take Harder Look at Traditional Test Methods." *Advertising Age* 43 (October 16, 1972): 3, 96.

Bengston, Roger, and Brenner, Henry. "Product Test Results Using Three Different Methodologies." *Journal of Marketing Research* (November 1964): 49-52.

"Can Success Spoil a Marketing Plan?" *Printer's Ink*, vol. 295, no. 4 (August 25, 1967): 17-22.

Clarke, T. J. "Product Testing in New Product Development." *Commentary* (July 1967): 135-46.

Claycamp, Henry J., and Liddy, Lucien E. "Prediction of New Product Performance: An Analytical Approach." *Journal of Marketing Research* (November 1969): 414-20.

"Computer in Test Marketing—Blazing New Dimensions." *Sales Management* 102 (March 1, 1969): 38-42.

Day, Ralph. "Methods of Estimating Distributions of Consumers' Preferences." *The Southern Journal of Business* (April 1966): 99-108.

"The Day the Test Marketing Stops." *Sales Management* 102 (March 1, 1969): 35-38.

Green, Paul E. "Bayesian Statistics and Product Decisions." *Business Horizons* 5 (Fall 1962): 101-109.

"Industrial Test Marketing—A Quickening Pace." *Sales Management* 102 (March 1, 1969): 31-33.

"Is the Chemistry Changing?" *Sales Management* 110 (April 16, 1973): 21-28.

Lipstein, Benjamin. "Test Marketing: A Perturbation in the Market Place." *Management Science* (April 1968): B437-48.

"Mathematics—Key to Product Tests." *Printer's Ink*, vol. 295, no. 4 (August 25, 1967): 22-27.

Mossman, Frank H., and Worrell, Malcolm L., Jr. "Analytical Methods of Measuring Marketing Profitability: A Matrix Approach." *Business Topics* (Autumn 1966): 35-45.

"New Products—The Push Is On Marketing." *Business Week* (March 4, 1972): 72-77.

"New SMSA Data Reveal Shifts in Test Marketing." *Advertising Age* 48 (October 8, 1973): 2.

O'Meara, John T., Jr. "Selecting Profitable Products. *Harvard Business Review* (January-February 1961): 179-84.

"Reducing the Risk of New Product Marketing." *Journal of Marketing Research* 6 (May 1969): 216-20.

Reitter, Robert N. "Product Testing in Segmented Markets." *Journal of Marketing Research* 6 (May 1969): 179-84.

"Research and Pseudo-Research in Marketing." *Harvard Business Review* vol. 52, no. 2 (March-April 1974): 73-76.

Richman, Barry M. "A Rating Scale for Product Innovation." *Business Horizons* (Summer 1962): 37-44.

"Test-Marketing." *Harvard Business Review*, vol 39, no. 2 (March-April 1961): 74-77.

"Test-Marketing—New Product Must." *Printer's Ink*, vol. 279, no. 2 (April 13, 1962): 21-31.

"Test Marketing Practices Are Documented in Private Survey." *Advertising Age* 43 (April 10, 1972): 30.

"Test Marketing—Think Small." *Sales Management* 101 (September 15, 1968): 39-40.

"Tighter Test Marketing Leads Rush to Payout." *Printer's Ink*, vol. 295, no. 4 (August 25, 1967): 7-15.

Tull, Donald S. "The Relationship of Actual and Predicted Sales and Profits in New Product Introductions." *Journal of Business* 40 (July 1967): 233-51.

"What's New." *Sales Management*, vol. 108, no. 1 (January 10, 1972): 34.

"When, Where, and How to Test Market." *Harvard Business Review*, vol. 53, no. 4 (May-June 1975): 96-105.

"Why Good Products Fail in Test Markets." *Printer's Ink*, vol. 279, no. 2 (April 13, 1962): 42.

Appendix to Chapter Five—
Experimental
Design in Test-Marketing

The *completely randomized design* is the simplest type of experimental design. In this design, the experimentation applied to the levels of the test variable is completely random. The number of observations for each level of the test variable (which is called the treatment) is determined by both cost considerations as well as the strength of the test. Analysis of variance is used to determine whether or not the treatment means differ significantly from the control means. The general model for the completely randomized design is:

$$x_{ij} = \lambda + T_j + E_{ij} \tag{1}$$

where

x_{ij} = the ith observation ($i = 1,2,3, \ldots , n_j$) of the jth treatment ($j = 1,2,3, \ldots , k$) levels

λ = common effect for entire experiment

T_j = the effect of the jth treatment

E_{ij} = the error in the ith observation on the jth treatment (this is considered to be a normally and independently distributed effect with a mean value of 0 and a similar variance for any treatment or level)

The analysis of this single-factor, completely randomized experiment involves a one-way analysis of variance test where the following null hypothesis (H_0) is tested. There is no effect on sales of the new product caused by the treatment variable. The test is accomplished through the use of the following analysis of variance (ANOVA) table:

Table 1. General ANOVA Table for Completely Randomized Design

Source of variation	Degrees of freedom	Sum of squares	Mean square	Calculated F ratio	Table F ratio	Conclusion
Between variables (T_j)						
Within variables or error (E_{ij})						
Total	___	___	___	___	___	___

Table 1 indicates that the degrees of freedom and sums of squares for the between, within, and total must first be calculated. The formulas for the sums of squares (SS) of each are given below:[1]

$$SS_{\text{between treatments}} = \sum_{j=1}^{k} \frac{T^2_{\cdot j}}{n_j} - \frac{T^2_{\cdot\cdot}}{N} \qquad (2)$$

where

$$T_{\cdot j} = \text{the total of each treatment in the experiment}$$

$$n_j = \text{the number of levels of each treatment}$$

$$T_{\cdot\cdot} = \text{the grand total of all treatments}$$

$$N = \text{the total number of observations}$$

$$SS_{\text{total}} = \sum_{j=1}^{k} \sum_{i=1}^{n_j} x^2_{ij} - \frac{T^2_{\cdot\cdot}}{N} \qquad (3)$$

[1] The derivation of these formulas as well as the formulas for randomized block, Latin square, and factorial designs can be found in Charles R. Hicks, *Fundamental Concepts in the Design of Experiments* (New York: Holt, Rinehart and Winston, 1964).

where

$$x_{ij} = \text{the individual observation for each treatment level}$$

$$T_{..} = \text{the grand total of all treatments}$$

$$N = \text{the total number of observations}$$

$$SS_{\text{within treatment (error)}} = SS_{\text{total}} - SS_{\text{between treatments}} \quad (4)$$

$$= \sum_{j=1}^{k} \sum_{i=1}^{n_j} x_{ij}^2 - \sum_{j=1}^{k} \frac{T_{.j}^2}{n_j}$$

The degrees of freedom for the between treatments are $k - 1$; for the total $N - 1$; the degrees of freedom for within treatments are equal to the degrees of freedom for the total minus the degrees of freedom for between, or $N - k$. After calculation of the sum of squares and degrees of freedom for each, the mean square is found by dividing the respective sum of squares by the degrees of freedom. For example, the mean square between is found by:

$$\text{mean square}_{\text{between}} = \frac{\text{sum of squares}_{\text{between}}}{\text{degrees of freedom}_{\text{between}}} \quad (5)$$

Each of the other two mean squares is found in a similar manner.

The final calculation is the F ratio. This is the ratio of two estimates of the sample of the universe variance and is found by dividing the mean square$_{\text{between}}$ by the mean square$_{\text{within}}$:

$$F \text{ ratio} = \frac{\text{mean square}_{\text{between}}}{\text{mean square}_{\text{within}}} \quad (6)$$

If the treatment variable of the new product being tested has almost no effect on sales, then the mean square estimate between and the mean square estimate within will differ only as a result of sampling error. It will be approximately unity. The more effect the treatment variable has on sales, the larger the F ratio becomes.

Now all the columns in Table 1 have been covered except for the last two: table F ratio and conclusion. The table F ratio is found by looking up the value in any table of F ratios for the desired confidence level is selected, e.g., 90% confidence level, 95%,

97.5%, or 99%. The degrees of freedom for the numerator in equation 6 are column headings. The degrees of freedom for the denominator are the row headings. These are the same degrees of freedom corresponding to the numerator and denominator of the calculated F ratio. The intersection of a particular column and row in the body of the table gives the critical table F value for the analysis.

Finally, the conclusion column of Table 1 is filled in by comparing the table F ratio and the calculated F ratio. If the calculated F ratio is less than the table F ratio, then the null hypothesis (H_0) is true; the conclusion is that the variable being tested does not significantly affect sales at the confidence level selected. However, if the calculated F ratio is greater than the table F ratio, then the null hypothesis (H_0) is rejected and the alternative hypothesis (H_1) is accepted. The conclusion is that the variable being tested does significantly affect sales at the chosen confidence level.

The use of the completely randomized design can be illustrated by the following. Kelly's Toys and Games, Inc. is interested in determining whether or not point-of-purchase displays significantly affect the sales of their new game *Impeachment*. Because this is the only variable the company wants to test, a completely randomized design is established in the appropriate number of stores. The sales results for each of the three point-of-purchase displays tested are given in Table 2. The top management of Kelly's is interested in knowing whether or not point-of-purchase

Table 2. Sales for the Three Point-of-Purchase Displays for *Impeachment*

Replications (i)	Treatments (j)		
	Point-of-purchase display 1 (T_1)	Point-of-purchase display 2 (T_2)	Point-of-purchase display 3 (T_3)
Week 1	10	5	3
Week 2	12	6	5
Week 3	8	7	4
Treatment totals ($T_{.j}$)	30	18	12
Treatment means $\bar{x}_j$	30/3 = 10	18/3 = 6	12/3 = 4
Overall grand total = 60			

displays significantly affect sales of the game at the 95% confidence level.

Using the formulas for the completely randomized design (equations 2, 3, and 4), the effect on sales is calculated as follows:

$$SS_{\text{between treatment}} = \sum_{j=1}^{k} \frac{T_{\cdot j}^2}{n_j} - \frac{T_{\cdot\cdot}^2}{N} \tag{7}$$

$$= \frac{(30)^2 + (18)^2 + (12)^2}{3} - \frac{(60)^2}{9}$$

$$= 56$$

$$SS_{\text{total}} = \sum_{j=1}^{K} \sum_{i=1}^{n_j} x_{ij}^2 - \frac{T_{\cdot\cdot}^2}{N} \tag{8}$$

$$= (10)^2 + (12)^2 + (8)^2 + (5)^2 + (6)^2 + (7)^2$$

$$+ (3)^2 + (5)^2 + (4)^2 - \frac{(60)^2}{9}$$

$$= 68$$

$$SS_{\text{within treatment(error)}} = SS_{\text{total}} - SS_{\text{between treatment}} \tag{9}$$

$$= 68 - 56$$

$$= 12$$

These results are indicated in Table 3.

Table 3. ANOVA for Point-of-Purchase Display

Source of variation	Degrees of freedom	Sum of squares	Mean square	Calculated F ratio	Table F ratio	Conclusion
Between variables	2	56	28	14	5.14	Reject H_0; point-of-purchase displays do affect sales of new product
Within variables	6	12	2			
Total	8	68				

The degrees of freedom for the between variables is $3 - 1 = 2$. The degrees of freedom for the total is $9 - 1 = 8$. Finally, the degrees of freedom for within is $8 - 2 = 6$.

Similarly, the mean square for each source of variation is found by dividing each sum of squares by its corresponding degrees of freedom. Therefore, the mean square for between is $56/2 = 28$ and for within is $12/6 = 2$.

Dividing the mean square between by the mean square within, we have a mean square calculated of 14 ($28/2 = 14$) for the problem. This then is compared to the appropriate table F ratio. Because we are interested in knowing whether or not point-of-purchase displays significantly affect sales at the 95% confidence level, we look at the F ratio table. The degrees of freedom are those corresponding to the numerator and denominator used to determine the calculated F ratio. In other words, the appropriate degrees of freedom are 2 degrees of freedom between and 6 degrees of freedom within. The table F ratio ($F_{.05,2,6}$) is 5.14.

Since 14 is greater than 5.14, we can conclude that we should reject the null hypothesis (H_0) and accept the alternative hypothesis (H_1). At the 95% confidence level, we are sure that point-of-purchase displays significantly affect sales of the new product.[2]

In the completely randomized design previously discussed, all sources of variation except those caused by the variable being tested are assumed to be constant over all observations. However, in test-marketing new products there is often at least one source of distortion. In order to isolate this source of variation or test for the significant effect of two variables on new product sales, the *randomized block design* must be employed. Again, analysis of variance is employed to test the significance of the two variables. The only difference between the analysis of variance for the randomized block design compared with the completely randomized design is the increase of one more variable and the mathematics of the computation. The general model for the randomized block design is:

$$X_{ij} = \lambda + B_i + T_j + E_{ij} \tag{10}$$

---

[2] The relative effect of each of the point-of-purchase displays can also be determined through two methods. If the decision to determine which of the treatment means are different before the new product experiment is run and the data collected, then the *method of orthogonal contrasts* can be used. However, if the decision to determine whether or not the treatment means are different is made after the experiment has been run, then the *Duncan Multiple Range* test is used. See Charles R. Hicks, *Fundamental Concepts*, pp. 28-31 for a description of the method of orthogonal contrasts; and D. B. Duncan, "Multiple Range and Multiple F Tests," *Biometrika*, 1956 for a description of the Duncan multiple range test.

where

$$\lambda = \text{common effect for the entire experiment}$$

B_i = the effect of ith block

T_j = the effect of the jth treatment

E_{ij} = the error in the ith observation on the jth treatment (this is considered to be a normally and independently distributed effect with a mean value of 0 and a similar variance for any treatment or level)

A similar ANOVA table is used to test the null hypothesis as was used in the completely randomized design. The only difference occurs under the column "source of variation." There are three sources of variation making up the total in the randomized block design: treatment variable, block variable, and error. The formulas for calculation of the sums of squares are, of course, different as follows:

$$SS_{\text{treatment}} = \sum_j \frac{T_{\cdot j}^2}{n} - \frac{T_{\cdot\cdot}^2}{N} \tag{11}$$

where

$T_{\cdot j}$ = the total of each treatment in the experiment

n_j = the number of levels of each treatment

$T_{\cdot\cdot}$ = the grand total of all treatments

N = the total number of observations

$$SS_{\text{block}} = \sum_{i=1}^{n} \frac{T_{i\cdot}^2}{K} - \frac{T_{\cdot\cdot}^2}{N} \tag{12}$$

where

$T_{i\cdot}$ = the total of each block effect in the experiment

K = the number of levels of each block

$T_{\cdot\cdot}$ = the grand total of all treatments

N = the total number of observations

$$SS_{total} = \sum_{j=1}^{K} \sum_{i=1}^{n_j} x_{ij}^2 - \frac{T_{..}^2}{N} \qquad (13)$$

where

X_{ij} = the individual observation for each treatment and

$T_{..}$ = the grand total of all treatments

N = the total number of observations

$$SS_{error} = SS_{total} - SS_{treatment} - SS_{block} \qquad (14)$$

The degrees of freedom for each of these sums of squares is $(nk - 1)$ for the total; $n - 1$ for the block effect; $k - 1$ for the treatment effect; and total – treatment – block for the error.

Kelly's Toys and Games, Inc. can illustrate the use of the randomized block design with the game of *Impeachment*. This time, let us assume that management is interested in determining the effect of point-of-purchase displays on the sales of the game but is interested in controlling for the effect of the place within the store where the display is located. Management believes that the effect of the display will be greatly influenced by the location of that display within the store; that is, sales of the new product would be significantly better if the displays were in a heavy traffic area such as near the checkout counters. The sales for two point-of-purchase displays tested in two different store areas are shown as an aggregate sales figure for the test period in Table 4. Kelly's management is interested in determining whether or not point-of-purchase displays significantly affect sales of the game, eliminating the location effect at the 90% confidence level.

This is accomplished through the use of formulas discussed previously.

$$SS_{treatment} = \sum_{j} \frac{T_{.j}^2}{n} - \frac{T_{..}^2}{N} \qquad (15)$$

$$= \frac{(918)^2 + (889)^2}{2} - \frac{(1807)^2}{4}$$

$$= 210$$

Table 4. *Impeachment* Sales for Two Displays in Two Locations

Block (i)	Treatment (j)		Block totals (T_i)
	Point-of-purchase display 1 (T_1)	Point-of-purchase display 2 (T_2)	
Location 1 (B_1)	434	430	864
Location 2 (B_2)	484	459	943
Treatment total ($T_{.j}$)	918	889	1807

Overall grand total = 1807

$$SS_{block} = \sum_{i=1}^{n} \frac{T_{i.}}{K} - \frac{T_{..}^2}{N} \qquad (16)$$

$$= \frac{(864)^2 + (943)^2}{2} - \frac{(1807)^2}{4}$$

$$= 1560$$

$$SS_{total} = \sum_{j=1}^{K} \sum_{i=1}^{n_j} x_{ij}^2 - \frac{T_{..}^2}{N} \qquad (17)$$

$$= (434)^2 + (430)^2 + (484)^2 + (459)^2 - \frac{(1807)^2}{4}$$

$$= 1881$$

$$SS_{error} = SS_{total} - SS_{treatment} - SS_{block} \qquad (18)$$

$$= 1881 - 1560 - 210$$

$$= 111$$

These sums of squares as well as other appropriate data are given in the ANOVA table (Table 5).

Table 5. ANOVA for Point-of-Purchase Display at Different Store Locations

Source of variation	Degrees of freedom	Sum of squares	Mean square	Calculated F ratio	Table F ratio	Conclusion
Treatment	1	210	210	1.9	8.5	Accept H_0; point-of-
Block	1	1560	1560			purchase displays do
Error	1	111	111			not affect the sales
Total	3	1881				of new product

The degrees of freedom for each of the items are calculated using equations 15 to 18. Since there are two locations (blocks) and two point-of-purchase displays (treatments), the degrees of freedom are:

$$\text{Total} = nk - 1 = (2)(2) - 1 = 3$$

$$\text{treatment} = k - 1 = 2 - 1 = 1$$

$$\text{block} = n - 1 = 2 - 1 = 1$$

$$\text{error} = \text{total} - \text{treatment} - \text{block} = 3 - 1 - 1 = 1$$

The mean squares are found in a manner similar to that of the completely randomized design. The sum of squares is divided by the corresponding degrees of freedom. The mean square treatment is then divided by the mean square error to determine the calculated F ratio of 1.9 (210/111 = 1.9). The corresponding table F ratio is found in the table for the 90% confidence level and 1 degree of freedom for the numerator and 2 degrees of freedom for the denominator ($F_{0.10,1,2}$). This table F ratio is 8.5.

When comparing the calculated F ratio to the table F ratio, it is evident that the null hypothesis (H_0) must be accepted since the calculated F ratio is less than the table F ratio. Therefore, Kelly's management would conclude that both point-of-purchase displays tested do not affect new product sales at the 90% confidence level.

We have been concerned with testing only one aspect of the new product (completely randomized design) and either one aspect of the new product, controlling for an extraneous variable, or two aspects of the new product (randomized block design). What happens if we are interested in either controlling two non-interacting sources of extraneous variation while testing one aspect of the new product or testing three aspects of the new product?

For either of these two situations, the *Latin square design* is used. In this design each treatment appears once and only once in each row and once and only once in each column. It is only possible to use this design when the number of levels of the treatment and the restrictions are equal; that is, it must be a square. Examples of the various types of Latin square designs for testing aspects of new products are shown in Table 6. Note that each design is square and that each treatment (*A*) appears once and only once in each row and position.

Table 6. Selected Latin Square Designs for New Product Testing

3 x 3 Design			4 x 4 Design				5 x 5 Design				
C	A	B	D	A	B	C	A	B	C	D	E
A	B	C	C	D	A	B	B	C	D	E	A
B	C	A	B	C	D	A	C	D	E	A	B
			A	B	C	D	D	E	A	B	C
							E	A	B	C	D

   Analysis of the data from testing aspects of the new product is merely an extension of that of the randomized block design. The data in the Latin square design has one more dimension—the positions effect (λ_k). This is reflected in the general model:

$$X_{ijk} = \mu + B_i + T_j + \lambda_k + E_{ijk} \qquad (19)$$

where

μ = the common effect for the entire experiment

B_i = the effect of the *i*th block

T_j = the effect of the *j*th treatment

λ_k = the effect of the *k*th positions

E_{ijk} = the error in the *i*th row and *k*th column subject to the *j*th treatment (this is considered to be a normally and independently distributed effect with a mean value of 0 and similar variance for any treatment, row, or position)

Again, the usual ANOVA table is used to test the null hypothesis. The only difference from Table 5 is the number of sources of variation. In the randomized block design, there was a total of three sources of variation: treatment variable, block variable, and error variable. In the Latin square design, there are four sources of variation: treatment, block, positions, and error. The formulas for the calculations of the respective sums of squares are expanded to include the new variable:

$$SS_{\text{treatment}} = \sum_j \frac{T_{\cdot j}^2}{n_j} - \frac{T_{\cdot\cdot}^2}{N} \tag{20}$$

where

$T_{\cdot j}$ = the total of each treatment in the experiment

n_j = the number of levels of each treatment

$T_{\cdot\cdot}$ = the grand total of all treatments

N = the total number of observations

$$SS_{\text{block}} = \sum_i \frac{T_{i\cdot}^2}{k} - \frac{T_{\cdot\cdot}^2}{N} \tag{21}$$

where

$T_{i\cdot}$ = the total of each block effect in the experiment

k = the number of levels of each block

$T_{\cdot\cdot}$ = the grand total of all treatments

N = the total number of observations

$$SS_{\text{positions}} = \sum_k \frac{T_{k\cdot}^2}{n_k} - \frac{T_{\cdot\cdot}^2}{N} \tag{22}$$

where

$T_{k\cdot}$ = the total of each position's effect in the experiment

$$n_k = \text{the number of levels of each position}$$

$$T_{..} = \text{the grand total of all treatments}$$

$$N = \text{the total number of observations}$$

$$SS_{total} = \sum_i \sum_j \sum_k x_{ijk}^2 - \frac{T_{..}^2}{N} \tag{23}$$

where

$$X_{ijk} = \text{the individual observation for each treatment,}$$
$$\text{block, and position}$$

$$T_{..} = \text{the grand total of all treatments}$$

$$N = \text{the total number of observations}$$

$$SS_{error} = SS_{total} - SS_{treatment} - SS_{block} - SS_{positions} \tag{24}$$

The corresponding degrees of freedom for each are $(nk - 1)$ for the total; $n - 1$ for the treatment; $k - 1$ for the block; $n - 1$ for the positions; and total – treatment – block – positions for the error.

Returning to Kelly's Toys and Games, Inc. test-marketing of *Impeachment*, let us assume this time that management is interested in determining the effects of shelf height, number of facings of the product, and shelf fullness on the sales of the game. Management believes that eye-level shelving with more exposures due to more than one facing and having the shelves well stocked will increase the sales of *Impeachment*. To test this, sales of the product were obtained for four facings (T_j), four shelf heights (B_i), and four shelf fullnesses (λ_k) (see Table 7). Management is interested in determining whether or not any of these variables affect sales of the game at the 95% confidence level.

The effect of each can be determined by using the formulas to determine the sum of squares:

$$SS_{treatment} = \frac{\sum_n T_{.j}^2}{n} - \frac{T_{..}^2}{N} \tag{25}$$

$$= \frac{(51)^2 + (69)^2 + (71)^2 + (74)^2}{4} - \frac{(265)^2}{16}$$

$$= 80.8$$

$$SS_{block} = \frac{\sum\limits_{i} T_{i.}^2}{k} - \frac{T_{..}^2}{N} \tag{26}$$

$$= \frac{(59)^2 + (66)^2 + (71)^2 + (69)^2}{4} - \frac{(265)^2}{16}$$

$$= 20.8$$

Table 7. Sales of *Impeachment* for Four Shelf Heights, Four Facings, and Four Shelf Fullnesses

Block (B_i)	Treatments (T_j)				Block totals $(T_{i.})$
	One facing T_1	Two facings T_2	Three facings T_3	Four facings T_4	
Lowest shelf height B_1	$\lambda_1 = 13$	$\lambda_2 = 16$	$\lambda_3 = 16$	$\lambda_4 = 14$	59
Next-to-bottom shelf height B_2	$\lambda_4 = 19$	$\lambda_1 = 17$	$\lambda_2 = 20$	$\lambda_3 = 20$	66
Eye-level shelf height B_3	$\lambda_3 = 14$	$\lambda_4 = 19$	$\lambda_1 = 17$	$\lambda_2 = 21$	71
Top shelf height B_4	$\lambda_2 = 15$	$\lambda_3 = 17$	$\lambda_4 = 18$	$\lambda_1 = 19$	69
Treatment total $(T_{.j})$	51	69	71	74	265

Positions totals $\Sigma\lambda_1 = 66$, $\Sigma\lambda_2 = 72$, $\Sigma\lambda_3 = 67$, $\Sigma\lambda_4 = 60$

Overall grand total = 265

$$SS_{positions} = \frac{\sum\limits_{k} T_{k\cdot}^2}{n} - \frac{T_{\cdot\cdot}^2}{N} \qquad (27)$$

$$= \frac{(66)^2 + (72)^2 + (67)^2 + (60)^2}{4} - \frac{(265)^2}{16}$$

$$= 18.2$$

$$SS_{total} = (13)^2 + (9)^2 + (14)^2 + (15)^2 + (16)^2 + (17)^2 \qquad (28)$$

$$+ (19)^2 + (17)^2 + (16)^2 + (20)^2 + (17)^2 + (18)^2$$

$$+ (14)^2 + (20)^2 + (21)^2 + (19)^2 - \frac{(265)^2}{16}$$

$$= 144$$

$$SS_{error} = SS_{total} - SS_{treatment} - SS_{block} - SS_{positions} \qquad (29)$$

$$= 144 - 80.8 - 20.8 - 18.2$$

$$= 24.2$$

The corresponding degrees of freedom are also needed. This is a 4 × 4 square matrix, so each of the treatment, block, and positions has 3 degrees of freedom (4 − 1 = 3). The total has 15 degrees of freedom (4 × 4 − 1 = 15). Finally, the degrees of freedom for the error term are found by subtracting the degrees of freedom for the treatment, block, and error from the total. This gives 6 degrees of freedom for the error. The mean square terms are again found by dividing the respective sum of squares term by its degrees of freedom. Then, the calculated F ratio for each term is found by dividing the mean square for that term by the mean square of the error. In other words, for the treatment, the calculated F ratio is 26.9/4.9 or 6.7; for the block, it is 6.9/4.0 or 1.7; and for the positions, it is 6.1/4.0 or 1.5. All these values are given in Table 8. The calculated F ratios are then compared with the table F ratio, which is found in the table for 95% confidence level. Using 3 degrees of freedom for the numerator (the degrees of freedom for the treatment, block, and positions, respectively) and 6 degrees of freedom for the denominator (the degrees of

Table 8. ANOVA Table for Facings, Shelf Height, and Shelf Fullness

Source of variation	Degrees of freedom	Sum of squares	Mean square	Calculated F ratio	Table F ratio	Conclusion
Treatment (facings)	3	80.8	26.9	6.7	4.76	reject H_0
Block (shelf height)	3	20.8	6.9	1.7		accept H_0
Positions (shelf fullness)	3	18.2	6.1	1.5		accept H_0
Error	6	24.2	4.0			
Total	15	144				

freedom for the error), the table F ratio ($F_{0.05,3,6}$) is 4.76. When comparing the calculated F ratio with the table F ratio, it is evident that different conclusions will be drawn. Because the table F ratio is greater than the calculated F ratio for both the shelf height and shelf fullness, we accept the null hypothesis (H_0): neither shelf height nor shelf fullness affect sales of *Impeachment* at the 95% confidence level.

However, this is not the case for the number of facings. Here, the calculated F ratio is greater than the table F ratio. Therefore, the null hypothesis (H_0) is rejected and the alternative hypothesis (H_0) is rejected and the alternative hypothesis (H_1) accepted. Kelly's management can conclude that shelf facings indeed significantly affect sales of their new product at the 95% confidence level.

Thus far, managers have been only interested in testing the effect of one, two, or three variables on the sales of the new product. They have been assuming that the effect of the variables together has minimal, if any, impact on sales. However, in many new product situations, it is desirable to test two or more variables and obtain a measurement of how the variables together affect sales. *Factorial design* provides the methodology whereby two or more variables and their interaction can be evaluated for their effect on sales of the new product. As previously mentioned, many variables can be tested, but as we increase the number of variables, the number of interactions increases more rapidly. Because the general theory is the same, factorial design will only be discussed in terms of a two-variable test.[3] The general model for a two-factor factorial experiment is:

$$X_{ijk} = \lambda + A_i + B_j + AB_{ij} + E_{k(ij)} \tag{30}$$

where

λ = the common effect for the entire experiment

A_i = the effect of factor A ($i = 1, 2, \ldots, a$ levels of factor A)

B_j = the effect of factor B ($j = 1, 2, \ldots, b$ levels of factor B)

AB_{ij} = the interaction effect of factors A and B

$E_{k(ij)}$ = the error term (this is considered to be a normally and independently distributed effect with a mean value of 0 and a similar variance for any factor)

Factorial design employs the usual ANOVA table. As one would suspect, the sources of variation are different from those depicted in Table 1. These sources reflecting the terms in the general model are factor A, factor B, interaction ($A \times B$), error, and total. The sum of squares for these terms is obtained through the following formula:

$$SS_{\text{factor } A} = \sum_i^a \frac{T_{i..}^2}{nb} - \frac{T_{...}^2}{nab} \tag{31}$$

where

$T_{i..}$ = the total for each level of factor A in the experiment

n = number of observations per cell

b = the number of levels of factor B

$T_{...}$ = the grand total of the experiment

a = the number of levels for factor A

[3] For more than a two-factor factorial experiment, see Charles R. Hicks, *Fundamental Concepts*, Chapters 9-15.

$$SS_{\text{factor } B} = \sum_{j}^{b} \frac{T^2_{\cdot j \cdot}}{na} - \frac{T^2_{\cdots}}{nab} \qquad (32)$$

$T_{\cdot j \cdot}$ = the total for each level of factor B in the experiment

n = the number of observations per cell

a = the number of levels for factor A

$T_{\cdots}$ = the grand total of the experiment

b = the number of levels for factor B

$$SS_{\text{interaction}} = \sum_{i}^{a} \sum_{j}^{b} \frac{T_{ij\cdot}}{n} - \sum_{i}^{a} \frac{T_{j\cdots}}{nb} - \sum_{j}^{b} \frac{T^2_{\cdot j\cdot}}{na} + \frac{T^2_{\cdots}}{nab} \quad (33)$$

where

$T_{ij\cdot}$ = the total for each level of factors A and B together in the experiment

n = the number of observations per cell

$T_{j\cdots}$ = the total for each level of factor A in the experiment

$T_{\cdot j\cdot}$ = the total for each level of factor B in the experiment

b = the number of levels for factor B

a = the number of levels for factor A

$T_{\cdots}$ = the grand total of the experiment

$$SS_{\text{total}} = \sum_{i}^{a} \sum_{j}^{b} \sum_{k}^{n} X^2_{ijk} - \frac{T^2_{\cdots}}{nab} \qquad (34)$$

where

X_{ijk} = the individual observation for each replication of the experiment

$T_{...}$ = the grand total of the experiment

n = the number of observations per cell

a = the number of levels for factor A

b = the number of levels for factor B

$$SS_{error} = \sum_{i}^{a} \sum_{j}^{b} \sum_{k}^{n} X_{ijk}^2 - \sum_{i}^{a} \sum_{j}^{b} \frac{T_{ij.}^2}{n} \qquad (35)$$

where

X_{ijk} = the individual observation for each replication of the experiment

$T_{ij}\cdot$ = the total for each level of factor A and factor B together in the experiment

n = the number of observations per cell

The degrees of freedom breakdown is $a - 1$ for factor A, $b - 1$ for factor B, $(a - 1)(b - 1)$ for the interaction, $abn - 1$ for the total, and degrees of freedom for the total minus the degrees of freedom for factor A, factor B, and the interaction for the error.

Once again, let us use the test-marketing of *Impeachment* by Kelly's Toys and Games, Inc. This time the company is testing two different packages (factor A) and two different prices (factor B). However, management feels that the two variables will jointly affect sales as well as affect sales individually. For example, the most attractive package and price together will have an impact on sales in addition to the effect the most attractive package will have and the most attractive price will have. The total sales results are given in Table 9. Is there a significant effect on sales at the 95% confidence level?

Again, the first step in determining whether or not a significant effect is caused by the new packages, prices, or the interaction of the two is to calculate their respective sum of squares:

$$SS_{factor\ A} = \sum_{i}^{a} \frac{T_{i..}^2}{nb} - \frac{T_{...}^2}{nab} \qquad (36)$$

$$= \frac{(3976)^2 + (4407)^2}{5(2)} - \frac{(8383)^2}{5(2)(2)}$$

$$= 9287$$

$$SS_{\text{factor } B} = \sum_{j}^{b} \frac{T_{.j.}^2}{na} - \frac{T_{...}^2}{nab} \tag{37}$$

$$= \frac{(4302)^2 + (4081)^2}{5(2)} - \frac{(8383)^2}{5(2)(2)}$$

$$= 2442$$

$$SS_{\text{interaction}} = \sum_{i}^{a} \sum_{j}^{b} \frac{T_{ij.}}{n} - \sum_{i}^{a} \frac{T_{i..}^2}{nb} - \frac{\sum_{j}^{b} T_{.j.}^2}{na} + \frac{T_{...}^2}{nab} \tag{38}$$

$$= \frac{(2130)^2 + (1846)^2 + (2172)^2 + (2235)^2}{5}$$

Table 9. Sales of *Impeachment* with Two Prices and Two Packages

Factor A	Factor B		Total factor A
	Price 1	Price 2	
Package 1	430	398	3976
	423	341	
	425	369	
	426	369	
	426	369	
	$T_{ij} = 2130$	$T_{ij} = 1846$	
Package 2	393	433	4407
	495	446	
	462	476	
	437	456	
	385	424	
	$T_{ij} = 2172$	$T_{ij} = 2235$	
Total factor B	4302	4081	8383
Overall grand total = 8383			

$$- \frac{(3976)^2 + (4407)^2}{5(2)} - \frac{(4302)^2 + (4081)^2}{5(2)}$$

$$+ \frac{(8383)^2}{5(2)(2)}$$

$$= 6021$$

$$SS_{total} = \sum_{i}^{a} \sum_{j}^{b} \sum_{k}^{n} X_{ijk}^2 - \frac{T_{...}^2}{nab} \tag{39}$$

$$= (430)^2 + (423)^2 + (425)^2 + (426)^2 + (426)^2 + (398)^2$$

$$+ (341)^2 + (369)^2 + (369)^2 + (369)^2 + (393)^2$$

$$+ (495)^2 + (462)^2 + (437)^2 + (385)^2 + (433)^2$$

$$+ (446)^2 + (476)^2 + (456)^2 + (424)^2 - \frac{(8383)^2}{5(2)(2)}$$

$$= 3,543,371 - 3,513,735$$

$$= 29,636$$

$$SS_{error} = \sum_{i}^{a} \sum_{j}^{b} \sum_{k}^{n} X_{ijk} - \sum_{i}^{a} \sum_{j}^{b} \frac{T_{ij.}^2}{n} \tag{40}$$

$$= 3,543,371 - \frac{(2130)^2 + (1846)^2 + (2172)^2 + (2235)^2}{5}$$

$$= 11,886$$

The corresponding degrees of freedom are obtained by applying equations 36 to 40. The degrees of freedom are $a - 1 = 2 - 1 = 1$ for factor A, $b - 1 = 2 - 1 = 1$ for factor B, $(a - 1)(b - 1) = (2 - 1)(2 - 1) = 1$ for the interaction, $abn - 1 = (2)(2)(5) - 1 = 19$ for the total, and total $-$ factor A $-$ factor B $-$ interaction $= 19 - 1 - 1 - 1 = 16$ for the error. These, along with the mean square, calculated F ratios, and table F ratios (determined in the usual manner) are given in Table 10.

Table 10. ANOVA Table for Factorial Design

Source of variation	Degrees of freedom	Sum of squares	Mean square	Calculated F ratio	Table F ratio	Conclusion
Factor A package	1	9287	9287	13.8	4.49	reject H_0
Factor B price	1	2442	2442	3.3	4.49	accept H_0
Interaction	1	6021	6021	8.1	4.49	reject H_0
Error	16	11886	743			
Total	19	29636				

Again, when comparing the calculated F ratios to the table F ratios, different conclusions are reached. The calculated F ratio is greater than the table F ratio for the packages of the new product. Therefore, management can conclude that the packages significantly affect the sales of *Impeachment* at the 95% confidence level. A similar conclusion can be reached for the interaction between price and package as this term's calculated F ratio is also greater than the table ratio. However, price alone does not significantly affect sales of the new game at the 95% confidence level. Because the table F ratio is greater than the calculated F ratio for this term, the null hypothesis (H_0) is accepted.

Factorial design, as well as the three previously discussed designs (completely randomized, randomized block, and Latin square), provides the management of a company that is test-marketing its new product with the methods to statistically determine which variables of the new product significantly affect sales. With the increased capacities and software of computer operations, the use of experimental design will grow more and more in the test-marketing of new products.

Part Three

The New Product: Acceptance and Demand Estimation

CHAPTER
SIX

Market Segmentation
For New Products

A company must identify the group of customers toward whom it will direct the new product and all the associated marketing activities. If this is not done, the probability of success for the new product decreases significantly, if indeed, it continues to exist at all. This chapter explores the undifferentiated approach versus the market segmentation approach in target market selection. Then the various segmentation variables are discussed. The chapter concludes by presenting some new product segmentation strategies for various markets.

UNDIFFERENTIATED APPROACH

Some companies define the target market for their new product as the total market for this product. In other words, the company assesses the needs of all customers in the target market as very similar; therefore, there is no need to subdivide the market according to any product or market attribute. Although this undifferentiated approach is rarely used for new products, it may be useful for any new products that consumers would think of as being homogeneous.[1] New products similar to staple food items, such as sugar or salt, would be prime candidates for the undifferentiated strategy. This approach is illustrated in Figure 6-1.

[1] See, for example, Wendall R. Smith, "Product Differentiation and Market Segmentation as Alternative Marketing Strategies," *Journal of Marketing* (July 1956), pp. 3-8; and Alan R. Roberts, "Applying the Strategy of Market Segmentation," *Business Horizons* (Fall 1961), pp. 65-72.

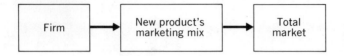

Figure 6-1. Undifferentiated Market Approach for New Products

OVERVIEW OF MARKET SEGMENTATION

Every company must determine not only which consumer needs its new product will service, but, equally important, what firm, group of individuals, or governmental unit has these needs. A balance must be achieved between the number of markets a firm appeals to and the new product ideas forthcoming. There are many sources for new product ideas (see Chapter 5) that produce many new product ideas. Yet, with the firm's limited resources, these new product ideas must be carefully analyzed so that the correct market for each is delineated and then evaluated.

Benefits of New Product Segmentation

The concept of market segmentation for new products is relatively new. Firms used to develop new products and market them without any thought of the people who would possibly buy them. Firms concentrated on the product and all its attributes but not on the characteristics of the market. There was little or no recognition of preference or need variations within the market; many firms felt that everyone would want the new product being proferred.

As competition became more intense, as consumers became more educated, and as communications systems improved, this nonsegmentation approach no longer assured market success for new products. This was evidenced in the high failure rate of new products discussed in Chapter 1. Some firms felt that perhaps a better method would be to look to the market, define its needs, and design the new product and all its attributes based on this analysis. Figure 6-2 indicates this market-oriented concept. This market can then be evaluated on a very definitive basis. In other words, customer groups could be distinguished. *Market segmentation* is the process of dividing a total market into smaller groups composed of entities (people, firms, governmental units) with similar needs and characteristics. Through market segmentation, various

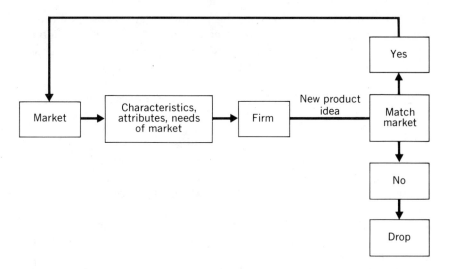

Figure 6-2. Market-Oriented Approach for New Product

groups of potential buyers of the new product, each with its own
set of buying desires or requirements, are identified.

By identifying the market and its characteristics for new products in this manner, a firm benefits in two ways. First, the needs
of the market are identified and therefore can be matched with the
proposed new product; the market needs can be examined in terms
of the degree to which products currently on the market are ful-
filling these needs. Needs of market segments that have low levels
of satisfaction can be evaluated in terms of the proposed new product. Second, if a certain market is clearly identified, then specific
characteristics for the new product can be developed. These desired
attributes can be emphasized to the buyer. In addition, the entire
marketing program can be designed and funded to satisfy the different parts of the market.

Conditions for Product Segmentation

It may appear that the golden rule for new product success is
No Matter What Else You Do, Be Sure to Segment. Although market segmentation is important, there is such a thing as oversegmen-
tation. It is probably better to segment than not to segment, but
market segmentation for a new product should be done only when
the factors, benefits, and costs allow. For example, there is no
benefit in determining that the only market for a new dog treat

(a snack food given a dog when he performs) are owners of mongrel
dogs who can do a one-and-a-half gainer dive from a 1000 meter
board, if there is no such dog in existence. This, of course, is an
absurd case, but the point is that there is no reason to break a
market down further than the benefits derived warrant. The goal
of market segmentation is to achieve maximum segmentation information per segmentation base. This goal for a new product is
achieved when certain demands and/or conditions are met.

The first is *size.* The market segments identified must be
large enough to be worth considering. The smallest segment that
should be considered is one that, if saturated, would result in
meeting the sales and/or profit goals established for the new
product. Effective segmentation does require considerable time
and costs; therefore, it would not be worthwhile to isolate a
market segment for the new product that is not large enough to
afford the expense.

The second condition is *the firm's capabilities.* The market
segment must be such that the firm has the capability of successfully marketing the new product to this segment. If the chosen
segment cannot be effectively serviced by the firm, then it is not
worth the cost of identification. For example, one small elec-
tronics firm in Boston determined that its best market segment
for a particular new product was in Los Angeles. Yet the company had no distributors, service outlets, or any familiarity with
this region. This particular market segment was totally inacces-
sible to the firm, given its budget constraints.

The final condition is *quantifiability.* The segmentation
criteria for the final market segment must be such that information
is either available or can be obtained through primary research.
There is no value in delineating a market segment based on unquan-
tifiable characteristics. If the success of a gas barbecue grill
depends on ease of cleaning it up, ease of starting, or status, then
some more measurable segmentation criteria should be selected to
replace status.

BASES FOR NEW PRODUCT SEGMENTATION

A large number of variables can be used in effective segmentation for most new products. Most of them and their categories
for consumer products are listed in Table 6-1. As indicated, these
can be grouped into four major classes: 1. Demographic 2. Geographic 3. Psychological 4. Product-related variables.[2] Of course,

[2] There are other possible classification schemes available. For example, one good alternative classification scheme can be found in Philip Kotler,
Marketing Management: Analysis, Planning, and Control, 3rd ed. (Englewood Cliffs, N.J.: Prentice-Hall, 1976).

Table 6-1. Major New Product Segmentation
Variables and Corresponding Breakdowns

Variable	Segmentation breakdown for new products
Demographic	
Age	5 and under, 6-10, 11-17, 18-24, 25-34, 35-49, 50-65, over 65
Educational level	Some high school or less, graduated high school, some college, graduated college, advanced college degree work
Family life style	Single, married with no children, married with children under six, married with children over six living at home, married with adult children living out of home, widowed
Family size	1, 2, 3, 4, 5, more than 5
Income	Under $10,000; $10,000-$14,999; $15,000-$19,999; $20,000-$29,999; $30,000-$49,999; $50,000 and over
Nationality	American, British, French, German, Italian, Spanish, other
Occupation	Executive or managerial; professional or technical; teacher or professor; salesperson; government or military; secretarial, clerical, or office worker; craftsman, mechanic, or factory worker; housewife; student; retired
Race	Caucasian, Black, Asian
Religion	Catholic, Protestant, Jewish, Other
Residence	Rent, own condominium, own home
Sex	Male, female
Social class	Lower-lower, upper-lower, lower-middle, middle-middle, upper-middle, lower-upper, upper-upper
Geographic	
City (SMSA) size	Under 19,999; 20,000-99,999; 100,000-249,999; 250,000-499,999; 500,000-999,999; 1,000,000-3,999,999; 4,000,000 and over
Climate	Northern; Southern
County size	A, B, C, D
Market density	Urban, suburban, rural
Region of country	New England, Atlantic, Central, Mountain, Pacific
Terrain	Mountains, plain
Psychological	
Life style	Swinger, nonswinger, etc.
Motives	Emotional, economic
Personality attributes	Extrovert, introvert, dependent, independent, etc.

Continued

Table 6-1.—*Continued*

Variable	Segmentation breakdown for new products
Product-related	
Benefits desired	Durability, dependability, economy
Brand loyalty	Strong, minimal, none
Controllable marketing elements	Advertising, sales promotion, price, service
End use	Consumption, capital
Volume of consumption	Heavy, medium, light, none

not all variables are appropriate for every market. This relevancy by market type will be discussed later in this chapter.

To these segmentation classes, groups of people, firms, or governmental units can be assigned so that the total market is categorized into segments. As illustrated in Figure 6-3, the firm can then develop a new product and its marketing mix to appeal specifically to a particular segment or segments.

Selection of Variables

A segmentation variable and its components are the basis for the division of a market into segments. New product segmentation variables (indicated in Table 6-1) are characteristics useful for segmentation.

In deciding which segmentation variables should be used for a particular market, several factors should be considered. In evaluating these factors, one should keep in mind that the choice of the appropriate segmentation variable is a critical step in sound market segmentation for the new product.[3] Its importance

[3] The concept of selection of the best segmentation variable has been evaluated in many ways. It is, of course, a variant with at least the product, market, and usage rate. For example, see Robert D. Hisrich and Michael P. Peters, "Selecting the Superior Segmentation Correlate," *Journal of Marketing* (July 1974), pp. 60-63; H. Lee Mathews and John W. Slocum, Jr., "Social Class and Commercial Bank Credit Card Usage," *Journal of Marketing* (January 1969), pp. 71-79; John W. Slocum, Jr., and H. Lee Mathews, "Social Class and Income as Indicators of Consumer Credit Behavior," *Journal of Marketing* (April 1970), pp. 69-74; James H. Myers, Roger R. Stanton, and Arne F. Haug, "Correlates of Buyer Behavior: Social Class versus Income," *Journal of Marketing* (October 1971), pp. 8-15; James H. Myers and John F. Mount, "More on Social Class versus Income as Correlates of Buying Behavior," *Journal of Marketing* (April 1973), pp. 71-73.

Figure 6-3. Market Segmentation Approach for New Products

becomes even more evident when one considers the need for good
market segmentation for new product success. The factors previously discussed with respect to conditions for product segmentation are similarly important in variable selection. The variables
should be selected for market size. It would not be beneficial
to use segmentation variables that would indicate a market of
insufficient size to be profitable. In other words, a sufficient
market size should be delineated through any segmentation used.
It should be selected in terms of the firm's ability to successfully
market the new product if the segment identified so warrants. If
it is not within the firm's capabilities and resources to market to
the segment indicated, then the segmentation variable should not
have been used. Also, the segmentation variable selected should
lead to quantifiable results. In other words, information should
be available so that sales can be realistically estimated for each
of the market segments defined. Finally, underlying each of the
factors previously discussed, the segmentation variable has to be
selected for the needs, desires, and product use by the total
market of consumers, industrial concerns, or governmental units;
that is, the total market and its characteristics should be the
prime determinant in the selection of a particular segmentation
variable.

Types of Variables

A company that wishes to use a segmentation approach to
successfully market a new product can select from a wide variety
of segmentation variables. *Demographic segmentation variables*
are the broadest and most widely used set of characteristics to
segment markets. They include age, family size, education level,
family life style, income, nationality, occupation, race, sex, and
social class for dividing the consumer market (see Table 6-1). In
the industrial market, commonly used demographic variables are

number of employees, volume of company sales, amount of profit, and product line. Wide use of this group of variables also occurs in the government market, such as type of agency, degree of autonomy in decision-making, and size of budget.

These variables are very often used in all markets because they are generally closely related to the needs as well as the purchasing behavior of the market; that is, they generally correlate very closely to sales of many product categories. As we would expect, sales of major durable consumer goods, such as high quality furniture, are highly correlated with income. Similarly, sales of any of the automobile manufacturers are highly correlated with the purchase of their raw materials, such as steel. Another reason for the widespread use of demographic variables is the fact that most demographic variables are easier to quantify than other types of variables. In fact, a significant amount of published data exist for many variables. Both the *Census of the Population* as well as the *Census of Business* provide data on many categories of these variables.

For example, DuPont used demographic segmentation when analyzing the market for a new plastic resin—a resin the company believed to be the most rugged plastic developed to date. With this quality characteristic as well as an initial price of $1.45/pound for orders of 40,000 pounds or more, DuPont felt that the new resin had uses in products such as helmets, agricultural equipment, sporting goods, high-impact gears, toys, and the housings of power tools.[4] The company segmented its market for the new tough, clear plastic on the basis of the type of product line of companies in the industrial market.

Geographic variables are probably the next most widely used segmentation variables. Besides being easily quantifiable and having data available, geographic segmentation can provide potential customer categories on the basis of sales force or manufacturer's representatives' locations. In other words, because the sales force must know what the target market is, it will have to be divided on the basis of existing sales territory divisions. In addition, through geographic variables, a firm can choose a market in which it enjoys a comparative advantage. A beautician will distinguish between his or her "local" clientele and more distant customers. Until recently, Coors Brewery served primarily Denver and the surrounding area. The Boston Symphony primarily serves the Boston area when playing at Symphony Hall but all of New England when playing at Tanglewood during the summer.

The various breakdowns of this variable as well as the others discussed are summarized in Table 6-1. As indicated, geographic

---

[4] "DuPont Unveils Plastic It Terms Toughest Ever," *Wall Street Journal* (December 17, 1975), p. 17.

variables, such as region of the country, market density, and city size, are used in the consumer market. Markets for new products are often divided into regions of the country according to sales territories so that target customers can be introduced to the new product. In addition, one or more geographic factors may cause one region to differ from another. A company marketing a product to the consumer market could divide the United States into five regions: New England, Atlantic, Central, Mountain, and Pacific. An even more precise breakdown could also be done. A firm operating in a smaller-than-national market could also use geographic segmentation variables, such as counties or zip code areas.

Market density indicates the number of potential customers for the new product per unit of land area such as a square mile. Although market density is related to city size, it is not necessarily a proportional relationship. For example, in two different geographic markets of about equal size and population, the market density for a new baby's toy may be much higher in one of the areas if that area contains a significantly greater number of babies. Division of the consumer market by density may help the company decide on the advertising, distribution, and sales activities necessary for the new product to reach low-density markets as contrasted with high-density ones.

City size (standard metropolitan statistical area—SMSA) can also greatly influence the amount of exposure per advertising dollar. In addition, a firm can evaluate cities for inclusion in test market selection (discussed in Chapter 6) by sorting the cities into categories according to population such as under 19,999; 20,000-99,999; 100,000-249,999; 250,000-499,999; 500,000-999,999; 1,000,000-3,999,999; and 4,000,000 and over. The size of the city may influence the need for a new product. For example, the demand for a new security device may increase as the city size increases.

The final geographic segmentation variable commonly used in the consumer market is climate. Climate often has a significant impact on customer behavior and needs for new products. Examples of such new products include air conditioning and solar heating equipment, new types of skis, and new building materials.

For the industrial and government markets, fewer geographic variables are used. Region of the country is commonly used for the industrial market. This is due in part to sales territory divisions of the company as well as to the geographic clustering that tends to occur for some types of businesses. For example, a large part of the textile industry is located on the east coast. The center of the automobile industry is Detroit, Michigan.

The government market, on the other hand, can be divided accordingly on a regional basis or on a federal, state, or local basis, depending on the uses of the new product being marketed. The latter results in different buying practices because the federal, state, and local governments each have individual procurement procedures.

Although there are many different *psychological segmentation variables* that could be used, perhaps the three most common in the consumer market are life style, motives, and personality traits. Although a psychological variable can be used alone to segment a market, it is usually combined with other types of segmentation variables, such as demographic and geographic ones. It should be kept in mind that when psychological variables are used in market segmentation, it almost always requires primary research because little, if any, published data exist.

When using life style, the firm is evaluating market possibilities for its new product on the basis of the orientation that the market group has toward consumption, work, and play. This can result in delineating such groups as "swingers" who may seek the latest in new products of various product lines that reflect a high status in society; and "straights" who primarily seek new products that accomplish what they are supposed to. In spite of the fact that life style segmentation usually requires a significant expenditure on research, firms are using it increasingly to define markets for their new products.[5] For example, Volkswagen introduced that it termed "life-styled automobiles." For the conservationist there is a Volkswagen that is economical, safe, and ecologically sound. In addition, there is a car that handles well and is sporty for the car buff.

Aside from life style, motives are another commonly used psychological variable. Motive is the force that moves an individual toward a goal. Obviously, motives influence in varying degrees whether or not a person will buy the new product. The motives can vary from emotional ones (prestige, belonging, love) to economic ones (product dependability, economy, and convenience). For example, if convenience is the primary motivating factor in whether or not a new product is purchased, then the number of stores that carry the new product becomes extremely important. Although motives are an excellent basis for psychological segmentation in that their use depicts the forces behind a person's new product purchase, the accurate quantification of these is, at best, very difficult, and in some cases, virtually impossible.

[5] See Mark Hanan, *Life-Styled Marketing* (New York: American Management Association, 1972).

The final commonly used psychological segmentation variables are embodied in the general term *personality traits.* Many different personality traits can be used to define potential markets for new products, such as extroversion, introversion, degree of dependency, aggressiveness, ambitiousness, or competitiveness. Personality traits are most useful in segmenting the market for a new product when the new product is very similar to competing products already on the market. However, the usefulness of this as a segmentation variable has not been effective in every case. One example is the case of whether or not different personalities were attracted to buying Ford versus Chevrolet automobiles.[6]   In the 1950s Fords and Chevrolets were promoted as having different personalities; Ford buyers were considered independent, masculine, and self-confident, and Chevrolet buyers were considered conservative, thrifty, and middle of the road. In an attempt to measure whether or not this was true, owners of the two car types were given an Edwards' personal preference test. The Ford owners did not differ to a significant extent from the Chevrolet owners on any attribute except dominance. Therefore, it was concluded that "the distribution of scores for all needs overlap to such an extent that [personality] discrimination is impossible." However, critics have disputed this finding on the basis of the small, localized sample and the statistical methodology employed. Indeed, even though it appears reasonable that personality characteristics would affect buyers' product choice, numerous research efforts since the Evans study have yielded very little supporting evidence.[7]

The usefulness of these psychological variables in the industrial and government markets has had virtually no statistical evidence.   However, it is possible that the degree of industrial

[6] The whole series of articles dealing with this study include Franklin B. Evans, "Psychological and Objective Factors in the Prediction of Brand Choice: Ford vs. Chevrolet," *Journal of Business* (October 1959), pp. 349-369; Gary A. Steiner, "Notes on Franklin B. Evans' 'Psychological and Objective Factors in the Prediction of Brand Choice'," *Journal of Business* (January 1961), pp. 57-60; Charles Wineck, "The Relationship Among Personality Needs, Objective Factors, and Brand Choice: A Reexamination," *Journal of Business* (January 1961), pp. 61-66; Franklin B. Evans, "You Still Can't Tell a Ford Owner from a Chevrolet Owner," *Journal of Business* (January 1961), pp. 67-73; Alfred A. Kuehn, "Demonstration of a Relationship Between Psychological Factors and Brand Choice," *Journal of Business* (April 1963), pp. 237-241; and Franklin B. Evans and Harry V. Roberts, "Fords, Chevrolets and the Problem of Discrimination," *Journal of Business* (April 1963), pp. 242-249.

[7] See Ralph Westfall, "Psychological Factors in Predicting Product Choice," *Journal of Marketing* (April 1962), pp. 34-40; *Are There Consumer Types?* (New York: Advertising Research Foundation, 1964); and W. T. Tucker and John J. Painter, "Personality and Product Use," *Journal of Applied Psychology* (October 1961), pp. 325-329.

leadership of the industrial market and the degree of ability to change for the government market could prove to be useful psychological segmentation variables for a new product for each of these markets.

Although psychological variables can provide a very effective mechanism for delineating market segments for the new product, their function as segmentation variables will probably continue to have limited use. These variables are very difficult to measure accurately. Sorely needed, for example, is a better set of tests to measure personality. In addition, the relationship between a given psychological variable and actual purchase of a new product is often obscure and untested. Still, the theory behind the promotion of many products such as Smirnoff vodka and Schweppes tonic water is an appeal to special personality types. Only time and statistical evidence will determine the real applicability of this group of segmentation variables for determining the new product's market.

The final class of segmentation variables for new products is *product-related variables*. This class of segmentation variables divides the new product market on the basis of the new product's attributes and the consumer's relationship to the product. Three main criteria are a part of this classification—benefits, volume of use, and controllable marketing elements.

One form of product-related segmentation is the use of various benefits the consumers expect from the particular product category. Although the needs of the customers underlie any segmentation variable used, consumers' needs in respect to product characteristics are the basis of benefit segmentation. In other words, consumers are identified according to the importance of the different benefits they may be seeking from the product.[8] For example, one group of automobile buyers may be seeking a product that is economical to maintain, easy to operate, and inexpensive to purchase and repair.

There may be various benefits for the consumer market. Some of these are durability, dependability, convenience, and status from ownership. Although some criteria, such as dependability and durability, are also useful in segmenting the industrial and government markets for new products, other bases take on importance in these markets. For example, in the industrial market, important benefits the buyer may be looking for in deciding whether or not to purchase the new product are reliability of the

[8] See, for example, Daniel Yankelovich, "New Criteria for Market Segmentation," *Harvard Business Review* (March-April 1964), pp. 83-90; and Russell J. Haley, "Benefit Segmentation: A Decision-Oriented Research Tool," *Journal of Marketing* (July 1968), pp. 30-35.

seller and support services, efficiency in operation or use, and/or enhancement of the firm's earnings. For the government market, reliability of the seller and the provision of support services as well as product dependability are very significant bases of segmentation.

Choosing the benefits to be used as the basis for market segmentation for the new product can be very difficult. This is particularly true in the consumer market. The benefits actually sought by the customers must be identifiable and these benefits must be the real reasons underlying new product purchase. Although home gardeners may indicate that they buy a particular new brand of fertilizer for ecological reasons, the real reason may be economy. In addition, the segment of the market determined through benefit segmentation must be quantifiable as well as accessible to the firm. For example, although a certain segment of the market may want an economical, dependable, no-frills watch, this market may not be accessible to a quality watch manufacturer because of its image and distribution system.

The second type of product-related variable is volume segmentation. In this type of segmentation the market is first divided on a use and nonuse basis. The use segment is further culled on the amount of product consumed; that is, the users of the new product can be divided according to heavy, medium, or light usage or some other more detailed consumption basis. This segmentation basis is applicable to all three markets.

Once determined, all breakdowns according to volume of use should be evaluated in terms of a viable potential market for the new product. For example, nonusers comprise two types of people: those who do not use any product at all in this product category and those who use one. Even those people who do not use any product at all in the product category should be dropped as a possible market segment only after careful deliberation. Similarly, just because a group potentially has the largest consumption rate for a new product, this segment may not be the most profitable to reach because of the required heavy expenditures, brand loyalty, or the high degree of competition. Regardless of the segment finally chosen as the target market for the new product, volume of use is a very useful criterion for new product market segmentation.

The final type of product-related segmentation variable commonly used for new products is controllable marketing elements segmentation. The firm divides the market into groups that are responsive to different marketing elements within the firm's control, such as price, advertising, sales promotion, warranty, guarantee, or service. As indicated in Table 6-2, the most important

Table 6-2. Market Segmentation for New Products by Type of Market

Segmentation Criteria	Basis for Type of Market		
	Consumer	Industrial	Government
Demographic	Age, family size, education level, family life cycle, income, nationality, occupation, race, religion, residence, sex, social class	Number of employees, size of sales, size of profit, type of product line	Type of agency, size of budget, amount of autonomy
Geographic	Region of country, city size, market density, climate	Region of country	Federal, state, local
Psychological	Personality traits, motives, life style	Degree of industrial leadership	Degree of forward thinking
Benefits	Durability, dependability, economy, esteem enhancement, status from ownership, handiness	Dependability, reliability of seller and support service, efficiency in operation or use, enhancement of firm's earnings, durability	Dependability, reliability of seller and support services
Volume of Use	Heavy, medium, light	Heavy, medium, light	Heavy, medium, light
Controllable Marketing Elements	Sales promotion, price, advertising, guarantee, warranty, retail store purchased service, product attributes, reputation of seller	Price, service, warranty, reputation of seller	Price, reputation of seller

marketing element will, of course, vary by type of market—consumer, industrial, or government. But regardless of the market, once the best market segment is determined on the basis of controllable marketing elements, then, of course, these elements will receive the most emphasis in the new product introductory marketing plan.

Market-Gridding in New Product Market Selection

A useful technique for evaluating the potential target markets for a new product is the *market grid*. A *market grid concept* depicts the total market in a two or three dimensional manner based upon selected, relevant market characteristics.[9] An example of a market grid is shown in Figure 6-4. Notice that only potential customers in the target market are shown in the lined area. Customers not part of the potential market for the new product but who are a part of the total market are in the "all-others" category. It should be kept in mind that the usefulness of the market grid as an evaluative technique is solely dependent upon the segmentation variables selected as well as their respective classifications. This is the most important part of successful market segmentation for the new product and should, therefore, be subject to a great deal of painstaking analysis.

This concept of market grid for selection of the target market(s) for a new product can be well illustrated in the banking market. The specific grids are shown in Figures 6-5 through 6-7. When looking at the market grids for this market, one should keep in mind that we are evaluating potential customers for a new banking concept, not the various bank offerings presently on the market.

To ensure that every possible customer is analyzed, customer characteristics are used first. As shown in Figure 6-5, the type of customers (a demographic segmentation variable) is analyzed by market density (a geographic segmentation variable). Assuming that the industrial market is the prime target for the bank, further analysis of this market is needed.

Two different approaches to the analysis of this market are shown in Figures 6-6 and 6-7. Figure 6-6 shows an analysis of the industrial market for the commercial bank by two demo-. graphic segmentation variables—size of business and by type of business. Note that the size of business is differentiated on a

---

[9] Although the concept of market-gridding can be found in most introductory marketing textbooks, a good overview with examples can be found in E. Jerome McCarthy, *Basic Marketing* (Homewood, Ill.: Richard D. Irwin, 1975), Chapters 4 and 6.

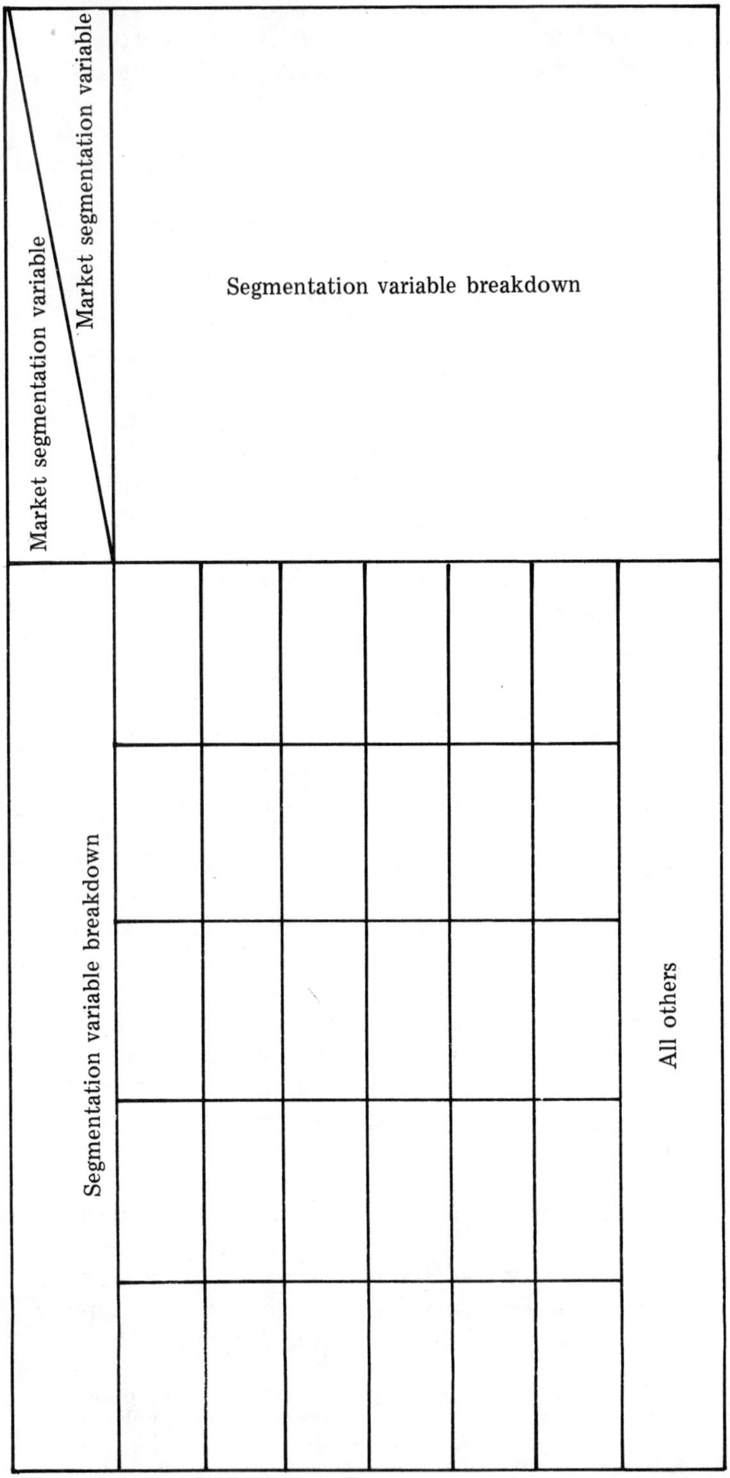

Figure 6-4. Market Grids for New Product Market Selection

Rural	Suburban	Urban	Region of country / Type of customer
			Consumer market
			Industrial market
			Government market
All Others			

Figure 6-5. General Market Grid for the Services of a New Commercial Bank

Large	Medium	Small	Size of business / Type of business
			Manufacturing
			Retail trade
			Service industries
			Transportation
			Utilities
			Wholesale trade
			Construction
			Insurance and real estate
All others			

Figure 6-6. Market Grid Example for the Services of a New Commercial Bank for the Industrial Market

Type of business / Bank service	Manufacturing	Retail trade	Service industries	Transportation	Utilities	Wholesale trade	Construction	Insurance and real estate
Commercial loans								
Checking accounts								
Savings accounts								
Safe-deposit box								
Branch banking								
After-hours depository								
Bank by mail								
Lock box plan								

Figure 6-7. Market Grid Example for the Service of a Bank for the Industrial Market

Type of business / Bank service	Insurance and real estate	Construction	Wholesale trade	Utilities	Transportation	Service industries	Retail trade	Manufacturing
Account reconcilement plan								
Freight payment plan								
Payroll accounting plan								
Commercial mortages								
Executive welcome service								
Industrial development services								
Corporate trust services								
Custodial services for securities								

Figure 6-7—*Continued*

Type of business → / Bank service ↓	Insurance and real estate	Construction	Wholesale trade	Utilities	Transportation	Service industries	Retail trade	Manufacturing
Credit inquiries								
Wire transfer of funds								
Foreign and domestic collections								
Payroll and excise tax depository								
Trust services								
Commercial real estate management								
Pension and profit-sharing plans								
All others								

Figure 6-7—*Continued*

very general basis: small, medium, and large. This categorization can be much more specific, such as categories by number of units sold, number of people employed, or dollar amount of profit. In addition, not all possible types of businesses in the industrial market are shown. Only those which are considered to have enough potential to be in the target market are included. Other businesses without this potential would be included in the all-others category.

On the other hand, Figure 6-7 illustrates another approach to the analysis of the industrial market as the potential target market for the commercial bank. In this example, a demographic segmentation variable (type of business) and a controllable marketing element segment variable (services that could be offered by the bank) are used. This grid is an attempt to determine the amount of use each type of business would have for each of the potential services of the bank. The resultant analysis would show the prime candidates in the business market for all of the bank's services as well as indicate the potential usage rate of each service. Note that neither of the sections of the selected segmentation variables are all inclusive, hence, the need for the all-other category.

SUMMARY

The importance of market segmentation for success in marketing new products cannot be overemphasized. This is particularly true as competition becomes heavier and more new products inundate the market.

The benefits of new product segmentation are many, particularly when the proper conditions for product segmentation are met. The markets for the new product can be segmented according to demographic, geographic, psychological, and/or product-related variables and the use of market grids. To be ultimately useful in the successful marketing of the new product, the segments must be of sufficient size, related to the firm's capabilities, and quantifiable. Indeed, the importance of segmentation for new products has never been greater.

SELECTED READINGS

Barnard, J. *American Community Behavior*, rev. ed. Chicago: Holt, Rinehart and Winston, 1962.

Britt, Steuart Henderson. *The Spenders.* New York: McGraw-Hill, 1960.

Coleman, Richard P. "The Significance of Social Stratification in Selling." *Marketing: A Mature Discipline*, ed. Martin L. Bell. Chicago: American Marketing Association, 1961.

Frank, Ronald E.; Massy, William F.; and Wind, Yoram. *Market Segmentation.* Englewood Cliffs, N.J.: Prentice-Hall, 1972.

Gottlieb, Maurice J. "Segmentation by Personality Types." *Advanced Marketing Efficiency*, ed. Lynn H. Stockman. Chicago: American Marketing Association, 1959.

Haley, Russell J. "Benefit Segmentation: A Decision-Oriented Research Tool." *Journal of Marketing* (July 1968):30-35.

Heidingsfield, Myron S. *Changing Patterns in Marketing.* Boston: Allyn & Bacon, 1968.

Holloway, Robert J., and Hancock, Robert S., eds. *The Environment of Marketing Behavior.* New York: Wiley, 1964.

Katona, George. *The Powerful Consumer.* New York: McGraw-Hill, 1960.

Reynolds, William H. "More Sense About Market Segmentation." *Harvard Business Review* (September-October 1965):111-18.

Twedt, Dik Warren. "How Important to Marketing Strategy Is the 'Heavy User'?" *Journal of Marketing* (January 1964):71-72.

Westfall, Ralph. "Psychological Factors in Predicting Product Choice." *Journal of Marketing* (April 1962):34-40.

Yankelovich, Daniel. "New Criteria for Market Segmentation." *Harvard Business Review* (March-April 1964):83-90.

7

Diffusion and
Adoption of New Products

One of the foremost reasons for new product failure is inadequate marketing strategy and planning (see Chapter 1). However, since it is one of marketers' prime roles to integrate new products into the cultural composition of the society, they must have a more comprehensive understanding of the process of new product adoption. This understanding can be manifested, in part, through research focusing on the factors governing the diffusion of new products introduced into the social system.

HISTORICAL PERSPECTIVE OF DIFFUSION RESEARCH

The process by which an innovation spreads from its inception to its ultimate or final user is referred to as diffusion. Diffusion research studies have been carried out for about 50 years in many different disciplines. Interest began with the rural sociologists attempting to understand how new farm technology could be more rapidly diffused in the farm community. This was necessary because of technological changes occurring in our society in the early 1940s. At that time the average American farmer had to support more and more people, thus necessitating large increases in the average crop yield through new technological development. With new innovations designed to improve yield, which required a considerable time lag before gaining wide acceptance, rural sociologists sought techniques and strategies by which diffusion of these innovations could be hastened.[1]

[1] For a comprehensive presentation of the diffusion and adoption process see Everett M. Rogers, *Diffusion of Innovations* (New York: The Free Press, 1962); and Thomas S. Robertson, *Innovative Behavior and Communication* (New York: Holt, Rinehart and Winston, 1971).

Although taking the initiative in diffusion research, rural sociology is not the only discipline that has contributed to the process of understanding the diffusion process. Research studies have focused on innovations in anthropology, sociology, education, medicine, economics, and industrial and consumer goods marketing.[2] Marketing's interest in diffusion stems from an attempt to increase the probability of success of a new product through an increased understanding of the factors governing the diffusion process. However, until recently research in the marketing area has been minimal. Its importance as a means of improving the new product development process is only now beginning to be recognized.

THE DIFFUSION PROCESS

The diffusion process is often confused with the adoption process. The adoption process is the mental process by which individuals pass from the point where they first become aware of a new product's existence to when they actually use or adopt the product on a regular basis. Hence, the diffusion process is the aggregate of all individual adoptions over time.

Elements of Diffusion

Four crucial elements are identified in the diffusion process: (a) the innovation, (b) the communication from one individual to another, (c) the relevant social system of which these individuals are a part, and (d) the time dimensions in the process.

Innovation   An innovation is an idea or a product perceived as new by the buyer. Chapter 1 discussed the difficulty in defining what is meant by *new*. The basis of defining *new* seems to depend on the disrupting effects the new product has on established behavioral patterns. It appears that more meaningful theory development could occur if research studies in marketing were classified according to the relative newness of the product. Then marketers could refer to research findings categorically related to the new product they are introducing. These findings would be useful to

---

[2] A listing of all published diffusion research in all disciplines is maintained at the Documents Center at Michigan State University. These publications are listed in Everett M. Rogers, *Bibliography on the Diffusion of Innovations* (East Lansing, Mich.: Department of Communication, Michigan State University, 1971).

their new product introduction since similar results may be expected with products having similar degrees of newness.

The Communication   The essence of the diffusion process involves human interaction in which one person transmits information regarding an innovation to another person. This communication, which can be transmitted through formal or informal channels, is necessary in order for diffusion to take place.

The Social System   A social system is defined as a population of individuals who are functionally differentiated and engaged in collective problem-solving behavior. Thus, the social system for a new product would be all those individuals or firms in a specified area who can use the product. This specified area may represent a test market in which a new product is being tested for possible large-scale market introduction.[3] The information on the diffusion of a new product in the test market could be quite useful in the design of a marketing plan by the firm attempting to achieve large geographical or national distribution. When all individuals or units in a specified area have adopted the innovation under study, the diffusion process is complete.

Some confusion exists as to what is meant by the adoption unit in the social system. There actually exists a continuum of adoption units ranging from an individual choice to a group decision. At one extreme we find innovations that are adopted by an individual; although this individual may be influenced by others in the social system, he or she basically makes the final choice. At the other extreme are innovations that are adopted by a group. Many community decisions would fall into this latter class.

The Time Dimension   Not all people adopt an idea or new product at the same time. Thus, time in the diffusion process refers to when or how long after introduction an individual or unit decides to adopt an innovation. For example, Figure 7-1 shows housewife A hearing a commercial on the product Bounce, a new static remover and fabric softener in May 1976. However, housewife A did not actually begin using this product on a regular basis until September 1976. Housewife B hears of Bounce from her neighbor in June 1976. She begins to purchase this product on a regular basis in July 1976. It can be seen that the time needed to adopt a new product by each housewife differs significantly. Marketers would be quite interested in knowing not only why it took housewife A so long to adopt the innovation, but any individual and environmental variables distinguishing A from B.

[3] A full discussion of test-marketing new products is found in Chapter 5.

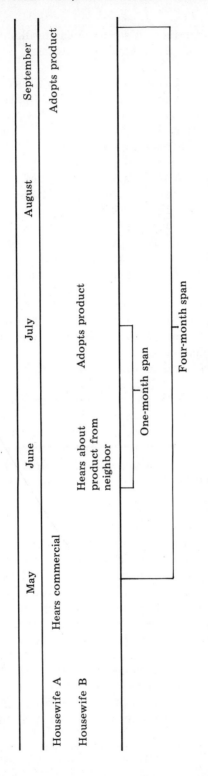

Figure 7-1.   Examples of Time Spans Incurred Before Actual Adoption

One attempt to establish adopter categories was developed by rural sociologists classifying buyers according to when they adopt an innovation.

Adopter Categories

Figure 7-2 depicts the diffusion curve partitioned into categories of adopters over time. The distribution of adoption of any innovation over time has been found to resemble a normal distribution. This is supported by Rogers, who found that in eight different studies adopter distributions all approached normality.[4] The categories established by the rural sociologists assume this normality condition since each category is represented as an area that is a specified number of standard deviations from the mean. Thus, the area under the curve is used to determine the percentage of people or units who have adopted in that time span. The innovators represent the first 2.5% to adopt, the early adopters the next 13.5%, and so on. Although this categorization is arbitrary, it has been meaningful to rural sociologists in studying the adoption of agricultural innovations. However, much of the marketing diffusion research deviates from the percentages as well as from labels established by rural sociologists that identify each adopter category. For example, marketing researchers have been mainly concerned with such distinctions as innovators compared to noninnovators or early adopters compared to later adopters. In each case the categories were identified using different percentages. The use of any percentage is strictly arbitrary and is usually chosen for its convenience to the researcher.

The diffusion process can also be depicted as a cumulative curve, as seen in Figure 7-3. The cumulative curve resembles an S-shape pattern very similar to the familiar product life cycle discussed in Chapter 1. However, the cumulative curve is based on the proportion of consumers in any given potential market who adopt the innovation, whereas the vertical axis for the product life cycle represents absolute dollars of sales.[5] The identification of the potential market (depicted as 1.00 in Figure 7-3) would depend on what the firm felt it could achieve given certain market conditions. One way of not only determining this percentage but also of studying the nature of the cumulative diffusion pattern would be to use test markets and then make projections based on an analysis of the sample data.[6]

[4] Rogers, *Diffusion of Innovations*, p. 158.

[5] For a more detailed discussion of the product life cycle and cumulative diffusion curve see Robertson, *Innovative Behavior*, p. 30.

[6] A discussion of this is presented in Chapter 6.

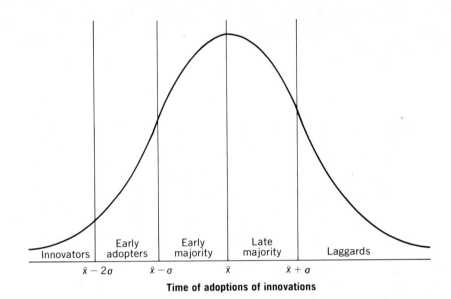

Figure 7-2. Market Segments Identified by Time of Adoption of New Product
(From Everett Rogers, *Diffusion of Innovations* [New York: The
Free Press, 1962], p. 162. Copyright © 1962, The Free Press.)

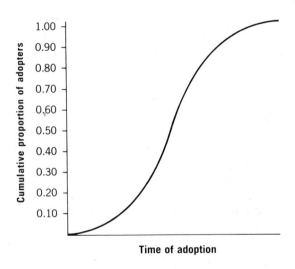

Figure 7-3. Cumulative Diffusion Curve

THE ADOPTION PROCESS

As stated earlier the adoption process is concerned with the individual, whereas the diffusion process is concerned with aggregate behavior. In studying the individual, certain behavioral tendencies or mental patterns have been discerned that have enhanced the understanding of why and how consumers adopt new products.

Before some of these mental and/or behavioral tendencies are discussed, it is necessary to clear up some confusion as to the actual meaning of adoption. Adoption in some situations may refer to the single purchase of a product, and in other situations it may refer to a series of purchases of the innovation in question by the same person. The key to identifying adoption appears to depend on the commitment made by the consumer. For example, a consumer who purchases any large-ticket item is actually committed to that product for an extended period of time. However, the single purchase of a new household cleaner may not represent actual commitment since the consumer could switch brands without ever repurchasing the new product in question. Thus, for a product of this type it is necessary to identify some commitment on the part of the consumer by determining the number or frequency of purchases of the new product made by that person. Of concern is what number of repeat purchases represents adoption. Some researchers have distinguished adopters on the basis of usage rate of any new product. For example, Frank and Massy categorized buyers of Folger's coffee according to the proportion of total pounds of coffee purchased in a given period of time that were Folger's.[7] The definition of adoption for frequently purchased products varies according to the parameters established by the researcher.

Stages in the Adoption Process

From the point in time when an individual first hears of an innovation to the point in time when adoption occurs has been recognized as consisting of five sequential stages:

1. *Awareness stage.* The individual is exposed to the innovation but lacks complete information about it. The individual is aware of the innovation but is not yet motivated to seek further information.

---

[7] Ronald E. Frank and William F. Massy, "Innovation and Brand Choice: The Folger's Invasion," *Proceedings of the American Marketing Association* (December, 1963), p. 102.

2.   *Interest stage.* The individual becomes interested in
the new idea and seeks additional information about
it. The innovation is favored in a general way but is
not yet judged in terms of its utility to a specific
situation.

3.   *Evaluation stage.* The individual mentally applies
the innovation to his or her present and anticipated
future situation and then decides whether or not to
try it.

4.   *Trial stage.* The individual uses the innovation on a
small scale in order to determine its utility in his or
her own situation.

5.   *Adoption stage.* The individual decides to continue
the full use of the innovation.

It should be noted that any innovations may be rejected at
any stage of the adoption process. For example, a housewife may
hear about Bounce, but she does not own a clothes dryer; thus, she
would be rejecting the innovation at the awareness stage.

Rejection of an innovation can also occur after an individual
has adopted it. This behavior is referred to as a discontinuance. A
discontinuance is the cessation of using an innovation after previously adopting it. Discontinuances in marketing are quite common, especially since consumers often purchase everyday items
without any special loyalty to one brand. Thus, in marketing the
importance of defining adoption as a function of the commitment
made by the consumer becomes more critical.

A consumer could conceivably move through several of these
stages simultaneously, such as in an impulse decision or when a free
sample of a new product is received. These instances do not destroy the argument for the existence of these stages, but merely
collapse them into a shorter time span. Criticism has been made
concerning the strict sequencing of these stages. The beginning
stage, for example, may be the perception of a problem that seems
to concur with the interest stage discussed earlier. Thus, it is possible in these circumstances that problem or interest could precede
awareness.

Increased understanding of the sequencing of these stages and
the types of communication most effective in each stage will enable
the firm attempting to market a new product to develop a promotional campaign consistent with the behavior of the consumer.
Initially, more mass media should be employed to relay product
awareness and information on product utility. As time passes, the
appeal should be modified to include a more personal appeal, since

the consumer generally becomes more dependent on others for evaluating, trying, and adopting the new product. The strategy employed, however, must give some consideration to the nature of the new product. The characteristics of the new product will affect the adoption process, and it may be a necessary part of the promotional considerations to alleviate any negative characteristics of the product that may deter its rate of adoption in the marketplace.

Characteristics of the Innovation

In marketing a new product, special emphasis must be given to particular product attributes and the brand image created by the manufacturer. The perceived attributes or characteristics of the innovation may regulate the rate at which diffusion occurs. These characteristics are: (a) relative advantage, (b) compatibility, (c) complexity, (d) divisibility, and (e) communicability.

Relative Advantage   This is the degree to which an innovation is superior to one it supersedes or competes with in the marketplace. Removal of phosphates from detergents represented a likely perceived relative advantage over the old product it replaced or any competitive product that still maintained its traditional formula. However, the addition of green crystals to a detergent was less likely to be perceived by the consumer as having any relative advantage. The strategy used by most firms is to seek product differentiation by employing tactics that would result in a relative advantage over any existing products. A new wonder drug that could cure a sore throat within hours would certainly have a superior edge or advantage over any other available product, thus likely increasing the rate at which this product would be diffused. It should be emphasized, however, that the relative advantage of an innovation depends extensively on the perception of the members of a given social system.

Compatibility   This refers to the degree to which a new product is consistent with existing values and experiences of the consumers. A new product whose perceived image is not consistent with cultural norms will diffuse less rapidly than one that is consistent. Also, new products that are similar to other products that have been failures will negatively affect the rate of diffusion.

For example, instant coffee experienced some initial barriers in achieving its predicted success. The product was promoted as a time saver for housewives. The housewife during this period often associated the use of time-saving products with lazy people and thus tended to reject the product. Research revealed this error, and advertising was corrected to be more compatible with existing norms and values.[8] When it was introduced, television was found to be more consistent with the values of lower classes, and hence diffused more quickly at that level.[9]

It appears that the marketer should give some emphasis in assuring that any new product is consistent or compatible with existing norms or values so that the probability of its success and rapid diffusion may be enhanced.

Complexity   This terms refers to the degree of difficulty in understanding or using an innovation. A new product that is confusing to consumers so that they are unable to evaluate (evaluation stage) the product's utility will generally take longer to diffuse in a given market. Products that require new knowledge also apparently take longer to diffuse. For example, Graham concluded that one reason that canasta and television diffused at different rates was the difference in complexity of the two ideas.[10] Canasta generally required some personal explanation, whereas television usage was relatively simple and required little explanation.

Divisibility   This is the degree to which a new product may be tried on a limited basis. The ability of consumers to purchase small, trial-size packages of new products at a low cost may encourage the rate of adoption. The amount of risk associated with such a small-scale purchase is minimal and allows consumers to examine an alternative to their present brand. Other products that are sold with the added feature of a ten-day, free home trial attempt to accomplish the same effect as the small trial size. Many other products, however, cannot be sold on a small scale or with the ten-day, free home trial. Industrial products, such as computers and machines, are difficult to move and thus are more permanent purchase decisions.

In recent years marketers have offered more trial sizes for their new products than in the past. Free samples given by manufacturers have also shown substantial increases. One example of this increase occurred in 1967 when Colgate-Palmolive mailed free sample boxes of Axion to 50 million of the nation's 60 million households. In its introduction of Maxim coffee, General Foods also mailed out about the same number of free samples. Indications are

[8] M. Haire, "Projective Techniques in Marketing Research," *Journal of Marketing* 14 (1950), pp. 649-52.

[9] Saxon Graham, "Cultural Compatibility in the Adoption of Television," *Social Forces* 33 (1954), p. 169.

[10] S. Graham, "Class and Conservatism in the Adoption of Innovations," *Human Relations* 9 (1956), pp. 91-100.

that this approach costs less than the same dollar amount of advertising needed to get the consumer to the trial stage in the adoption process. Marketers must be concerned with making it as easy as possible for the consumer to try a new product with little risk so that the rate of diffusion may possibly be enhanced.

Communicability   This refers to the degree to which information regarding a new product may be easily communicated to other people in the marketplace. Products that are visible to others, such as clothing and automobiles, and products that can be easily demonstrated, such as television, phonographs, and other small appliances, generally fall into the high communicability category. Generally, products that are very complex will be most difficult to communicate to others.

Evidence regarding some of these five factors is still not clear, as is shown in Table 7-1. Research studies relating to divisibility, communicability, and complexity are limited, and thus, their conclusions are not definite. More research must be completed before any conclusions may be drawn regarding the relationship of these product characteristics to adoption. It is imperative, however, that the firm give serious consideration to determining if any of these characteristics are especially inherent in their product such that the rate of adoption may be slowed. Promotional strategy can be designed to accommodate negative product attributes, such as complexity, by incorporating as much explanatory information as

Table 7-1. New Product Characteristics Related to Innovativeness

Characteristic	Percentage of findings indicating relationship to innovativeness					Total number of findings
	Positive	None	Negative	Conditional	Total	
Relative advantage	79	15	3	3	100	66
Compatibility	86	14	0	0	100	50
Complexity	19	37	44	0	100	16
Divisibility	43	43	14	0	100	14
Communicability	75	25	0	0	100	8

SOURCE: Based on Everett M. Rogers and David J. Stanfield, "Adoption and Diffusion on New Products: Emerging Generalizations and Hypotheses," *Applications of the Sciences in Marketing Management*, ed. Frank M. Bass et al. (New York: Wiley, 1968), pp. 227-250. Copyright © 1968 John Wiley & Sons, Inc. Reprinted by permission of John Wiley & Sons, Inc.

possible. Marketing strategy may also be developed to improve communicability and divisibility of the new product. Free maintenance may act as a substitute for new products that cannot be sold on a smaller scale. Promotional strategies, such as demonstrations, may also improve the communicability problem. Effective advertising may be able to alleviate compatibility problems, such as the approach used in the instant coffee case discussed earlier. Nevertheless, it is apparent that the new product must be carefully analyzed to identify any of the above attributes so that marketing strategies to remedy these consumer perceptions can be employed.

CORRELATES OF INNOVATIVENESS: EMPIRICAL FINDINGS

The findings pertinent to the development of a diffusion research tradition in marketing are categorically discussed below. These contributions should enhance the success of new product introductions, particularly in developing a more effective marketing strategy, which in the past has been one of the major reasons for new product failures.

Rural Sociology

Most of the pertinent research in the diffusion area is found in the rural sociology literature. A general summary of these findings involving farm innovations indicates that: (a) earlier adopters are generally found to be younger in age than later adopters; (b) earlier adopters have higher social status than later adopters; (c) earlier adopters have a more favorable financial position than later adopters; (d) earlier adopters have more specialized farm operations than later adopters; (e) earlier adopters have a type of mental ability different from that of later adopters; (f) earlier adopters are more cosmopolitan than later adopters; and (g) earlier adopters have more opinion leadership than later adopters.

A study by Rogers specifically concerned with personality traits found that certain personality traits were statistically significant in relation to innovativeness.[11] Of seven personality variables that were studied in relation to adoption, rigidity, change orientation (general attitude toward new technological practices), innovative proneness (desire to seek out changes), and adoption self-ratings were found to be significantly related. Although change orientation, innovative proneness, and adoption self-ratings were positively related to adoption, rigidity was negatively related to adoption.

[11] Everett M. Rogers, "Personality Correlates of the Adoption of Technological Practices," *Rural Sociology* 22 (September 1957), pp. 267-68.

Economics

Most of the research concerned with industrial product adoption has been published by economists. However, the results are quite relevant to marketers for purposes of increasing their understanding of the diffusion of new industrial products.

In one study Mansfield found that the size of the firm and the profitability of an innovation to the firm explained about 50% of the variation in time of adoption.[12]   Brozen, on the other hand, suggested that a positive relationship between size of firm and innovativeness may not exist, and therefore the largest firms in an industry may not be the most innovative.[13]   Carter and Williams found that the firm's growth rate was positively related to the "technical progressiveness" of the firm. The higher the growth rate, the more likely the firm was to have adopted innovative management practices and policies.[14]   These studies focused strictly on environmental variables and not on the individual characteristics of the buyer(s).

Marketing

In the marketing diffusion literature, studies have focused on both consumer and industrial products. Although the majority of these studies were concerned with consumer goods, more attention is presently being given to industrial products. Empirical findings in both areas relevant to marketing will therefore be discussed separately.

Consumer Goods

Although the existence of stages has been researched extensively by rural sociologists, marketers have recognized that variations in diffusion theory do occur when crossing discipline boundaries. Thus, some research has focused on validating the existence of stages in the consumer goods adoption process. Robertson found that stages did exist and that innovators and noninnovators responded differently to information in each of these stages.[15]   In

[12] Edwin Mansfield, "The Speed of Response of Firms to New Techniques," *Quarterly Journal of Economics* 77 (May 1963) pp. 290-311.

[13] Yale Brozen, "Invention, Innovation, and Imitation," *American Economic Review* 41 (May 1951), pp. 239-57.

[14] C. F. Carter and B. R. Williams, "The Characteristics of Technically Aggressive Firms," *Journal of Industrial Economics* 8 (March 1959), pp. 87-154.

[15] Thomas S. Robertson, "Purchase Sequence Responses: Innovators vs. Non-Innovators," *Journal of Advertising Research* 8 (March 1968), pp. 47-52.

their study of a new drug called "gammanym" Coleman, Katz, and
Menzel found that stages did exist and that contrary to rural sociology findings personal sources of information were more important
at the awareness stage. In the first six months of the product's
existence, most doctors sought advice from their colleagues when
first becoming aware of the new drug. These networks seemed to
disappear after six months when the doctors were in the later stages
of the adoption process. During these later stages, the doctors
sought information from outside sources, such as medical journals
and detail people before actually adopting the product.[16]

Most of the research in marketing has focused on the correlates relevant to the adoption process. Bell studied two types of
innovations: strategic (color television and stereophonic equipment)
and functional (dishwashers and air conditioning). These two types
of products basically fit the continuous and dynamically continuous
categories described in Chapter 1. The first 10% to purchase the
products were labeled innovators, the next 40% were termed early
adopters, and the remainder called the mass market. When innovators were compared to early adopters and then to the mass market
for both types of products, significant differences were found regarding such variables as age, occupation, education, income, ethnic
group, home characteristics, and size of family. The differences on
these variables were also significant for innovators of strategic innovations compared to innovators of functional innovations.[17] Frank
and Massy reported that purchase characteristics exerted the greatest
effect in determining innovative behavior regarding Folger's coffee.
The most significant variables were number of pounds of coffee
purchased per week, number of stores shopped in, income, and
average pound purchase of coffee per shopping trip. Also relevant
was the wife's employment status.[18] Robertson's study of the diffusion of the Touch-Tone telephone indicated that the innovator
(first 10%) was characterized as venturesome, socially mobile, privi-
leged, socially integrated, and noncosmopolitan.[19] King's work
with fashions suggests that the early buyer (first 35% to buy) is
older, has higher education and change orientation, is involved in
social activities, and is very interested in personal appearance.[20]

[16] James Coleman, Eliha Katz, and Herbert Menzel, "The Diffusion of an
Innovation Among Physicians," *Sociometry* 20 (December 1957), pp. 253-70.

[17] William E. Bell, "Consumer Innovators: A Unique Market for Newness," *Proceedings of the American Marketing Association* (December 1963),
pp. 85-95.

[18] Ronald E. Frank and William F. Massy, "Folger's Invasion," p. 105.

[19] Thomas S. Robertson and James N. Kennedy, "Prediction of Consumer Innovators: Application of Multiple Discriminant Analysis," *Journal of
Marketing Research* 5 (February 1968), pp. 64-69.

[20] Charles V. King, "Fashion Adoption: A Rebuttal to the Trickle
Down Theory," *Proceedings of the American Marketing Association* (December
1963), pp. 108-25.

To a large degree these studies were concerned with demographic and shopping variables with little concern for risk-handling variables, such as perceived risk and generalized and specific self-confidence. A few studies have looked at these variables. In a study on the diffusion of Perky coffee, Arndt found that pioneers and early adopters of this product were significantly lower in perceived risk than nonadopters.[21] Popielarz found that there was a relationship between the willingness to try new products and willingness to accept different forms of risk. One type of risk was trying a new product that may be unsatisfactory and the other type of risk was restricting decisions so that more satisfying products may be missed.[22] Ostlund found that specific self-confidence appears to override generalized self-confidence in innovative willingness to adopt a new product.[23] Thus, if specific self-confidence is high, there appeared to be a greater likelihood of adoption regardless of the level of generalized self-confidence. Although these variables must be studied in more detail by marketing researchers, their importance to the adoption of a new product appears to be significant. Marketers must show more concern with the variables affecting the adoption of their new products. Increased knowledge of these variables may then appropriately be employed for decisions regarding packaging, branding, pricing, distribution, and promotion.

Industrial Goods

As previously mentioned, little research has focused on the diffusion process in the purchasing of new industrial products. Only one known published study looked at the existence of stages in the industrial product adoption process. This pilot study by Ozanne and Churchill found some evidence to validate the five-stage model. In a reversal of previous results, however, these researchers found that personal sources of information were more prevalent in the later stages.[24]

[21] Johan Arndt, "Role of Product-Related Conversations in the Diffusion of a New Product," *Journal of Marketing Research* 4 (August 1967), p. 294.

[22] Donald T. Popielarz, "An Exploration of Perceived Risk and Willingness to Try New Products," *Journal of Marketing Research* 4 (November 1967), pp. 368-72.

[23] Specific self-confidence is defined as the degree of faith one has in his or her ability to purchase a specific type of product. Generalized self-confidence refers to feelings a buyer has about his or her ability to cope with the general buying situation. See Lyman E. Ostlund, "The Interaction of Self-Confidence Variables in the Context of Innovative Behavior," *Proceedings of the American Marketing Association* (September 1971), pp. 351-57.

[24] Urban B. Ozanne and Gilbert A. Churchill, "Adoption Research: Information Sources in the Industrial Purchasing Decision," *Proceedings of the American Marketing Association* (August 1968), pp. 352-60.

A more recent study by Peters and Venkatesan also supports the existence of the stages. However, in this study involving a small computer, personal sources of information were important in all stages of the adoption process.[25] Therefore, it appears that the relevant sources of information at each stage may be dependent on the nature of the innovation.

Most of the limited research in this area is concerned with identifying the pertinent variables significant in the industrial product adoption process. A study conducted by Robinson, Faris, and Wind indicated that determinants of an industrial buyer's behavior include psychological and behavioral characteristics as well as organizational and environmental variables. Perceived risk and attitude toward the supplier were apparently relevant to the new industrial product adoption.[26] Cardozo found in a preliminary study that variables, such as perceived risk and self-confidence of the individual buyer, and environmental factors, such as profit margin, competitive advantage, and type of firm, were related to adoption behavior.[27] Webster also supports the importance of behavioral variables in the industrial product adoption process.[28]

More recently Peters and Venkatesan found that the adoption of a small computer was related to: (a) individual behavioral variables—perceived risk, specific self-confidence, attitude toward supplier, and open mindedness; (b) demographic variables—education, computer knowledge of buyer, and number of prior jobs held; and (c) environmental variables—size of firm, growth rate, industry type, and prior data processing (EDP) equipment or service used.[29] Doubts of validity and reliability, however, still surround much of this research. Future studies that duplicate the above research will give us more conclusive evidence regarding new industrial product adoption. Such evidence may then be used in the development of a marketing plan for the new industrial product.

Of particular significance to all research across these many disciplines is that the innovator in one product category does not tend to be innovative in other product categories. Innovativeness does

[25] Michael P. Peters and M. Venkatesan, "Exploration of Variables Inherent in Adopting an Industrial Product," *Journal of Marketing Research* (August 1973), pp. 312-15.

[26] Patrick J. Robinson, Charles W. Faris, and Yoram Wind, *Industrial Buying and Creative Marketing* (Boston: Allyn and Bacon, 1967).

[27] Richard N. Cardozo, "Segmenting the Industrial Market," *Proceedings of the American Marketing Association* (August 1968), pp. 433-40.

[28] Frederic E. Webster, Jr., "New Product Adoption in Industrial Markets: A Framework for Analysis," *Journal of Marketing* 33 (July 1969), pp. 35-45.

[29] Peters and Venkatesan, "Exploration of Variables Inherent in Adopting an Industrial Product," *Journal of Marketing Research* (August 1973), pp. 312-15.

appear, however, to exist within product categories; an early adopter or innovator for one type of new product may be an early adopter or innovator for another similar type of product. Therefore, any diffusion information that is to be applied to marketing a new product must be obtained from past research involving similar products. If this is not done, marketing decisions may be based on erroneous information regarding the correlates appropriate to the adoption of the new product in question.

The test market discussed in Chapter 5 should also provide management with valuable data as to the diffusion process for the new product. Assuming that the test market is representative and is retained over a number of repurchase cycles, the correlates related to adopter categories—that is, innovators, early adopters, early majority, late majority, and laggards—can be projected to the national market. This analysis will give the firm an opportunity to prepare for each adopter category over time and to modify its marketing strategy to enhance acceptance.

In addition to the adopter categories, various tests to determine the most effective means of communication to enhance movement through the stages of awareness to adoption may be conducted. In particular, this promotion should consider the problems of the new product's relative advantage, compatibility, complexity, divisibility, and communicability.

The overall benefit from diffusion research is the ability of the firm to now effectively develop and time marketing strategy modifications to enhance consumer acceptance.

SUMMARY

This chapter has synthesized a substantial portion of the diffusion of innovation literature. Many of the important findings relevant to each research tradition were discussed. The chapter looked at both the diffusion process, which involves aggregate behavior, and the adoption process, which involves individual behavior. The diffusion process includes four crucial elements: the innovation, communication, the social system, and time. Adopter categories are identified in the diffusion process and are depicted as fitting a normal distribution. Categories are labeled and identified differently in different disciplines. Of most significance are the factors or correlates that are related to each adopter category. These correlates generally relate individual behavioral variables and/or environmental variables where appropriate.

Characteristics of the product also appear to affect the rate of diffusion. Factors, such as the relative advantage, compatibility, complexity, divisibility, and communicability, may determine the ease with which consumers accept a new product.

The adoption process is believed to follow a five-stage sequential process beginning with actual awareness of a product's existence and ending with adoption or commitment to that product. Information sources that are relevant to each stage appear to differ in each discipline and hence may be a function of the nature of the innovation in question.

The foremost reason for studying the diffusion and adoption process is to increase the level of understanding of how, when, and why new products are accepted or rejected. It is believed that a more comprehensive understanding of this process will enhance the success of future new product introductions.

SELECTED READINGS

Feldman, Lawrence P., and Armstrong, Gary M. "Identifying Buyers of a Major Automotive Innovation." *Journal of Marketing* (January 1975):47-53.

Malecki, Edward J., and Brown, Lawrence A. "The Adoption of Credit Card Services by Banks: A Case Study of Innovation Diffusion." *Bulletin of Business Research* (August 1975):1-4.

Mason, Joseph Barry, and Bellenger, Danny. "Analyzing High Fashion Acceptance." *Journal of Retailing* (Winter 1973-1974):79-88.

Ozanne, Urban B., and Churchill, Gilbert A. "Five Dimensions of Industrial Adoption Process." *Journal of Marketing Research* (August 1971): 322-25.

Peters, Michael P., and Venkatesan, M. "Exploration of Variables Inherent in Adopting an Industrial Product." *Journal of Marketing Research* (August 1973):312-15.

Robertson, Thomas S. *Innovative Behavior and Communication.* New York: Holt, Rinehart and Winston, 1971.

Rogers, Everett M. *Diffusion of Innovations.* New York: The Free Press, 1962.

_____, and Shoemaker, F. Floyd. *Communication of Innovations.* New York: The Free Press, 1971.

Scott, Carol A. "The Effects of Trial and Incentives on Repeat Purchase Behavior." *Journal of Marketing Research* (August 1976):232-65.

8

Forecasting
New Product Sales

Through a product's development stages, each decision regarding the new product is based on some forecast whether or not formal techniques are used. In the course of planning the future for the new product, several sales forecasts may be made, each giving an estimate of probable sales when a certain marketing plan is initiated and when a set of controllable elements prevails.

This chapter discussed the many favorable and unfavorable factors affecting new product sales forecasting as well as the relationship of series indicators to accurate sales forecasting. Then several methods are presented. An evaluation of the problems in forecasting accurate sales follows the discussion of the actual forecasting of new product sales on a short-term and long-term basis.

FACTORS AFFECTING NEW PRODUCT FORECASTING

Two sets of variables are involved in making any new product forecast: uncontrollable variables and controllable elements in the new product's marketing plan that will affect its sales. There are favorable and unfavorable factors in each of these two sets of variables that directly influence the sales forecast. Each of these should be listed for every new forecast situation.

Favorable Factors

Favorable factors are those the effect of which are likely to help the new product achieve good sales. By carefully analyzing

the new product and market situation, management can identify
factors that would be beneficial to sales. These are highly dependent on the type of product as well as on whether its primary
market is consumer, industrial, or government. Certain indicators
of sound business activity will help the sales of new products to
varying degrees. For example, when increased capital expenditures
are planned, the more favorable climate could provide an optimistic
buying setting that could help the new product's sales. This could
occur regardless of how closely the new product ties in with
capital goods. Other indicators are increased demand for goods;
low unemployment rate; increasing consumer, industrial, and
government purchases; reasonable balance of trade, and inventories
in line with sales.

Unfavorable Factors

On the other side, there are factors that will probably have a
negative effect on the sales of the new product. These elements
should be even more carefully analyzed than favorable ones since
they increase the rate of new product failure. Again, the effect of
these items will vary depending on the product and market characteristics of the new offering. The following indicators generally
have a negative effect on sales: high interest rates, rising prices
and threat of inflation, decline in construction (particularly home
building), decline in automotive sales, labor discontent and strikes,
restrictive monetary policy, and decline in the stock market.

Judgment must be used to assess the degree of impact each
factor, both beneficial and detrimental, will have on the new product. Those factors that have a significant effect on the sales
should be studied for their future trends. This analysis is particularly helpful in forecasting new product sales because it requires a
thorough investigation of the current market situation and an
evaluation of the future of important components.

SERIES INDICATORS

One major factor influencing the sales of any new product,
regardless of its market, is the general economic condition confronting the product. It is always necessary to have at least a
broad gauge of general business activity. For successful launching,
it is equally important to have an accurate prediction of future
business conditions. This prediction requires more than having an
understanding of the mechanisms of the economy and the interrelationships among them.

Each company establishes favorite indices of those general economic conditions most relevant to its product category. These indices should be examined for any indicators that may affect the sales of the new product. Although indicators are product specific, there are three categories of indicators, shown in Table 8-1. Naturally, the group of indices that lead general business activity is usually examined most closely. A leading index is one the movement of which (upward or downward) precedes that of the sales of the new product. Unfortunately, these do not consistently mean an upswing or downturn in new product sales. It is particularly difficult to interpret the meaning of leading indicators when there is some inconsistency or contradiction among several indicators, as there often is.

Simultaneous (coincident) and lagging indicators have little importance in the decision to launch a new product. Coincident indicators are those that are in harmony with the peaks and

Table 8-1. Principal Business Indicators for Predicting New Product Sales

Leading indicators

Average work week of production workers
Value of manufacturer's new orders (durable goods industries)
Construction contracts awarded for commercial and industrial
  buildings
Contracts and orders for plant and equipment
Newly approved capital appropriations
Net change in the business population (new businesses incorpo-
  rated and failures)
Corporate profits after taxes
Index of stock prices
Change in business inventories
Value of manufacturers' new orders

Simultaneous (coincident) indicators

Unemployment rate
Index of help-wanted advertising in newspaper
Index of industrial production
Gross national product
Personal income
Sales of retail stores
Index of wholesale prices

Lagging indicators

Business expenditures on new plant and equipment
Book value of manufacturers' inventories
Consumer installment debt
Index of labor cost per unit of output

troughs in the new product's sales. Although these will be of value in establishing marketing strategies in various stages of the product life cycle, after the new product has been on the market, they have little value in the initial go, no-go decision. Similarly, for a number of important economic indicators, peaks and troughs follow turning points in general business. Although the activities of these lag behind the general level of business activity, in a few instances they can have some predictive value for new products. For example, a firm that must borrow funds to launch the new product should be aware that interest rates usually go up some time after a coincident series peak has been reached. If a trough occurs, then interest rates will often reach their lowest level a few weeks later.

MARKET SIZE DETERMINATION

Throughout the entire new product development process from conception to market introduction, the primary concern is the size of the market. This size must be determined on both a present and projected basis.

The problem of measuring market size for the new product varies with the degree of newness of the product. It is easier to determine the market potential for a continuous innovation, particularly if it is very similar to products the company is currently marketing. Market size determination becomes easiest when the new product is a line extension. For discontinuous innovations, market determination is more difficult. For such products, the company lacks experience, and, of course, no published data exist.

Companies often overestimate the sales of the new product. This is attributable to underestimation of competitive reaction, to being too optimistic about the new product's marketing plan, and to consumers overstating their opinion and degree of buying interest when queried about the new product.

The market size must also be evaluated for its growth potential. When the new product is in a growth market, the probability of success greatly increases. However, measuring long-term growth potential poses even more difficulties than determining the initial market size. Again, the degree of difficulty increases with the newness of the product; that is, the more discontinuous and revolutionary, the more difficult it is to establish the growth potential. Even when the overall growth pattern for a product class can be estimated, it still may be difficult to estimate the growth for a single product within that class. This is especially the case in rapidly changing markets. Because of these difficulties, the first one-year estimate often occurs late in the development of the new product.

In determining market size for the new product, it is often valuable to use a standardized form. Table 8-2 is one form useful in forecasting not only sales volume, but profit and market share as well. The form can be filled out by sales personnel and product managers. Their estimates can be pooled either by straight averaging or by a weighted averaging method if certain estimates are considered more valid. It is important to note that the price per unit is requested for each year that a sales volume estimate is made. This forces the estimator to more carefully and realistically appraise the sales.

Another useful form is shown in Table 8-3. The rating scale provides a succinct means for sales people, product managers, or members of the new product committee to evaluate the potential sales and profits of the new product. Each of the individuals would rate every category from 0% to 100%. Each of the ratings (column 2) is then multiplied by its respective weight (column 3) (preassigned by a management committee) to obtain its weighted rating (column 4). When all the weighted ratings are summed, an overall product rating is obtained for each product being evaluated. The sum of weights (column 3) should be 100%.

The total weighted rating can be used to estimate the new product's sales volume. An example of sales volume determination for several new products is shown in Table 8-4. The rating of each product (A) is obtained from Table 8-3. These total 400. The preference ratio (B), the number that indicates which product is best, is found by dividing each product rating by the total of all product ratings—that is, by 400. For example, the preference ratio for product 104 is 80/400 = 0.20. The total sales expected for the next period (C) is a very difficult but essential estimate to make. It can be in either dollar or unit figures. It is often obtained from data on similar new products or from the sales of other products in the same product class. In this case, total new product sales were estimated to be $10,000.

This total sales expected ($10,000) can now be allocated to each of the new products under consideration by multiplying it by the respective preference ratios. For example, for product 104, the total product sales is $2,000 ($10,000 × 0.2) For the sake of contingencies, three sales forecasts are calculated: the most optimistic, the most likely (calculated above), and the most pessimistic. In the case at hand, from examination of past new product sales, management felt that most optimistically, sales could exceed the most likely forecast by as much as 20% (E). Therefore, multiplying each new product's sales by 1.2 will yield the most optimistic estimate of sales for each new product under consideration.

Table 8-2. New Product Sales and Profit Determination

Product experience and forecast			Forecast years		
Categories determining value of product	Unit of measurement	Test market and sales	1	2	3
Price per unit	$				
Sales volume	No. of units				
Sales volume	$				
Variable margin per unit	$				
Variable margin per year	$				
Net profit per unit	$				
Net profit per year	$				
Market share	%				
Sales as percentage of firm's total volume	%				

SOURCE: Adapted from Norbert Lloyd Enrick, *Market and Sales Forecasting*, ed. 2 (Huntington, N.Y.: R. E. Krieger Pub. Co., Inc. In press).

Table 8-3. New Product Sales and Profit Determination

Future expectations for the product	Rating of future potential of a new product												Weight W (%)	Weighted rating $W \times R_1$ (%)
	Rating R_1 (%)													
	Low										High			
	0	10	20	30	40	50	60	70	80	90	100			
Market potential that can be realized														
Required amount of promotional expense														
Profit per unit														
Contribution to sales of other products														
Other contributions to firm's overall program														
Total														

SOURCE: Norbert Lloyd Enrick, *Market and Sales Forecasting*, ed. 2 (Huntington, N.Y.: R. E. Krieger Pub. Co., Inc. In press).

Table 8-4. New Product Sales and Profit Determination

| | Conversion of rating to volume | | | | | | | |
| Procedure | Product number | | | | | | | Total |
	101	102	103	104	105	106	107	
A. Rating of product (%)	40	80	50	80	60	20	70	400
B. Preference ratio = $\dfrac{\text{Product rating (\%)}}{\text{Total of ratings (\%)}}$	0.10	0.20	0.125	0.20	0.15	0.05	0.175	1.0
C. Total sales expected for next period ($)								10,000
D. Product sales expected $ = B \times C$	1,000	2,000	1,250	2,000	1,500	500	1,750	
E. High expectation $ = 1.20 \times D$	1,200	2,400	1,500	2,400	1,800	600	2,100	12,000

SOURCE: Norbert Lloyd Enrick, *Market and Sales Forecasting*, ed. 2 (Huntington, N.Y.: R. E. Krieger Pub. Co., Inc. In press).

For product 104, this figure is 2400 (2000 × 1.2). A pessimistic expectation sales figure is also calculated so that profit determinations can be made for low, best, and high sales.

(One important determinant of the new product's sales that warrants very careful consideration is competing companies, in general, and their products in particular.) As discussed in Chapter 1, misunderstanding competition is often the cause for new product failure. To help reduce the possibility of misunderstanding, it is often desirable to analyze each competitor individually. Specifically a determination should be made regarding whether or not the new product can be competitive on the basis of various controllable marketing elements. Is the new product deficient, equal, or superior in terms of quality, utility, convenience, versatility, reliability, durability, serviceability, and safety? This analysis is very helpful in ensuring that the new product does not have "quality features" that the market does not want and therefore is unwilling to pay for. Analysis of competition, if done in all stages of the development process, is particularly beneficial in orienting research and development efforts toward the market.[1]

This analysis of competitive products for their design and performance features must take place throughout all stages of product development. In the latter stages of development, it becomes increasingly important to compare the promotion, pricing, and timing of the introduction of new products to competing products. The purpose is to delineate opportunities or deficiencies. Factors of the new product, such as advertising (both consumer and trade), packaging, cost, and price must be measured against those of competing products. Through a careful appraisal of competition, a more accurate determination of the market size for the new product can be made.

Aside from analyzing the competition's product, it is beneficial to evaluate the competing company itself. Such areas as management risk-taking ability, production and engineering capability, and distribution and sales strength of each competitor should be compared to determine whether any comparative advantages or disadvantages exist. The assessment of management of major competitors is very important, especially in determining the competitive reaction to one of the most vulnerable areas of the new product: price. This is fully developed in Chapter 11.

---

[1] This problem in developing the best possible product for the market through proper orientation of research and development is discussed in Chapter 2.

SPECIFIC FORECASTING METHODS

No single forecasting method gives accurate forecasts in all situations. The most favored technique used in obtaining estimates of new product sales is to use several methods simultaneously. Not only are better forecasts obtained, but each forecast acts as a check on the results of another.

Probably the most important factor is the amount of data available on or related to product sales. This amount is usually dependent on whether or not some type of market test was undertaken (discussed in Chapter 6). A recent corporate survey identified four criteria for selecting a forecasting method. Aside from cost and the characteristics of the specific product situation, other identified criteria were the user's technical ability and the characteristics of the methods considered.[2] The user's technical ability indicates that in order for a company to use a particular forecasting method, it must have an understanding of the method. This was also reflected in the fourth criterion: the method's individual characteristics. These delineate the preference of the forecaster as well as his or her skills and background.

Among the methods most commonly used in new product forecasting are jury of executive opinion, sales force composite, buyers' expectation, Delphi, correlation and regression analysis, models, and other specialized techniques. Each of these forecasting methods will be discussed separately with the exception of models. Models for new product evaluation and forecasting were discussed in Chapter 3.

These methods are used to varying degrees depending on the specific product/market situation. The acceptance and use of various techniques in general forecasting situations are indicated in Table 8-5. The companies participating in the survey were asked the number of different forecasting methods they used. Not only did over half of the responding companies account for seven of the eight techniques mentioned, but the "survey also determined that once a company tries a specific method, it is likely to continue to use it."[3] The results may not be exactly the same if the companies were asked specifically about new product forecasting, but there is little reason to believe that there would be a great deviation. The major difference for new product forecasting is in the amount of data available.

---

[2] These results as well as others are found in Steven C. Wheelwright and Darral G. Clarke, "Corporate Forecasting: Promise and Reality," *Harvard Business Review* (November-December 1976), pp. 40-60

[3] Ibid., pp. 41.

Table 8-5. Acceptance and Use of Alternative Forecasting Methods

Method	Use of the method by those familiar with it (%)	Ongoing use of the method by those who have tried it (%)	Those unfamiliar with the method (%)
Jury of executive opinion	82	89	6
Regression analysis	76	91	8
Time series smoothing	75	84	13
Sales force composite	74	82	10
Index numbers	67	85	33
Econometric models	65	88	12
Customer expectations	57	78	15
Jenkins box	40	71	39

SOURCE: Steven C. Wheelwright and Darral G. White, "Corporate Forecasting: Promise and Reality," *Harvard Business Review*, (November-December 1976), p. 41. Copyright © 1976 by the President and Fellows of Harvard College; all rights reserved.

Jury of Executive Opinion

The jury of executive opinion—one of the oldest and simplest techniques known—asks top executives of the firm about future sales. Averaging these views, a broad base forecast is usually obtained, possibly leading to a more accurate forecast than by using only a single estimate. In the jury of executive opinion method, estimates of sales are generally obtained from executives of functional areas, such as marketing, finance, production, and purchasing. The more factual information these executives have at their disposal, the more accurate their estimate of sales.

Table 8-6 and Table 8-7 show the advantages and disadvantages of four forecasting methods, respectively. The advantage most often cited for the jury of executive opinion method is that it is quick and easy. Perhaps the major disadvantage is that it relies on the opinions of executives who may be only slightly associated with the new product and therefore could only guess its sales. Some new product managers felt that this method of forecasting the sales of the new product should only be used in the total absence of internal and external data when no other means is available.

Sales Force Composite

The sales force composite method compiles the sales force's estimates of future sales. The salespeople sometimes make these

Table 8-6. Advantages of Techniques for Forecasting New Products

Jury of executive opinion	Sales force composite	Buyer's expectation	Delphi
1. Can provide forecasts easily and quickly 2. May not require the preparation of elaborate statistics 3. Brings a variety of specialized viewpoints together for a pooling of experience and judgment 4. May be the only feasible means of forecasting, especially in the absence of adequate data	1. Uses specialized knowledge of people closest to the market 2. Places responsibility for the forecast in the hands of those who must produce the results 3. Gives sales force greater confidence in quotas developed from forecasts 4. Tends to give results greater stability because of the magnitude of the sample 5. Lends itself to the easy development of product, territory, customer, or salespeople breakdowns	1. Bases forecast on information obtained direct from product users whose buying actions will actually determine sales 2. Gives forecaster a subjective feel of the market and of the thinking behind users' buying intentions 3. Bypasses published or other indirect sources, enabling the inquiring company to obtain its information in the form and detail required 4. Offers a possible way of making a forecast where other methods may be inadequate or impossible to use—e.g., forecasting demand for a new industrial product for which no previous sales record is available	1. Can provide relatively accurate short- and long-term new product sales 2. Uses experts in the field 3. Keeps any "bandwagon effect" from occurring 4. Can be very effective in forecasting sales of new high technology products

SOURCE: The first three techniques are found in *Forecasting Sales* (New York: National Industrial Conference Board, 1964), pp. 13, 21, and 31.

Table 8-7. Disadvantages of Techniques for Forecasting New Products

Jury of executive opinion	Sales force composite	Buyer's expectation	Delphi
1. Is inferior to a more factual basis of forecasting, since it is based so heavily on opinion	1. Salespeople are poor estimators, often being either more optimistic or more pessimistic than conditions warrant	1. Is difficult to employ in markets where users are numerous or not easily located	1. Requires a great deal of time to implement
2. Requires costly executive time	2. If estimates are used as a basis for setting quotas, salespeople are inclined to understate the demand in order to make the goal easier to achieve	2. Depends on the judgment and cooperation of product users, some of whom may be ill-informed or uncooperative	2. Accuracy somewhat dependent upon ability of coordinator
3. Is not necessarily more accurate because opinion is averaged	3. Salespeople are often unaware of the broad economic patterns shaping future sales and are thus incapable of forecasting trends for extended periods	3. Bases forecast on expectations, which are subject to subsequent change	3. Estimates can be made without insight into the market
4. Disperses responsibility for accurate forecasting	4. Since sales forecasting is a subsidiary function of the sales force, sufficient time may not be made available for it	4. Requires considerable expenditure of time and manpower	4. Can be somewhat costly
5. Presents difficulties in making breakdowns by products, time intervals, or markets for operating purposes	5. Requires an extensive expenditure of time by executives and sales force		
	6. Elaborate schemes are sometimes necessary to keep estimates realistic and free from bias		

SOURCE: The first three techniques are found in *Forecasting Sales* (New York: National Industrial Conference Board, 1964), pp. 13, 21, and 31.

estimates alone, using a specially designed form. Other times, the sales estimates for the new product are made in consultation with the sales manager. The latter approach is generally preferred for new products because the salespeople may have limited familiarity with the product concept. The sales manager can provide such information. In addition, the sales manager can evaluate the forecast with the salesperson and any necessary modifications can then be made jointly.

The results are totaled for the district or region. The district (or regional) managers then evaluate this estimate by comparing it with the accuracy of past estimates of new product sales. Their own experience also enters into their evaluation before the district's estimate is forwarded to the home office, where a total sales estimate is compiled.

The forecast for the new product is made up of a composite of individual estimates by the salespeople. However, this does not mean that individual forecasting errors will be negated. A common bias is usually operative in the sales force causing forecasting errors, usually resulting in low forecasts. Believing the estimate they give for the new product's sales will be the basis of their sales quota when the product is introduced, members of the sales force tend to underestimate the sales potential of the new product. This can occur even when the sales force is assured that this will not be the case.

Understatement of the sales potential of the new product can cause the firm to lose potential profits by not introducing the new product or by having insufficient production capacity to meet the demand. This can be corrected by establishing an index of pessimism for each salesperson. The index is derived from comparing all previous estimates of new product sales with the actual sales. The difference, when divided by the estimate, becomes the salesperson's index. By averaging all the indices from previous new product sales estimates, an index of pessimism is established. Multiplying this index by the understated estimate of the new product can yield a proportionately increased estimate, which more accurately reflects the probable sales. In one company the estimates for about 90% of the sales people were within ±10% of actual sales when indices of pessimism were used.

The sales force composite method allows the new product's sales forecast to be estimated by knowledgeable people who are closest to the market. However, it still has two problems in producing accurate forecasts. First, the structure of the market is an important factor in the ability of the sales force to accurately forecast sales. If the salespeople are selling to relatively few accounts or if relatively few accounts comprise the predominant proportion of the salesperson's business, then the new product forecasts are usually more accurate than when the salesperson is selling to many small, nondominating customers. In the former situation the salesperson usually has intimate knowledge of key accounts and can better estimate their purchasing behavior with the new product. The second problem with the sales force composite method is that salespeople's evaluation, compensation, and promotion are based on sales, not on their forecasting accuracy. Therefore, they usually spend as little time as possible in making the forecast. This problem can be somewhat alleviated if directions from upper level management indicate the importance of new product forecasts. By establishing a bonus system, the accuracy of new product forecasts by the sales force can increase dramatically.

Buyer's Expectation

Many companies planning the introduction of a new industrial product often ask present, past, and potential customers about their possible purchases if the new product were introduced. This approach can be best implemented when there are relatively few potential customers. These potential customers can be queried about their purchasing plans by mail, telephone, or in person for more accurate and detailed estimates. A major problem occurs if potential buyers really like the new product and overstate their buying intention. When this happens, there may be an oversupply of the new product. One technique for discounting artificial demand is called an index of optimism. This is based on the past purchases of new products; it is similar to the index of pessimism discussed in the sales force composite technique. However, this index has far more limited use because buyers change so often that there is seldom a buying history upon which to establish the index.

The buyer's expectation method can also be used for consumer products in conjunction with consumer panels. By employing a consumer panel within a test market, not only can sales of the new product within that area be predicted, but the market test results can be projected to the entire area of final distribution.[4] Under the buyer's expectation method, data on individual purchases of the new product are collected from the panel members in as many test areas as are established. Socioeconomic characteristics and general buying behavior patterns as well as abnormalities in

---

[4] The ability to make this projection as well as its accuracy is dependent on the degree the test market reflects the area of final distribution. This aspect of test market selection is discussed in Chapter 6.

reporting information are noted. Growth in the purchase of the
product class due to the introduction of the new product into the
test market, as well as the repeat purchase rate, can be determined.
By extrapolating and then multiplying the growth rate by the
repeat purchase rate, a prediction of the market share for the new
product in the long run can be obtained. To obtain the total market forecast for the new product, the panel forecast is projected to
the test market and, in turn, the test market to the whole market
area.[5] Consumer panels can provide a very accurate forecast of
new product sales when carefully monitored.

Delphi

The Delphi method has been used recently to forecast sales for
new product concepts as well as to predict future trends. This
method employs a panel of experts who answer elaborate question-
naires on the new product's sales potential. Their responses are
summarized and used as a basis for establishing the next set of elaborate questions. This process is repeated until a reliable estimate of
the sales potential of the new product is obtained. This method,
which gained wide attention in 1964 when it forecasted a manned
lunar landing by 1970, is particularly useful for determining sales of
high technology products.

Correlation and Regression Analysis

Where data exist from test market results, correlation and regression analysis are probably the most widely used procedures to
forecast new product sales. These procedures establish the mathematical relationship between sales of the new product and at least
one other variable. Correlation analysis measures the magnitude of
the relationship between sales and at least one other variable. Both
have the underlying assumption that sales as well as the values of
the other variable(s) are chosen at random. It is often used to
detect any relationship between sales and any other variable(s) in
the market test data.

After one or more associations is found, regression analysis is
used to predict the value of the dependent variable—the sales of the
new product. In regression analysis it is assumed that the independent variables (those related to the sales of the new product) are

---

[5] A useful procedure for estimating new product sales through consumer
panels can be found in David H. Ahl, "New Product Forecasting Using Consumer Panels," *Journal of Marketing Research* (May 1970), pp. 160-67.

predetermined and selected with foresight and judgment. On the other hand, the Y value (new product sales) associated with these independent variables is selected at random—that is, it is distributed around the independent bariables.

To illustrate the use of regression analysis, let us assume that we are trying to determine the potential sales of Lifecard. This new product is a plastic card that has a tiny microfilm insert containing the bearer's entire medical history. The information can be used as a reference by doctors or hospital staff. There is space on the card to record information such as health insurance, eyeglass prescription, allergies, and the names and phone numbers of people to contact in case of an emergency. The card is being market tested for $9.95.[6] The market test results as well as the number of heart attacks in the test market area are given in Table 8-8.

Table 8-8. Market Test Results of Lifecard

Time in test market (biweekly results)	Sales (in thousands of dollars) Y	Number of heart attacks (in hundreds of units)	XY	Y^2	X^2
1st	7.0	6.0	42.0	49.0	36.0
2nd	6.0	7.0	42.0	36.0	49.0
3rd	5.0	5.0	25.0	25.0	25.0
4th	4.0	4.0	16.0	16.0	16.0
5th	5.0	4.0	20.0	25.0	16.0
6th	6.0	5.0	30.0	36.0	25.0
7th	5.0	6.0	30.0	25.0	36.0
8th	6.0	4.0	24.0	36.0	16.0
9th	7.0	8.0	56.0	49.0	64.0
10th	8.0	7.0	56.0	64.0	49.0
11th	6.0	7.0	42.0	36.0	49.0
12th	7.0	8.0	56.0	49.0	64.0
Total	72.0	71.0	439.0	446.0	445.0

It is believed that the sales of Lifecard are a function of the number of heart attacks occurring. Therefore, regression analysis can be used to find the relationship, if any, between the number of heart attacks and the sales of Lifecard. There are many types of regression equations to show the application of regression analysis in forecasting new product sales. We will assume, however, that a

[6]This Lifecard was described in "A Wave of New Products for Work, Play, Travel," *U.S. News and World Report* (November 29, 1976), pp. 73-76.

linear regression will be the one that best fits the data. This linear regression equation is of the form:[7]

$$Y_c = a + bx \qquad (1)$$

The values of a and b are calculated by solving the following two equations:

$$b = \frac{n\Sigma xy - x\Sigma Y}{n\Sigma x^2 - (\Sigma x)^2} \qquad (2)$$

$$a = \overline{Y} - b\overline{x} \qquad (3)$$

where

n = number of observations in sample

x = independent variable (number of heart attacks)

Y = dependent variable (sales of Lifecard)

a = equation's intercept of Y axis when $x = 0$

b = slope of equation

$\overline{x}$ = mean of $x(\overline{x} = x/n)$

$\overline{Y}$ = mean of $Y(\overline{Y} = Y/n)$

Using the data in Table 8-8, the regression equation for Lifecard can be substituted as follows:

$$b = \frac{n\Sigma xY - \Sigma x\Sigma Y}{n\Sigma x^2 - (\Sigma x)^2} = \frac{12(439) - (72)(71)}{12(445) - (71)^2} \qquad (4)$$

$$= 0.521$$

$$\overline{x} = \Sigma x/n = 71.0/12 = 5.92$$

---

[7] A discussion of regression analysis can be found in N. R. Draper and H. Smith, *Applied Regression Analysis* (New York: Wiley, 1966); and Charles W. Gross and Robin T. Peterson, *Business Forecasting* (Boston: Houghton Mifflin 1976). The formulas presented here are taken from the latter text.

$$\overline{Y} = \Sigma Y/n = 72.0/12 = 6.00$$

$$a = \overline{Y} - b\overline{x} = 6.00 - (0.521)5.92 = 2.92$$

$$Y_c = 2.92 + 0.521(x)$$

This sample regression equation shows that the forecasted sales for the new product is a function of the number of heart attacks occurring. For example, if 900 heart attacks were to occur then Lifecard sales would be:

$$Y_c = 2.92 + 0.521(9.0) = \$6,609$$

Although we have established the regression equation for predicting sales of the new product Lifecard, we will still have to determine the standard error of the regression, the significance of b, and the confidence level for the prediction of sales. The standard error of the regression ($\hat{\sigma}_{y \cdot x}$) is dependent upon the strength of the association between the dependent and independent variables. When no association exists at all between the sales of the new product and the independent variable, then the standard error of the regression is the same value as the standard deviation of Y. On the other hand, when a strong association exists, there is a small standard error of the regression, with perfect association producing a standard error of the regression equal to zero. In this latter case, the regression equation of heart attacks to sales explains everything of the dependent variable (sales).

The standard error of the regression is calculated by using the following equation:

$$\hat{\sigma}_{y \cdot x} = \frac{\Sigma Y^2 - a\Sigma Y - b\Sigma xY}{n - 2}$$

$$= \frac{446 - 2.92(72) - 0.521(439)}{12 - 2} \tag{5}$$

$$= 0.843$$

Aside from the standard error of the regression, we must determine whether or not the slope of the regression equation is statistically significant. As previously stated, one assumption in regression analysis is that the Y value is normally distributed about the true regression line, allowing the basic assumption to be made that b. also has a normal sampling distribution.

To test the significance of b, the t statistic is used.[8] The t statistic is found by using the following formula:

$$t = \frac{b - B}{\hat{\sigma}_b} \qquad (6)$$

where

b = the slope for the regression function

B = the population parameter ($B = 0$ when testing the significance of b)

$\hat{\sigma}_b$ = unbiased estimate of the standard error of b

$$\hat{\sigma}_b = \frac{\hat{\sigma}_{y \cdot x}}{\sqrt{\Sigma x^2 - \frac{(\Sigma x)^2}{n}}}$$

This $\hat{\sigma}_b$ value is then compared with the critical value of t at the specified confidence level with $n - 2$ degrees of freedom. The null hypothesis is $H_0(B) = 0$ and the alternative hypothesis is $H_a(B) \neq 0$. If the calculated t is greater than the table t, the null hypothesis is rejected and an significant association does exist.

Calculating the significance for Lifecard at the 95% confidence level:

$$\hat{\sigma}_b = \frac{\hat{\sigma}_{y \cdot x}}{\sqrt{\Sigma x^2 - \frac{(\Sigma x)^2}{n}}} = \frac{0.843}{\sqrt{445 - \frac{(71)^2}{12}}} \qquad (7)$$

$$= 0.168$$

$$t = \frac{0.521 - 0}{0.168} = 3.10$$

The table t value is found from using any table of critical values of t using $12 - 2 = 10$ degrees of freedom and the 95% con-

---

[8] When n is small, the t distribution is used instead of the standard normal distribution. For larger samples, the standard normal distribution is approached, and a z value is computed. The computational procedure of the two methods is very similar. In forecasting new product sales from market test data, there is usually only a small number of observations so the t distribution is used.

fidence level. The table value is 2.228. Since our calculated value (3.10) is greater than the table t value (2.228), b is significant and is the best estimate of the population.

A final calculation for the confidence interval is needed when using regression analysis. The confidence interval gives the range around the true regression line within which the predicted sales value (Y) will fall. The confidence interval is determined through the following formula:

$$Y_c \pm (t \text{ value at specified confidence level})(\hat{\sigma}_{y-y_c})$$

where

$$\hat{\sigma}_{y-y_c} = \hat{\sigma}_{y \cdot x} \sqrt{1 + \frac{1}{n} + \frac{(x_p - \bar{x})^2}{\Sigma x^2 - \frac{(\Sigma x)^2}{n}}} \tag{8}$$

x_p = the value of the independent variable used to predict sales of the new product

The confidence interval for the forecasted value of Lifecard is:

$$\hat{\sigma}_{y-y_c} = 0.843 \sqrt{\frac{1 + 1/12 + (9.0 - 5.9)^2}{25}}$$

$$\hat{\sigma}_{y-y_c} = 1.02$$

$$6.61 \pm 1.02(2.228)$$

$$4.34 \leqslant y \leqslant 8.88$$

With 95% confidence, the company can be sure that when heart attacks are at a 900 level, sales of Lifecard will be between $3,290 and $9,930. Other confidence interval estimates can be established for other values of the independent variable.

Specialized Techniques

Company or product specific techniques are often employed in addition to the above techniques and new product models for forecasting the sales of the new product. One of these is Data Development Corporation's Sales Waves.[9] Sales Waves provides a measurement of repeat purchasing and the usage characteristics of the new product by offering it for sale at a company-established selling price. After being screened to ensure that they have recently used the product category, qualified consumers in five cities

> are exposed to a concept board and asked their intention to buy on a four-point buying scale. Those who respond favorably to the top two boxes are given the product to use for two weeks. After the so-called home placement test concludes, respondents are given the opportunity to purchase the product at a retail price set by the manufacturer. The product is offered in this way for several purchase occasions or 'waves'—intervals of approximately three months.[10]

Although the technique provides an estimate of the market for the new product, the data are not obtained by measuring sales when a consumer selects the product among competing products on the shelf. It is based on noncompetitive usage and then purchase of the product at a price established by the company.

Another method to forecast new product sales is the test market laboratory. Various measures of intention to buy and current purchasing behavior are used to predict sales. Several "laboratory" methods are Yankelovich Laboratory Test Market, Management Decisions Systems "Assessor," and Elrick and Lavidge "Comp."[11] Most of these methods are similar in the way in which new product sales are projected. After being exposed to a commercial, consumers are involved in a shopping situation in which they can decide to purchase (or not to purchase) the new product. Measurements of consumer awareness and attitude toward competitive products, the degree of satisfaction with the new product, and the effects of alternative prices, containers, or labels are obtained. Laboratory tests give an indication of the degree of interest in the new product and its competitive edge by allowing the consumer to select it from among competing products and try the product in the home. Their limitation in forecasting new product sales is that no indication is given of the adoption and repeat purchase behavior beyond the first purchase.

---

[9] For a more indepth description of this technique, see Alexandre Ivahnenke, "Two Forecast Ways Offer Good Rough Estimates of Market," *Marketing News* (November 19, 1976), p. 4; and *Marketing News* (December 31, 1976), p. 6.

[10] *Marketing News*, December 31, 1976, p. 6.

[11] These techniques are described in Edward M. Tauber, "Forecasting Sales Prior to Test Market," *Journal of Marketing* (January 1977), pp. 80-84.

PROBLEMS IN NEW PRODUCT FORECASTING

Even forecasting the sales of established products is often a difficult task but forecasting new product sales is more difficult still. With the exception of a case in which a test market was conducted, there is no sales record or company experience upon which the forecast can be based. This is particularly true when the new product is either discontinuous or has little similarity with other products in the company's product line. In some cases, a reliable forecast is impossible. Because of the uncertainty in forecasting the sales of the new product and the high risks involved, early sales are closely monitored, and forecasts are continually revised to conform to actual market conditions. Regardless of the product/market situation, the best estimates are usually obtained when a variety of forecasting techniques are used. This allows cross referencing for the accuracy of the new product's sales forecast.

SUMMARY

One of the most important yet difficult tasks is the estimation of the new product's sales at various stages in the development process. In forecasting sales it is important to establish and evaluate the relevant factors that will affect sales. Although different for every new product, these factors should be identified to the extent possible and classified according to their degree of favorableness. Then the impact on sales of all factors, favorable and unfavorable, should be assessed along with the probability that each will occur.

The business climate into which the new product will be introduced must be analyzed. This can be best accomplished by establishing a relationship between the company and the general product category's sales with leading economic indicators. Although the appropriate indicators are different for every product, leading and lagging indicators should be viewed as indicating the business climate for the new product, not only at its launching but also in the future.

In establishing the probable market size for the new product, it is often beneficial to use forms. Several forms were presented in this chapter that are helpful in assessing not only the probable sales and profit for the new product but also the competition.

Many specific forecasting methods can be used to estimate the sales of the new product. Methods, such as jury of executive opinion, sales force composite, buyer's expectation, Delphi, and correlation and regression analysis can be used to estimate the new product's sales. Since sales forecasting is such an uncertain task, it is usually best to use several methods concurrently. This can provide better forecasts, and each forecast acts as a check on the results of another.

SELECTED READINGS

Braden, J. H. C. "A Systems Approach to the Introduction of a New Product." *Business Quarterly* 36 (Autumn 1971):58-64.

Chambers, J. C. "How to Choose the Right Forecasting Technique." *Harvard Business Review* 49 (July-August 1971):45-74.

Dhalla, N. K., and Yuspeh, S. "Forget the Product Life Cycle Concept." *Harvard Business Review* 54 (January-February 1976):102-12.

Dodds, W. "Application of the Bass Model in Long Term New Product Forecasting." *Journal of Marketing Research* 10 (August 1973):308-11.

Konson, A. "The Forecasting of Demand for New Products." *Problems of Economics* 11 (June 1968):16-24.

Kovac, F. J., and Dague, M. F. "Forecasting by Product Life Cycle Analysis." *Research Management* 15 (July 1972):66-72.

Reinmuth, J. E. "Forecasting the Impact of a New Product Introduction." *Jounal of the Academy of Marketing Science* 2 (Spring 1974):391-400.

Shoemaker, R., and Staelin, R. "Effects of Sampling Variation on Sales Forecast for New Consumer Products." *Journal of Marketing Research* 113 (May 1976):138-43.

Tauber, E. M. "How Market Research Discourages Major Innovation." *Business Horizons* 17 (June 1974):22-26.

_____ . "Why Concept and Product Tests Fail to Predict New Product Results." *Journal of Marketing* 39 (October 1975):69-71.

Wheelwright, S. C., and Clarke, D. G. "Corporate Forecasting: Promise and Reality." *Harvard Business Review* vol. 54, no. 6 (November-December 1976):40-64.

Part Four

The New Product's Marketing Program

9

Planning the
New Product Mix

This chapter introduces the marketing mix for the new product by giving an overview of each of the factors in the mix and providing an analytical framework to guide management decisions. The product planning process discussed in previous chapters provides the basis for the core activity of new product management—designing a marketing plan for the new product that will appeal to the selected target markets. The chapter then deals with evaluating alternative mix possibilities and their evaluation using return on investment criteria. Program Evaluation Review Technique (PERT) is presented by demonstrating its application to the development of the new product's marketing plan and introduction. The chapter concludes by discussing the importance of establishing a product information system for control and evaluation.

INTEGRATING MARKETING MIX DECISIONS

The main objective of the new product manager is to formulate a marketing strategy that will contain the correct mix of product features, branding and packaging, price, distribution network, and promotion for the particular product/market situation. Establishing the best mix is not easy because of the various relationships that are possible between sales and mix levels, the initial level of satisfaction and subsequent repeat purchase patterns of the consumer, and the potential and nature of competitive response. Additional complications can occur due to changes in business conditions, shifts in the economic environment, and changes in legal regulations.

Figure 9-1 shows aspects of developing the marketing plan for the new product. The starting point is the development of the

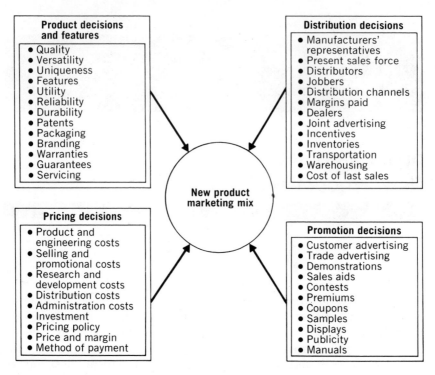

Figure 9-1. Designing the New Product's Marketing Mix

various characteristics of the product. Decisions on the product's uniqueness, quality, reliability, and durability must be made. These decisions must take into account consumer desires, the contribution to the overall profitability and stability of the firm, and the competition. The length and coverage of warranties (if any), guarantees, as well as servicing are often important additions to the product that could affect the success of its introduction.

Closely related to decisions regarding the characteristics of the new product is the price. Inflation, shortages of resources and materials, and consumer awareness have contributed to new product price decisions. Cost serves as the floor for all price decisions, but allocating costs is often a difficult process. Research and development costs, product and engineering costs, and administrative costs must be equitably allocated to the new product. Then the costs of selling, distribution, and promotion efforts should be delineated. The price of the new product must also take into consideration competitive reaction and consumer acceptance. The product has to be priced to meet the company's objectives yet not entice competitive reaction. At the same time, the price must appeal to the consumer to stimulate sales.

The distribution system for the new product allows the firm to reach the government, industrial, or consumer markets. When the new product is very unusual, it is important to keep in mind the firm's corporate and product objectives when establishing the distribution strategy for the new product and when developing distribution systems for all products. Such factors as the nature of the market, margins required, available channel systems, and the degree of market exposure must be determined so that the new product will be available to meet demand. Specific decisions regarding the use of dealers, jobbers, distributors, sales force, or manufacturers' representatives must be made.

Promotion is another area of the new product's marketing plan. The choice of media and messages must be made in terms of the budget. Decisions regarding promotion require considerable interaction among the new product manager, the technical staff in the firm, and outside personnel. Aside from advertising, decisions about the use of contests, premiums, samples, displays, and manuals must be made. The availability and the method of using publicity should not be overlooked. It is particularly important for the firm to use a great deal of monetary and managerial resources to measure the effectiveness of the new product's promotion.

USE OF FINANCIAL CRITERIA

The optimal new product mix must be established in terms of the profits and the relative return on investment that will occur. A sound procedure for establishing the marketing mix/profit relationship was developed by Kotler.[1] This method allows the new product manager to develop various sales and cost estimates for given new product mixes. These estimates are then used to determine the best new product mix.[2]

In designing and developing the new product and its mix, several financial criteria enable management to select the best possible option. These include the effect the new product will have on cash flow and the return on investment of the amount of income obtainable from the particular investment.

[1] Philip Kotler, "Marketing Mix Decisions for New Products," *Journal of Marketing Research* (February 1964), pp. 43-49.
[2] These same methods can also be used to evaluate the profitability of new product alternatives throughout the product planning process discussed in Chapters 3-5.

Effect of Cash Flow

Tight capital markets, decreasing profits, and high interest rates have compelled new product managers to evaluate more carefully the cash flow characteristics of new product propositions. Accurate estimation of all monies spent and earned, given implementation of the mix being considered, requires an assessment of noncash elements, such as depreciation, and all opportunity costs as well. Although cash flow analysis does ensure that sufficient working capital will be available to implement the new product mix, it tends to favor the mix that will allow the new product to reach its break-even point in the shortest time. Proposals requiring an extended development and test period are often shelved until liquidity problems have eased.

Return on Investment

It is necessary to evaluate the attractiveness of each product mix in terms of the return on investment. There are five basic approaches that can be used: payback method, average rate of return method, net present value method, internal rate of return method, and profitability index.[3]

The payback method is probably the most frequently used method to evaluate new product mix proposals. Management is always interested in knowing how long it will take to recover the initial investment. The payback period divides the total investment by the annual cash inflows for the recovery period. If the new product mix had an initial investment of $90,000 with annual revenues of $25,000, it would have a payback period of:

$$\text{Payback Period} = \frac{\text{Total Investment}}{\text{Annual Cash Inflows}} = \frac{90{,}000}{25{,}000} = 3.6 \text{ years}$$

It is good for a company to establish a maximum accepted payback period against which all new product mixes are compared. If the payback period for the new product mix is less than the maximum, it is accepted. If not, the mix is rejected. When several new product mixes with payback periods that are less than the maximum are evaluated simultaneously, each payback period is compared with the projected life of the product. Although one mix may return its investment in a shorter period than others, the product

[3] This discussion assumes that the expected cash flows are realized at the end of the time period being used (i.e., month, quarter, or year). The formulas used can be found in most financial management textbooks. For a good in-depth discussion of this, see James C. Van Horne, *Financial Management and Policy* (Englewood Cliffs, N. J.: Prentice-Hall, 1974).

may have such a short life that only a break-even situation will occur if that new product is introduced.

The payback method gives management some insight into the liquidity and risk of the new product mix. However, the method has several shortcomings. It does not take into account interest income or other investment possibilities. It also neglects the size or the timing of the cash inflows during the recovery period. The major shortcoming of the payback method is that it does not consider any revenues occurring from the new product mix after the payback period is reached. In spite of these deficiencies, the payback method is probably the most widely used for evaluating new product mixes, perhaps because it is well understood and easy to calculate.

Another method used to evaluate new product mixes is the average rate of return. This accounting method indicates the ratio of the average annual profits (after taxes) to either the average investment or the total investment in the product mix. For example, a new product mix with an expected product life of four years is projected to have annual profits of $4000; with a total investment of $40,000, it would have a 10% (4000/40,000) average rate of return on the total investment and a 40% (4000/10,000) average rate of return on the average investment. As was the case with the payback method, a required rate of return is usually established by a firm so that each new product mix can be rated. Although the method is simple to use, it fails to take into account the timing of the cash inflows as well as the time value of money. It assumes benefits are the same regardless of whether they occur during the first year or last year of the product's life.

Three other methods of determining return on investment are present value methods that overcome some of the deficiencies of the payback and average rate of return methods. One of these, the net present value method, subtracts the present value of the total investment from the expected future cash inflows, which are discounted at the required rate of return.[4] The net present value of a product mix is found through the following formula:

$$\text{Net present value} = \sum_{t=0}^{n} \frac{A_t}{(1 + k)^t} \qquad (1)$$

[4] The required rate of return is an important part of this evaluation process. When evaluating various product mixes, it is important to consider the effect of the particular mix on the firm as a whole. Its marginal contribution is dependent on the correlation of the mix with both existing projects as well as other new product mixes being considered. For simplicity we will assume that the firm has only one mix under consideration at a time, and all

where $\qquad A_t$ = cash flow for period t

k = required rate of return

If the product mix generates cash flows that, when discounted, are equal to or greater than zero, that mix is accepted. If the discounted cash flows are less than zero, the product mix is rejected. In other words, the product mix will be implemented if the present value of inflows is greater than the present value of outflows. If a firm wants a required rate of return of 10% after taxes on a product mix that will have cash inflows of $10,800 for each year of a five-year life, after an initial cash outlay of $20,000, the net present value is:

$$\text{Net present value} = -20,000 + \frac{10,800}{(1.10)} + \frac{10,800}{(1.10)^2} + \frac{10,800}{(1.10)^3} \quad (2)$$

$$+ \frac{10,800}{(1.10)^4} + \frac{10,800}{(1.10)^5}$$

$$= -20,000 + 40,940.64$$

$$= \$20,940.64$$

Since this net present value is greater than zero, the new product mix should be adopted.[5]

The internal rate of return method is similar to the net present value method in evaluating alternative product mixes. Under the net present value method, the cash flows and the required rate of return are given so that the net present value can be found. Under the internal rate of return method, the cash flows are given so that the discount rate can be found that will equate the present

---

have the same degree of risk. For a discussion of the evaluation of risk, see Donald I. Tuttle and Robert H. Litzenberger, "Leverage, Diversification and Capital Market Effect on Risk-Adjusted Capital Budgeting Framework," *Journal of Finance*, 23 (June 1968), pp. 427-43; John Lintner, "The Valuation of Risk Assets and the Selection of Risky Investments in Stock Portfolios and Capital Budgets," *Review of Economics and Statistics*, 47 (February 1965), pp. 13-27; Robert H. Litzenberger and Alan P. Budd, "Corporate Investment Criteria and the Valuation of Risk Assets," *Journal of Financial and Quantitative Analysis*, 5 (December 1970), pp. 395-420; Mark E. Rubinstein, "A Mean-Variance Synthesis of Corporate Financial Theory," *Journal of Finance*, 28 (March 1973), pp. 167-82.

[5] An easier way to solve this problem would be to use a present value table. Look up the appropriate discount factor and multiply it by the annual cash inflow. For our problem, we would multiply the appropriate discount factor (3.7908) by the annual cash inflow (10,800). The resulting $40,940.64 has the cash outlay ($20,000) subtracted from it giving $20,940.64.

value of the cash inflows with that of the cash outflows. The resulting internal rate of return is compared with the required rate (established by the firm) to see if the new product mix should be adopted. If more than one product mix is being considered, then the internal rates of return can be used to rank the proposals. The internal rate of return (r) is the following rate:

$$\sum_{t=0}^{n} \frac{A_t}{(1 + r)^t} = 0 \tag{3}$$

where A_t = the cash flow for period t

r = internal rate of return

This formula can be expressed as follows when the initial cash outlay for the product mix occurs at time 0:

$$A_0 = \frac{A_1}{(1 + r)} + \frac{A_2}{(1 + r)^2} + \frac{A_3}{(1 + r)^3} + \ldots + \frac{A_n}{(1 + r)^n} \tag{4}$$

Using the previous example of product mix evaluation, we have:

$$20{,}000 = \frac{10{,}800}{(1 + r)} + \frac{10{,}800}{(1 + r)^2} + \frac{10{,}800}{(1 + r)^3} + \frac{10{,}800}{(1 + r)^4} + \frac{10{,}800}{(1 + r)^5}$$

Solving for r yields a rate of return of approximately 45%. When comparing this internal rate of return with the required rate of return of 10%, the product mix would be accepted.

The profitability index is another present value method for evaluating the return on investment of various product mixes. This benefit/cost ratio or a product mix is actually the present value of future cash flows divided by the initial cash outlay:

$$\text{Profitability index} = \frac{\displaystyle\sum_{t=1}^{n} \frac{A_t}{(1 + k)^2}}{A_0} \tag{5}$$

where A_t = cash inflow in period t

k = required rate of return

The profitability index for our problem would be:

$$\text{Profitability index} = \frac{\$20,940.64}{\$20,000} = 1.04$$

This product mix would be accepted because its profitability index is greater than 1. Again, as with the net present value method, various new product mix alternatives can be ranked according to the amount the indices exceed 1. Although for any new product mix being considered the profitability index and the net present value methods would yield similar results, the net present value method is somewhat preferred when choosing between two alternatives because the expected economic contribution is expressed in absolute terms.

PROGRAM EVALUATION REVIEW TECHNIQUE (PERT)

Timing is crucial during all aspects of the product planning and development process. It is especially important for successful commercialization of the new product. Sales and goodwill can be lost if the new product is not available at the time indicated by promotion. One useful method to achieve optimal coordination is PERT.[6] By identifying the critical operations in the commercialization process as well as producing status reports, PERT is an effective technique to reduce or eliminate delays.

PERT requires the development of a detailed activity network depicting all important aspects of the commercialization process. By listing all activities that must be performed and their interrelationships, the network for commercialization can be derived along with estimates of completion times. These estimates of the most likely completion times are prepared by individuals involved in completing the activity. In order to account for uncertainty about the time required to accomplish a particular activity, three time estimates for each activity are used:

$$t_e = \frac{t_o + 4t_m + t_p}{6} \tag{6}$$

where t_e = expected time for completion

t_o = optimistic time for completion

[6] This procedure is thoroughly developed in *An Introduction to* PERT/ *Cost System for Integrated Project Management,* Special Project Office, U.S. Navy Department, October 15, 1961.

t_m = most likely time for completion

t_p = pessimistic time for completion

An example of a PERT system for introducing a new product is shown in Figure 9-2. The number 6 in parentheses located below the arrow concerning purchase equipment was the expected required time in weeks to complete the activity. This was arrived at based on an optimistic time of four weeks, a most likely time of seven weeks, and a pessimistic time of 14 weeks:

$$t_e = \frac{4 + (4)(7) + 14}{6} = 6$$

In addition to the times in parentheses, each activity (task) is represented by a series of arrows that begin and end at points called events. These are indicated by circles with numbers inside.

The most important path in the new product introduction network is the path that represents the longest (in time) sequence of activities that must be completed. This *critical path* shows the earliest possible time that the new product can be introduced. The critical path in Figure 9-2 indicates that it will take 20 weeks to introduce the new product once a definite decision has been made. This path (and its related time) is critical because any delay in the activities along it will mean delays in the entire introduction process. PERT can be used to successfully control the entire new product development and introduction process. This process will be discussed in Chapter 15.

ESTABLISHING A NEW PRODUCT INFORMATION SYSTEM

As the new product mix is being planned and implemented, there is a need to establish a product information system. This system will provide relevant information so that the planned performance of the new product can be compared with actual results. Corrective actions can then be immediately undertaken to offset any deviations between projections and actuality. The basic characteristics of a product information system (PIS) are the same as those of a marketing information system:

A structured, interacting complex of persons, machines, and procedures designed to generate an orderly flow of pertinent information, collected from both intra and extra-firm sources, for use as the basis for decision

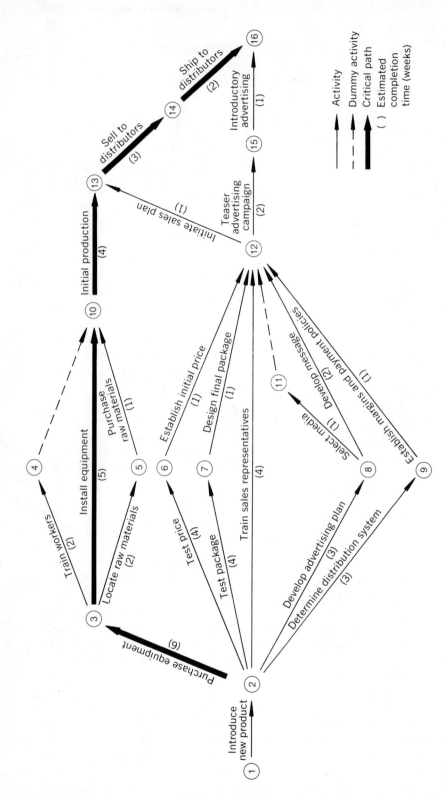

Figure 9-2. A New Product Introduction Network

Activity
Dummy activity
Critical path
( ) Estimated completion time (weeks)

Introduce new product
Purchase equipment (9)
Train workers (2)
Install equipment (5)
Locate raw materials (2)
Purchase raw materials (1)
Test price (4)
Test package (4)
Establish initial price (1)
Design final package (1)
Train sales representatives (4)
Develop advertising plan (3)
Determine distribution system (3)
Select media (1)
Develop message (2)
Establish margins and payment policies (1)
Initial production (4)
Initiate sales plan (1)
Teaser advertising campaign (2)
Sell to distributors (3)
Ship to distributors (2)
Introductory advertising (1)

making in specified responsibility areas of marketing management.[7]

In other words, a new product information system is a mechanism designed to gather and distribute data on the new product for the manager. By using this data base and the resulting detailed marketing reports, the new product manager can recognize trends and problems more quickly and implement any necessary changes in the new product's marketing mix.

SUMMARY

The main problem confronting the new product manager is to orchestrate a marketing mix that will achieve the goals of the firm. This composite of various aspects of brands, packages, price, promotion, and distribution must satisfy not only the target customer but ward off competitive reaction.

In formulating an optimal mix, it is necessary to consider the new product's impact on the financial resources of the firm. Of particular concern is the effect the new product mix will have on the cash flow and the return on investment. Several approaches can be used to determine the return on investment that the new product mix will achieve. Each of these evaluation methods (payback, average rate of return, net present value, internal rate of return, and profitability index) indicates the relative attractiveness of each new product mix under consideration.

Once the optimal mix has been selected, it is important to coordinate all the activities needed to successfully introduce the new product and establish a mechanism by which current information is available to management. PERT provides a means by which the critical path for successful introduction can be established. This network, combined with a sound product information system, will greatly help the introduction and evaluation process.

SELECTED READINGS

Bailey, Earl L., ed. "Marketing Strategies: A Symposium." *Conference Board Record*, report no. 629, annual report, 1974.

Banting, Peter M., and Ross, Randolph E. "The Marketing Mix: A Canadian Perspective." *Journal of the Academy of Marketing Sciences* 1 (Spring 1973): 1-11.

[7] Samuel V. Smith, Richard H. Brien, and James E. Stafford, eds., *Readings in Marketing Information Systems* (Boston: Houghton Mifflin, 1968), p. 7.

Baver, Judith. "Balanced Marketing Planning in a Period of Sudden Change." *Conference Board Record* 12 (May 1975): 14-17.

Finn, R. H. "Analyzing a Marketing Strategy." *California Management Review* 17 (September 1975): 84-86.

Hopkins, David S. "New Emphasis in Marketing Strategies." *Conference Board Record,* 13 (August 1976): 35-39.

Nickels, W. G., and Jolson, M. A. "Packaging the Fifth P in the Marketing Mix?" *SAM Advanced Management Journal* (Winter 1976): 13-21.

Rowan, Bayard F. "Effective Relationships Between Marketing and Other Corporate Functions." *AMA Management Briefing* (1976): 76-844.

Taylor, James D. "What a Chief Executive Should Know About Marketing." *Price Waterhouse Review* 17 (Spring 1972): 42-49.

"The Brand Manager: No Longer King. The Old and the New in the Management of Brand Marketing." *Business Week* (June 9, 1973): 58-62.

"The Squeeze on Product Mix: The Energy Crisis, Shortages, Price Controls Force Major Changes," *Business Week* (January 5, 1974): 50-55.

Walker, K. R. "How to Draw Up a Marketing Plan That Will Keep You on the Track." *Industrial Marketing* 61 (September 1976): 126-128.

10

Branding and
Packaging the New Product

Consumers distinguish between alternative goods and services by learning the meaning attributed to each alternative. Meaning is learned from actual experience or environmental influences, such as advertising and friends. This symbolic meaning is attached to the brand name of the product by the consumer to help in the recognition and decision-making process. Thus, the brand name develops a personality of its own that is interpreted by consumers and judged as to whether the image of the product will satisfy their needs. In some instances, the brand name itself can imply meaning without advertising or other external information. Such brand names as Mustang, Cling, My Sin, Rabbit, Captain Kelley, Janitor in a Drum, Mr. Muscle, and White Rain symbolize images to consumers without giving any information about the product. If the brand name can connote an image that is congruent to what the manufacturer is trying to convey, then the brand name can be a valuable asset in the introduction of a new product.

In many instances, management considers branding a new product to be one of the least important decisions. Most industrial products are given brand names without consideration of their psychological implications. In fact, most industrial product brand names are numbers, letters, or meaningless names. For example, computer manufacturers have traditionally used the corporate name and a model number to identify new computer systems. These numbers may be part of a series, such as the IBM series 360 or Honeywell 100.

There are many industrial product brands that have meanings to only certain groups within the industry. These groups represent the potential market segments for the product and would have a great interest in the product. However, these technical brand names do have a favorable psychological effect on the marketing effort in that they provide some means of product differentiation.

IMPORTANCE OF BRAND NAME

The obvious and most simple advantage of a brand name is to help the consumer or industrial user identify the most desirable product or service. The brand name may also provide protection to consumers; they are able to identify who the manufacturer of the product is. This ensures customers of being able to replace the product with another one of equal quality.

IMPORTANCE TO MANUFACTURER

In addition to their importance to consumers, brand names can be used by manufacturers to achieve certain marketing objectives.

Aid in Building a Company Image

New products are developed, tested, and launched because they satisfy a significant consumer need and will return a profit to the manufacturer. The new product is generally positioned in the market with some distinct characteristics over competitive products. In order to position the new product effectively, the manufacturer must use advertising and promotion to build a brand image that is acceptable to the target market. Thus, the brand name becomes the center of promotion and advertising strategy. It can establish acceptance, preference, or loyalty of the new product.

Reduce Price Comparisons

With a brand name, the manufacturer can establish a price that is different from competition. This is largely possible because the brand image will differentiate the product from competition, allow a price differential, and reduce consumer price comparisons. Most firms prefer to compete on a nonprice basis, and branding, to some extent, provides the manufacturer with the means to do so.

It has also been shown that branded products have more price stability than nonbranded or obscurely branded products. It is believed that price stability enhances the image of the product. However, this conclusion is still open to question.

Facilitate Expansion of Product Line

For the firm expanding its product line, a well-known brand name can be advantageous. It will facilitate consumer acceptance of the new product because of its existing brand reputation. For example, if Heinz were to introduce a new product, consumers would generalize that the new product would be similar in quality to other Heinz products, thus enhancing the adoption process. This advantage can easily become a disadvantage if the new product is a failure. This issue will be discussed later.

BRANDING POLICIES AND STRATEGIES

Prior to introducing any product, a branding policy or strategy should be established, especially in view of future new products. The manufacturer may decide to use a family or blanket branding strategy, an individual branding strategy, a mixed family and individual branding strategy or a combined trade name with an individual brand.

Family or Blanket Branding

In using a family or blanket branding strategy, the manufacturer chooses to apply the same brand name to all products. Firms such as Heinz, Hunt, Campbell, Green Giant, and General Electric use this strategy. This decision is adopted generally when the products are similar in terms of marketing mix strategies; that is, they use the same distribution channels, communication channels, and appeal to the same or similar target markets.

The family or blanket branding strategy has some important advantages, provided that the manufacturer is willing to maintain consistency in quality for all items in the line. First of all, it would facilitate the adoption process and acceptance of new products. Consumers will generalize that new products have the same quality level as existing ones. Secondly, the cost of branding the new product will be less since brand name research and extensive advertising for brand name awareness and preference will not be necessary. Thirdly, the consumer response to the new product will be faster, thereby reducing the introduction stage in the product life cycle where profits are negative.

There are also disadvantages in employing the blanket or family branding strategy. These disadvantages generally center on the ability of the manufacturer to maintain consistency in product quality and the similarity of the products. Lack of consistency in new product quality will result in consumer dissatisfaction, which may carry over to other successful products in the line. The reputation of all products and the manufacturer's image may be negatively affected by one product failure.

When products to be introduced are categorically different (for example, food versus nonfood), a family branding strategy will not be appropriate. For example, Swift and Company would not consider the same branding strategy for its hams and bacon as it uses for its fertilizer.

Individual Brands

When a firm produces or sells diverse products, it may not be appropriate to use one family or blanket brand name. Colgate, Procter and Gamble, General Foods, Bristol-Myers, Gillette, Johnson & Johnson, and many others market a wide variety of products that would not be amenable to family or blanket branding. Tide, a brand name for a detergent, would not be appropriate for a toothpaste or a mouthwash. Most consumers are relatively naive about what specific brands are produced by any one of the above listed firms. This individual branding strategy allows firms to develop different images and positions for each of their products without concern for the negative carryover on the entire product line if any new product should fail.

Individual brands, however, are more costly to introduce since each new product must be heavily advertised to establish brand awareness. Frequently, a firm's objective is to achieve a greater degree of market saturation. Specific, individual brands may appeal to one or a few market segments, thus constraining market share objectives. To increase the market share potential, the firm will introduce another product in the same category but appealing to a different market segment to attain broader market coverage and a larger market share. This is a multibrand strategy. For example, Procter and Gamble markets several detergents, such as Tide, Cheer, and Era. Each new detergent introduced by Procter and Gamble claimed somewhat different ingredients and characteristics. Each of these brands, when introduced, resulted in some reduction of market share of existing brands but overall, they increased sales volume, which was the immediate objective.

There are some important reasons for using a multibrand strategy. First, each brand occupies more shelf space, thus leaving less for competitors. Secondly, most consumers are not loyal to one brand and are likely to switch given the right circumstances, such as a price deal. If the manufacturer did not introduce new brands of the same type of product, it would eventually face a declining share of the market. In order to capture the brand switchers, a multibrand strategy is necessary. Thirdly, each new brand gives the firm an opportunity to appeal to different market segments.

The major problem with a multibrand strategy is the possibility that each new brand in a product category will only obtain a small market share, resulting in reduced profits for the company. For example, a firm with three marginally profitable detergents introduces a fourth brand to stimulate its total detergent sales. The new brand attains a small market share, but the reduction in the sales of the other three brands is equivalent to the sales attained by the new brand. The overall result of the new product introduction is no increase in total company sales but increased marketing and development costs. It is possible that total profits may now be negative since the company has spread its resources too thinly, resulting in a weak profit position.[1]

Mixed Branding Strategy

In many large companies, product line expansion occurs in different directions so that new families of products may be planned when a new product is conceived. In this case, the firm will use a mixed branding strategy with similar products carrying a family brand name and different products with individual brand names. For example, Sears, Roebuck & Co. employs a mixed branding strategy by using brand names such as Coldspot, Craftsman, and Kenmore as individual brand names, each with a family of products. Thus, each hardware item would be branded as Craftsman, yet all refrigerators and air conditioners are referred to as Coldspot.

This strategy is employed when the product line expands so that new products are quite different from other products, therefore requiring a unique name and marketing strategy.

Trade Name and Individual Brands

The last strategy that may be employed by the firm is to associate the company name with an individual brand for each product. In this case, the company name provides some legitimization and the individual name some differentiation for the new product. There are Johnson's Pride and Johnson's Glo-Coat; Post Raisin Bran, Post Cocoa Krispies, and Post Alpha Bits.

---

[1] For further discussion on multibrand strategy, see Robert W. Young, "Multibrand Entries," in *Plotting Marketing Strategy*, ed. J. Lee Adler (New York: Simon & Schuster, 1967), pp. 143-64.

This strategy, as in family or blanket branding, carries the risk of negative association of all products if the consumer rejects the new item. However, as mentioned earlier, the company may benefit from using its company name by enhancing the adoption process and reducing some of the heavy advertising costs in the introduction stage of the product life cycle.

Whatever branding strategy is employed, the advantages and disadvantages of each of the strategies discussed above should be carefully weighed. Future marketing objectives and target market strategy must also be considered when determining brand strategy.

BRAND NAME RESEARCH

In the packaged goods industries, the fact that the choice of the brand name is an inherent part of marketing strategy designed to result in a successful new product launch is well recognized. Research is often conducted to determine the image that a number of alternative brand names may convey to the end user. The objective of this research is to identify which brand name conveys the desired image before the new product is launched. A negative image conveyed during the product launch cannot be easily rectified and usually results in the product's withdrawal from the market. It may be reintroduced with a new brand name, but the firm would have already incurred damage to its reputation as well as financial losses. To avoid this outcome, it is beneficial to conduct brand name research to identify possible brand name image problems before they occur. In addition to image, the firm may be concerned with such aspects of the brand name as ease of recall, distinctiveness from competition, and relationship to corporate name.

Brand Name Research Techniques

Many different research techniques may be employed to test consumer reactions to alternative brand names. Some of the more widely used techniques are rank order, scaling, and various motivational research techniques.

Rank Order   In this technique, a sample of present users or potential users would be asked to rank the alternative brand names for a specified new product in their order of preference. The brand name that receives the highest preference rankings would then be adopted as the brand name. The major weakness of this technique is that the distance between ranked alternatives—that is, distance between rank 1 and rank 2 and between rank 2 and rank 3—may not be equal. However, the technique is simple to employ and can be completed quickly without great expense.

Scaling   Scaling techniques are often employed to determine end-user reactions to characteristics conveyed by the brand name. Table 10-1 shows a simplified example of the semantic differential scaling technique. It requires respondents to indicate on a seven-point scale the words that describe the image conveyed by the brand name.[2] If the firm wanted to convey an image of strength, aggressiveness, masculinity, etc., then it would select the brand name that consumers identify with these attributes. Many attributes should be listed in this type of test in order to determine all possible reactions. The semantic differential is the most popular technique among market researchers.

Other scaling techniques such as Likert's summated scale, Thurstone's differential scale and the Q-sort technique are also available but are not discussed here.[3]

Motivational Research Techniques   The objective of motivational research should not be to select the final brand name but to indicate which one or two words appeal most to the target market. Color, packaging, printing, and other factors used to display the brand name will all affect its performance. However, the use of these variables with the brand name in the research makes it difficult cult for the researcher to separate the actual causes of consumer reaction. Often firms wish to determine underlying psychological suggestions given by the brand name. This can be done through the use of motivational research. Techniques, such as word-matching, free association, cartoon tests, and narrative projections, are used for many different purposes in marketing. For brand name research, the word-matching or free-association techniques would be most appropriate to determine brand name image.

Free association is the best starting point for any brand name research. The tests provides consumers with a list of names, including those being tested, and asks them to identify what is associated with these words. New words can often be derived with this type of research. These are to be used as a brand name that would enhance the new product launch.

In a word-matching test, consumers are given a number of words and products, including the ones being tested, and asked to match them. From this test, the firm would be able to determine

[2] C. E. Osgood, G. J. Suci, and P. H. Tannenbaum, *The Measurement of Meaning* (Urbana: University of Illinois Press, 1957).

[3] For a discussion of these scales, see Paul E. Green and Donald S. Tull, *Research for Marketing Decisions*, 3rd ed. (Englewood Cliffs, N.J.: Prentice-Hall, 1975), pp. 167-208.

Table 10-1. Scaling Example to Measure Brand Name Image

Old fashioned							Modern
___	___	___	___	___	___	___	
Bland							Spicy
___	___	___	___	___	___	___	
Frigid							Sensual
___	___	___	___	___	___	___	
Aggressive							Passive
___	___	___	___	___	___	___	
Feminine							Masculine
___	___	___	___	___	___	___	
Powerful							Weak
___	___	___	___	___	___	___	
Light							Heavy
___	___	___	___	___	___	___	

the name or word that best describes the new product. Other products are used in the test to prevent bias by the respondents.

It is also necessary for the firm to determine whether or not consumers can remember the brand name easily and whether or not they differentiate the product from other brand names in the industry.

In general, a good brand name should be simple, easy to remember, and convey an image to the consumer that is congruent with marketing strategy to the target markets. Satisfaction of these objectives should eliminate some of the underlying causes of new product failure.

THE PACKAGING DECISION

Traditionally, the function of packaging was to protect goods. In some industries, this is still considered the primary function. However, in many industries, the package has become a promotional tool and image builder for the new product thereby enhancing its success in the market. This is especially true in cases where the consumer must choose from several alternatives on a shelf where the package then becomes a point of sale display. One of the first marketing decisions to be made is to determine how important the package is in developing a favorable appeal to the consumer.

PACKAGING DESIGN CONSIDERATIONS

The packaging decision must weigh each of four factors in the design phase: (a) marketing considerations, (b) product protection, (c) economic factors, (d) environmental factors. These four considerations are outlined in Table 10-2 and are discussed briefly below.

Marketing Considerations

The package design must consider the implications of the package on the manufacturer, the retailer (or other middlemen) and the consumer. As shown in Table 10-2, the retailer's major concerns are with the ability to get the product on the shelf with a minimum of difficulty and to prevent pilferage of high priced small items. The consumer, on the other hand, is most concerned with such factors as convenience and information provided on the package. The manufacturer must consider the ease of recognition and image conveyed by the package design.

Some of these factors may be contradictory, such as recognition and shelf stacking. For example, the manufacturer may decide to use an oddly shaped package to attract attention and to differentiate the new product from competition. However, the oddly shaped package presents problems to the retailer in terms of shelf space and stacking. Minimization of conflict in these marketing considerations will enhance channel acceptance of the new product.

Product Protection

Products subject to spoilage, physical damage, or contamination require laboratory testing prior to designing the final package. Food manufacturers work closely with paper companies, chemical manufacturers, metal processors, and other manufacturers of packaging materials to resolve packaging problems to satisfy the product protection objectives.

Industrial manufacturers are particularly concerned with physical damage if the product is fragile and expensive. Losses due to physical damage of the product are generally the responsibility of the manufacturer. Thus, it is necessary that the package be carefully

Table 10-2. Considerations in Design of Package

Marketing consideration	Product protection	Economic factors	Environmental factors
For management	Prevents contamination	Cost of materials	Biodegradable
Recognition	Prevents physical damage	Cost of fabrication	Ability to recycle
Color	Shelf life	Added or reduced manpower	Impact on pollution
Size	Effect of climate	Inventory, shipping and storage costs	Social pressures
Design	Safety	Refunds and allowances for damaged	Legislative pressures
Image	Effect of light	goods	Competition
Attitudes		Availability of raw materials	Impact on natural resources
		Equipment needs	
For retailer			
Shelf stacking characteristics			
Ease of price-marking			
Ease of case identification			
Quality of packages per case			
Ease of package removal			
Pilferage protection			
For consumer			
Consumer convenience			
Ease of storage			
Handling ease			
Directions for use			
Reusability			
Disposability			
Information			
Instructions for use			
Expiration date			
Alternative product uses			
Guarantees			
Nutritional components			

designed to protect the product from damage and subsequent
financial loss.

Economic Factors

Financial loss due to breakage or spoilage may be significant.
Thus, meeting certain product protection criteria may minimize
costs to the manufacturer. The manufacturer must also consider
the actual packaging costs for the new product. For high-value
products, the cost of an expensive package, since it is such a small
percentage of the value of the product, is relatively unimportant.
However, for many consumer and industrial products, the cost of
the package is significant. This is especially true when there is
competition and only a small profit margin.

From a strictly economic viewpoint, the manufacturer must
consider the costs of package materials, fabrication of the package,
manpower, inventory and storage, and equipment needs. To avoid
shortages for packaging, management should consider the future
availability of the material, especially if the need to change materials may negatively affect the image of the product. The availability of materials is reflected in the cost of these materials. When
the oil embargo took place, plastic material prices rose significantly
and forced many manufacturers to look for alternative packaging
materials.

Environmental Factors

Without question, one of the most significant trends in our
society is consumers' concern with pollution, particularly from discarded packaging. As a result of this trend, many state and local
governments have passed legislation to restrict the sales of throw-
away containers. Vermont, for example, now prohibits throw-away
bottles and requires consumers to pay a refundable deposit on all
bottled items.

Many manufacturers are now packaging their products in re-
usable containers as a means of recycling the packaging materials.
In addition, research is continually being carried out to develop new
packaging materials that are biodegradable or that minimize pollution problems. Consumable packages have been developed at high
cost but have received poor consumer acceptance. Efforts to
develop packaging materials that will ameliorate these environmental problems will continue, particularly in light of the growing
shortages of many of the important packaging materials.

PROMOTIONAL ADVANTAGE OF PACKAGING

Packaging offers the manufacturer an important promotional medium, particularly when many of the products are similar and difficult to differentiate. Packaging may be the dominant force in the consumer's choice when there is little product information available and the size and price are perceived as similar. The importance of the promotional impact of packaging is reflected in the battle by manufacturers to obtain shelf facings in retail stores. Exposure is increased by increasing the number of shelf facings. Thus, the package design that attracts the consumer's attention provides an important medium at the point of purchase.

ATTRIBUTES OF AN EFFECTIVE PACKAGE

In trying to satisfy the packaging design considerations and promotional advantages of the package, management must discern those attributes that make an effective package. First of all, an effective package should be attention-getting. The new product's package should stand out from competition, particularly at the point of purchase. Secondly, the package should be informative. It must identify the amount of the product in the package, the content's brand name, and other relevant information for the consumer. New labeling laws now require identification of the contents in order by amount. Thirdly, the package must be perceptually pleasing or appealing. Color, shape and texture, typography, materials, and illustrations should connote something pleasing to the consumer's senses. With the growing interest of mass merchandising in improving point-of-purchase information, the package will become a more significant means of providing this information. Lastly, the product package should protect the contents and be convenient for consumers to use.

In rating the above criteria, management must also determine the importance of each in meeting the firm's objectives. Continual evaluation is needed during the package design phase to determine how well the package is meeting these objectives so that modifications may be incorporated without excessive loss of time and money.

SUMMARY

Management frequently overlooks the importance of branding and packaging decisions. Both the brand name and package design contribute to the product's image and must be given consideration in the marketing mix decision-making process.

The brand name provides the manufacturer with the means to build a company image, reduces price comparisons, and facilitates expansion of the product line. In determining the brand name for the new product, management must decide whether or not to use a family or blanket branding strategy, individual branding strategy, mixed branding strategy, or combined trade name with the individual brand. Each of these policies should be considered in terms of the company's long-range objectives.

Brand name research techniques may be employed to test consumer reactions to various brand names. Some of the more widely used techniques are rank order, scaling, and motivation research.

The packaging decision must consider marketing, product protection, economic, and environmental factors. In trying to identify effective packaging attributes, management should determine whether the package is attention-getting, informative, perceptually pleasing, or appealing and functional. All packaging and brand name decisions are made in conjunction with the firm's marketing objectives.

SELECTED READINGS

Cook, Victor J., and Shutte, Thomas F. *Brand Policy Determination*. Boston: Allyn & Bacon, 1967.

Enzie, W. H. "Planning Your Package." *Modern Packaging* (November 1961): 26-29.

Gamble, Theodore R. "Brand Extension." *Plotting Marketing Strategy*, ed. Lee Adler. New York: Simon & Schuster, 1967.

Guss, Leonard M. *Packaging in Marketing*. New York: American Management Association, 1967.

Immermann, Milton. "Packaging—Integral Part of the New Product." *New Products New Profits*, ed. Elizabeth Marting. New York: American Management Association, 1964.

McMurry, Robert N. "How to Pick a Name for a New Product." *Sales Management* (August 15, 1954):102-5.

Mitchell, Jerome N. "The Secret Ingredient in Designing a Package." *Profitability and Penetration Through Packaging*. New York: American Management Association, 1965.

Morley, John, ed. *Launching a New Product*. London: Business Books Ltd., 1968.

Reynolds, William H. *Products and Markets*. New York: Appleton-Century-Crofts, 1969.

Scheuing, Eberhard E. *New Product Management*. Hinsdale, Ill.: The Dryden Press, 1974.

Schutte, Thomas F. "The Semantics of Branding." *Journal of Marketing* 33 (April 1969):5-12.

Shapiro, Ernest L. "The Responsibility for Package Design." *Package Design and Its Management.* New York: American Management Association, 1965.

Young, Robert W. "Multibrand Entries." *Plotting Marketing Strategy,* ed. J. Lee Adler. New York: Simon & Schuster, 1967.

11

Pricing the New Product

Price is an important variable in new product marketing decisions in part because of continuous product innovations and their
rapid imitation discussed in Chapter 3. The significance of pricing
the new product is confirmed by the fact that it tends to hold a
major position in corporate affairs (see Chapter 2). In addition, the
price of a new product is a major factor in determing the revenue
and the profits as well as the volume of sales.

Price is a complex variable because of the many people—manufacturers, wholesalers, retailers, consumers, and public policy
makers—who influence and are influenced by the price of a new
product. The relationships among these people as well as the relationship of the price with other elements of the marketing mix—
product, distribution, and promotion—must be fully considered
before setting the initial price. In order to answer the basic question of what the price of a new product should be, it is important
that carefully designed company objectives and policy be established. This chapter discusses the three fundamental concepts in
determining the price for the new product: cost, demand and market behavior, and competition. The chapter concludes with a discussion of the relationship of the initial selling price to other marketing variables that affect the new product.

COMPANY PRICE OBJECTIVES

Before establishing comprehensive pricing policies, a firm must
decide on pricing objectives since the policies are the means of

achieving the objectives. Table 11-1 indicates the variety of potential pricing objectives. Although specific pricing objectives will
vary from firm to firm as well as from product to product within
a given firm, depending on factors such as market position or competition and demand, pricing objectives can be classified into three
general groups: profit oriented, sales oriented, and other.[1]

Profit-Oriented Objectives

The ultimate objective of any firm is, of course, to make a
profit, pay dividends to shareholders, and provide a source of funds
for investing in research and development and plant and machinery
to ensure future growth and continued profitability. Most price
models have as a basic tenet that a firm will seek to maximize
profits in the short run. This is an uncommon approach due to the
inability to successfully maximize profits because of uncertainty
regarding relevant costs and demand. Another factor leading to
infrequent use of profit maximization objectives for a new product
is that a lower price might allow the new product to gain acceptance and develop a larger, more broadly based market. A profit
maximizing objective for a new product may cause new competing
products to be developed more quickly because the high margins
would be equally available to competing firms. In fact, some firms
formally monitor markets for complementary products to find one
in which the margins are attractive enough for them to enter.
Probably, the only case in which short-term profit maximizing concepts are practiced is in situations of competitive bidding.

Many firms seek a target profit for each new product. A price
is set that will achieve a specified rate of return based on the total
cost of the new product. In order to set this price, the total costs
at various levels of output are estimated. Then the most likely
level of production during the introductory stage is specified. For
example, let us assume a company is considering introducing a new
industrial adhesive. The company expects to use 80% of a total
plant capacity of 2 million during the introductory stage; that is, it
estimates it can sell 1.6 million units. The total cost of producing
this amount will be $20 million. Now the company must deter-
mine the associated total revenue curve by first specifying a target
rate of return. Due to the high research and development costs as
well as the uniqueness of the product, the company wants a 20%
profit over cost. Therefore, it wants to achieve net profits of $4

[1] For a comprehensive discussion of these and other pricing objectives
applied to all product pricing situations, see Robert A. Lynn, *Price Policies
and Marketing Management* (Homewood, Ill.: Richard D. Irwin, 1967).

Table 11-1. Potential Pricing Objectives

1. Maximum long-run profits
2. Maximum short-run profits
3. Growth
4. Stabilize market
5. Desensitize customers to price
6. Maintain price-leadership arrangement
7. Discourage entrants
8. Speed exit of marginal firms
9. Avoid government investigation and control
10. Maintain loyalty of middlemen and get their sales support
11. Avoid demands for "more" from suppliers—labor in practice
12. Enhance image of firm and its offerings
13. Be regarded as "fair" by customers (ultimate)
14. Create interest and excitement about the item
15. Be considered trustworthy and reliable by rivals
16. Help in the sales of weak items in the line
17. Discourage others from cutting prices
18. Make a product "visible"
19. "Spoil market" to obtain high price for sale of business
20. Build traffic

SOURCE: Alfred R. Oxenfeldt, "A Decision-making structure for Price Decisions," *Journal of Marketing* (January 1973), p. 50. Reprinted from *Journal of Marketing,* published by the American Marketing Association.

million during the introductory stage. This cost estimate of $24 million (cost plus profit) is the point on the total revenue curve at a volume of 80% of capacity. Another point on the total revenue curve will be zero at a volume of zero percent of capacity, as shown in Figure 11-1.

The slope of the total revenue curve indicates the price necessary to achieve the target rate of return. For the company in the example above, the slope is 2.5. Thus, selling 1.6 million units of the industrial adhesive, it will achieve its target rate of return of 20% or $4 million at a price of $2.50 per unit.

Another profit-oriented objective is a minimum profit objective. This goal is not one commonly considered by firms because if a new product cannot be sold at the price necessary to achieve the minimum profit desired, the new product should not be introduced.

Sales-Oriented Objectives

Sales-oriented objectives often guide the pricing of a new product. Although the adoption of such objectives in no way implies a complete abandonment of profit, sales-oriented objectives can lead

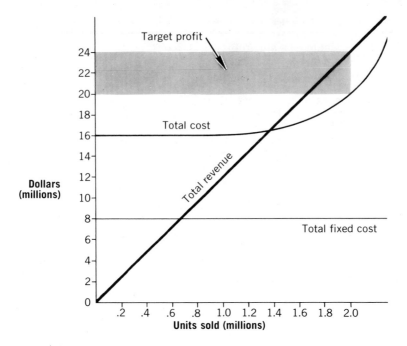

Figure 11-1. Target Rate of Return Pricing

to a price that is below what produces maximum profits. Usually, a sales-oriented objective is expressed in terms of attaining a specified market share. For example, a target market share may be 10%. A high volume of sales for the new product results from consumer acceptance. A low price can facilitate acceptance. This is not at all inconsistent with profit achievement.

Other Price Objectives

Other objectives such as meeting competition, conforming with product line, company image, and early cash recovery can be used to establish the price for the new product. Many firms adopt a somewhat passive pricing objective—that is, having the price of the new product meet the price of competing product(s) that are already being marketed. This is a particularly common pricing objective when the new product is not very new to the consumer.[2] In other words, if the product does not display distinct characteristics and/or does not seem as if it would have a dramatic effect on the

[2] The various aspects of newness as well as a classification system for products of varying degrees of newness can be found in Chapter 1.

life style of the consumer, then the new product may have to be priced close to products presently being marketed to stimulate sales. Studies have found such firms as National Steel, Republic Steel, Standard Oil of New Jersey, Gulf, and Goodyear to be price followers.[3] When using a meeting competition objective, a firm will rely on other aspects on the marketing mix, such as advertising and salespeople's commissions to differentiate the new product.

Instead of meeting competition, a new product can be priced using a product line objective. This means the new product is priced to fit into the product line and/or promote other products in the product line. The new product may not yield a profit itself but, rather, will enhance sales of other products of the firm.

Closely related to the product line objective is the range objective. A company's reputation or image is intangible, but it can still have a great deal of importance and value. Several methods for dealing with the image of the new product were discussed in the previous chapter. If the new product is identified with the company, then it may have to be priced in line with the prevailing company image. This will avoid any negative impact on the company's image as well as sales of the company's other products.

A new product must have a price that will be consistent with the image of the product itself. A major cause for poor sales is that the new product is priced too low relative to other products in that class.

Many firms price a new product so that rapid recovery of cash will result. This objective is becoming more widely adopted. For the most part, these firms are either short on capital or regard the future demand for the product and/or the economy to be too uncertain to slowly cultivate the market. Early cash recovery is a more frequent objective for new products in periods of high interest rates and uncertainty.

POLICY FORMULATION

The specific objectives in pricing new products must be formulated into general corporate policies. Of particular importance in formulating a company's pricing strategy and objectives is the long-term financial plan. In defining this financial plan, several key factors should be taken into consideration. First, the new product must be priced to yield an appropriate return on invested capital. This makes it necessary to delineate the capital requirements of

[3] See R. F. Lanzillotti, "Pricing Objectives in Large Companies," *American Economic Review* 48 (December 1958), pp. 924-27; and U. S., Congress, Senate, Subcommittee on Antitrust and Monopoly, *Administered Prices*, 88th Cong., 1st sess., 1963, p. 18178.

each new product. Once the capital requirements have been determined, the new product can be priced to yield a specified return on investment.

Another factor in formulating policy for pricing new products is the expected revenue. The revenue should not only be termed on a total basis but also on a percentage-of-profit basis as well. These ratios will indicate the level of flexibility to respond to a price maneuver by competitive products as well as rising costs.

The cash flow from the new product's sales, both its level and pattern, should be evaluated. This is a particularly important factor to consider in policy formulation because firms often find themselves with insufficient cash reserves to fund promotional efforts to stimulate the new product's sales.

A final area to consider in formulating new product pricing policy is the effect the new product will have on the company's present worth. Since the objective of any pricing strategy is to maximize the positive effect it will have on corporate earnings, this important factor should be the cornerstone of all new product pricing.

Within a general policy framework, two specific pricing policies can be implemented for the new product: skimming or penetration pricing policy.[4]   Under a skimming pricing policy, a company wants to take advantage of the fact that some consumers will pay a premium to be among the first to enjoy the new product. A company seeks to gain a larger profit from the higher price paid by buyers to whom the new product has a high present value. The price of the new product can be then reduced to appeal to the more elastic segments of the market.

Several conditions favor implementing a skimming pricing policy for the new product. The most important condition is that there is a sufficiently large number of buyers whose demand is relatively inelastic. This is more frequently the case for a novel product for which there are no comparable products on the market. With no comparable products, consumers are unable to make value comparisons and therefore tend to be relatively insensitive to price. The main question is how many is a sufficient number. This number must be carefully determined since the company plans to forego all sales to those who are price sensitive by setting a high initial price.

Another condition under which a skimming pricing policy is used is when no economies of scale would result; that is, the savings from producing and distributing a larger volume of the product

---

[4] For a detailed, indepth discussion of these two concepts, see Joel Dean, "Pricing Policies for New Products," *Harvard Business Review* (November-December 1976), pp. 141-53.

are not sufficiently high to offset the lower revenue from a low price. Therefore, a high price is mandatory.

A firm may not be financially able to produce a large volume of the new product. Since high cash outlays are needed in the introductory stages for production, distribution, and promotion, a firm often can only finance the production and distribution of an amount of product that is less than what is demanded at a higher price. In this situation skimming is the only feasible pricing policy.

Perhaps the greatest concern with a skimming pricing policy in the long run is the competition's reaction. When there is a high price resulting in high profits, the development of rival products is stimulated. The probability of this occurrence will decrease if the new product has strong patent protection or high development costs (see Chapter 10).

On the opposite end of the continuum from a market skimming policy is the market penetration policy. A firm will set a relatively low initial price for the new product in order to achieve relatively fast penetration of the market. This policy stimulates growth of the market for the new product and allows gaining of a large market share. A penetration pricing policy is most advantageous and is sometimes necessary when the market for the new product appears to be very price sensitive—for example, when a price-responsive market that brings in a large number of buyers at a lower price is forecasted.

Another condition favoring penetration pricing is when economies of scale are possible. By having a large market (and therefore increased output), the unit cost of both production and distribution would fall. A larger output would allow distribution of overhead costs as well as advertising expenses over more units, thus reducing the cost per unit.

Finally, a low initial price on the new product based on a penetration pricing policy would discourage actual as well as potential competition. Where high potential competition exists, a penetration policy can be beneficially employed to raise entry barriers for prospective competitors. Firms tend not to enter low-margin markets. This is especially true when the new product does not have a great deal of technological advantage and can therefore be easily duplicated.

COST CONSIDERATIONS

One of three cornerstones for pricing a new product is cost. Cost is the floor below which the price of the new product cannot fall, at least in the long run, in order for the firm to survive.[5]   Although it is possible to overemphasize the importance of cost in new product pricing and fail to consider other essential elements, it is necessary for management to know intimately the composition and behavior of product costs. Cost indicates whether or not the new product can be marketed profitably at alternative prices. It does not show the amount of markup that will be accepted by the buyers whether these be intermediaries or the final consumer. More importantly, accurate cost estimates can aid the design of a most profitable new product. The total cost of the new product should be computed before any significant investment in research and development takes place. The price of the new product based (and revised when needed) on cost should serve as a go or no-go guideline during the product's path toward the market.

Classification of Costs

The new product's costs can be classified into categories, such as direct and indirect, controllable and uncontrollable, manufacturing and nonmanufacturing, and most broadly, fixed and variable. It is important to determine the relationships between cost and quantity of output. Fixed costs are those that do not vary, regardless of output. Items such as property taxes, interest, some elements of depreciation, and exempt salaries are ordinarily fixed.

Variable costs are those related to output. Materials and labor are the most typical and important variable costs of the new product. Some costs are variable in one new product situation but not in another. A cost is variable not because of what the item is, but because it changes as a function of short-term output. Although economies of scale initially occur, reducing these costs, variable costs often rise more rapidly as the capacity of the plant is approached.

Cost Estimating

The cost of the new product in most cases is not an exact amount. It depends on concurrent manufacture of other products as well as the economies of joint distribution and/or advertising. For example, if a manufacturer locates a new branch outlet near an

---

[5] Although this is the case in a single-product firm, for multiproduct firms, a case can be made to have the price of the new product be below the costs in order to stimulate sales of other products in the product line. Yet, even here, care must be taken to ensure that the total corporate costs of doing business are covered.

existing branch, both outlets could jointly bear the cost of newspaper advertising since the newspaper serves the two adjacent towns.

New product costs are generally estimated by analyzing costs at various levels of sales of similar products. When a large number of observations exist at different volume levels, a cost function can be fitted to these data after adjustments for any variations. This is often done through regression analysis, which was discussed in Chapter 8.

The most difficult problem in cost estimation is in the allocation of those costs that cannot be traced to a particular product. Regardless of the allocation procedure, such nontraceable costs must be distributed among all products so that no one product, particularly a new one, bears more than its fair share of the burden. If it is uncertain how much of the general nontraceable costs should be allocated to the new product, they can be allocated based on a proportion of a traceable cost. For example, the nontraceable costs of the plant can be allocated in the same proportion as the traceable direct labor costs.

One way to forecast costs for the new product is to use the cost compression curve.[6] By relating manufacturing cost per unit of value added to the cumulative quantity produced, this curve is a consequence of intangible investments used to determine advantages or economies of production. Its use is particularly valuable in pricing technically advanced industrial products.

DEMAND AND MARKET CONSIDERATIONS

Although cost serves as the floor for any new product pricing, the basic concern is the response of the market to the new product's price. Demand is generally regarded as the amount of the new product that buyers would purchase at each of several possible prices. Some estimating techniques discussed in Chapter 8 are also applicable to assessing the demand at various prices. From this demand analysis, the price elasticity of the new product can be calculated.

Price Elasticity

Price elasticity describes the relationship between a change in price and the change in quantity demanded. It indicates the degree

---

[6] For a more thorough development see, for example, Joel Dean, "Pricing Policies for New Products." In addition, some of the techniques discussed in Chapter 5 can be used to establish this curve.

of sensitivity that the consumer has to the price of the new product. If the coefficient for the new product is less than 1, demand relatively inelastic. If the coefficient of elasticity is greater than 1, demand is relatively elastic. The formula for this determination is:

$$\text{coefficient of elasticity} = \frac{\%\ \text{change in quantity}}{\%\ \text{change in price}} = \frac{\dfrac{Q_2 - Q_1}{Q_2 + Q_1}}{\dfrac{P_2 - P_1}{P_2 + P_1}} \qquad (1)$$

When demand for the new product is relatively elastic, then if the price of the new product is increased, total revenue will fall. Conversely, if the demand is inelastic, total revenue increases if the price is raised.

Since it is usually very difficult and therefore expensive to get a measure of the elasticity of a new product, several factors can be used to give insight into the new product's price elasticity. First, if the new product is not truly unique and therefore a wide variety of acceptable substitute products already exist on the market, demand tends to be more elastic. However, if the need that the new product is designed to satisfy is easily filled, demand is inelastic.

Inelasticity of demand is in effect when the need is very urgent. In this case price has no effect on the purchase decision. For example, suppose it began to rain during a professional football game. A fan who had two pocket raincoats only needed one so the other was available to meet another fan's need. The price of this raincoat was indeed inelastic because the second fan needed it to stay dry and because there was no competition (the vendor had sold all his products).

A final determinant of elasticity is the durability of the new product. Since the purchase of durable goods can easily be postponed, this factor usually makes the demand for the new product elastic.

Regardless of whether or not the demand for a product is elastic or inelastic, it must be analyzed and related to production and distribution costs. One method for analyzing these relationships is through break-even analysis.

Break-Even Analysis

Break-even analysis is a clear and simple method to depict the effect of changes in prices and volume on profits. As indicated in Figure 11-2, the break-even point is the level of sales revenue at which profits are zero. Through use of this graph, management

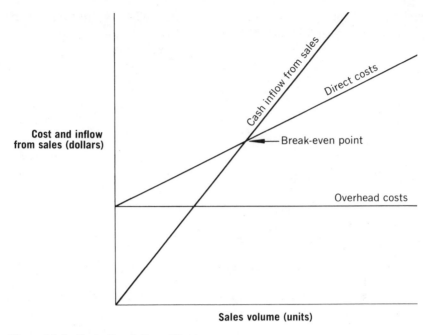

Figure 11-2. Basic Break-Even Chart

can evaluate decision that allocate costs between variable and fixed
as well as those that affect profits due to changes in the selling
price. The basic formula for break-even analysis is:

$$P(x) \;=\; FC + VC(x)\tag{2}$$

where

$$P \;=\; \text{selling price of the new product}$$

$$x \;=\; \text{break-even point}$$

$$FC \;=\; \text{fixed costs}$$

$$VC \;=\; \text{variable costs}$$

Equation 2 allows various prices to be substituted to determine various break-even points and indicate the way the fixed costs
are allocated over various quantities. The prices should be chosen
based on experience and judgment as well as the prices of competing products.

For example, let us suppose that a firm developed a new non-
fogging photochromic ski goggle. The fixed costs are $1,000,000

and the variable costs are $18.00 per unit. What is the break-even point at prices of $18.50, $20.50, and $22.50?

At a price of $18.50 per unit, the break-even point is:

$$18.50(x) = 1,000,000 + 18.00(x)$$

$$x = 2,000,000 \text{ units}$$

At a price of $20.50 per unit, the break-even point is:

$$20.50(x) = 1,000,000 + 18.00(x)$$

$$x = 400,000$$

At a price of $22.50 per unit, the break-even point is:

$$22.50(x) = 1,000,000 + 18.00(x)$$

$$x = 222,223$$

From this analysis, the firm can then estimate demand for the new product at the prices being considered to see which price should be charged to reach the new product's objective.

Price Determination Model

Closely related to break-even analysis is a price determination model, which requires determining the price/sales/quality relationship that will maximize profits.[7] Let us assume that a firm undertook a test market for its new product and found the following price/demand relationship:

Price	Estimated Demand (units)
$ 30	4100
60	3200
90	2300
120	1400
150	500

[7] For a discussion and application of this approach, see Donald V. Harper, *Price, Policy, Procedure* (New York: Harcourt, Brace and World, 1966), pp. 143-48.

This linear relationship can be expressed in a more general model:

$$Y = a + bx \qquad (3)$$

where

Y = quantity demanded

x = price

a = intercept (value of Y when x = 0)

b = slope of the line

Applying the market test data in the general model, it can be seen that when the price (x) is zero, the demand (Y) is 5000 units. The slope (b) of this equation is –30. Substituting the figures in the general model, the demand for the firm's new product can be expressed by the following equation:

$$D = 5000 - 30P \qquad (4)$$

where

D = new product demand (units)

P = price

The fixed costs for this product are $75,000 and the variable cost per unit is $30. Therefore, the total cost (TC) can be expressed as:

$$TC = 75,000 + 30D$$

Correspondingly, the revenue resulting from selling D units at a price of P is:

$$TR = (P)(D) = P(5000 - 30P) \qquad (6)$$

Expressing the total costs in terms of unit price and demand gives:

$$TC = 75,000 + 30D$$
$$= 75,000 + 30(5000 - 30P) \qquad (7)$$
$$= 225,000 - 900P$$

This expression (equation 7) for total costs indicates that if the price is zero, then 5000 units will be sold. Since each has a variable cost of $30, the total variable cost of $15,000, when added to the fixed cost of $75,000, gives the first term of equation 7: $225,000. In addition, since each dollar increase in price will produce 30 fewer units sold, a savings of $900 [demand (30) × variable cost ($30)] in cost will result for each dollar increase in price. This is indicated by the second term in equation 7.

Profit is equal to total revenue minus total cost:

$$\text{profit} = TR - TC$$

$$= P(5000 - 30P) - (225,000 - 900P)$$

$$= 5900P - 30P^2 - 225,000$$

Since the objective is to maximize profit, the optimal price can be found by taking the first derivative of price in equation 8 with respect to profit, setting the resulting expression (equation 9) equal to zero and solving for the price that maximizes profit.

$$\frac{d\text{ profit}}{dP} = 5900 - 60P = 0$$

$$P = \$98 \tag{9}$$

At this price, the quantity that will be sold is:

$$D = 5000 - 30(P)$$

$$= 5000 - 30(98) \tag{10}$$

$$= 2060 \text{ units}$$

Operational Approach to Demand

Another very useful approach to evaluate demand is the use of three sales volume estimates at each of the new product's prices under consideration. The three demand estimates at three different prices are: the most likely estimate of sales (Q_m), the most pessimistic estimate of sales (Q_p), and the most optimistic estimate of sales (Q_o). From these estimates and their probability of occurrence, the largest expected volume (Q_E) can be determined.[8]

CONSUMER CONSIDERATIONS

Regardless of what method is used to analyze demand, the consumer's value perceptions and expectations should be considered when determining the initial price for the new product. A buyer's reaction to various levels of any stimulus, such as price, is discontinuous. Therefore, only price differences greater than a specific percentage threshold or amount are perceived as being truly different. This noticeable difference is directly related to the overall price of the product category. For example, the noticeable difference for an automobile costing $5000 might be $300, but for an industrial machine costing $31,000, it is $500.

Buyers also have fair-price reference points for product categories. This means buyers view a new product's price with a reference price in mind as being the fair price to be charged. If the new product's price does not match this reference price, no purchase will occur.

A final yet very important consideration in looking at the demand aspect of pricing concerns a price/quality relationship. This can be easily illustrated by thinking about your reaction at the last good sale you attended. Did you not examine the items very, very carefully before purchasing because you felt that something must be wrong with the merchandise to allow such low prices? These same doubts are harbored by potential buyers of new products. A buyer judges the quality of the new product based, in part, on the price charged. Too low an initial price can be as detrimental to sales as too high an initial price. A low price can cause buyers to perceive the product to be of inferior quality. This price/quality relationship is very important to consider when introducing a new product in the market, particularly when simultaneously evaluating the product's present as well as future competition.

COMPETITIVE CONSIDERATIONS

Aside from cost and demand, a final important factor that must be considered in the pricing of every new product is competi-

---

[8] This approach is presented in detail in Bill R. Davden, "An Operational Approach to Product Pricing," *Journal of Marketing* 32 (April 1968), pp. 29-33.

tion. Competition must be considered in terms of the price of existing products as well as that of new products that may be forthcoming as a result of the present pricing strategy. Each and every product that can fulfill the same need should be evaluated for its ability to achieve sales the new product would otherwise achieve. In this analysis it is helpful to classify each product with respect to its degree of competitiveness to the new product. One classification scheme uses three major categories: direct competitors, near competitors, and indirect competitors.[9] Direct competitors are those products that offer direct substitutes for the new product. They are the ones to be the most concerned with in establishing the price of the new product because they offer the consumer the most apparent price comparisons. If the price of the new product is above the price of directly competitive products, then the new product must have enough differentiation to indicate its superiority and therefore higher price. On the other hand, if the new product is priced too much below a direct competitor, consumers may either appraise the offering as inferior, or the competitive product's price may be lowered to match the new product's.

Near competitors are products that partially meet, but not totally fulfill, the particular need of the buyer. Thus, since this type of product does not directly compete with the new product, their respective prices are not as comparable. Still, prices of near competitors should be evaluated as they do provide a frame of reference for the buyer. In addition, these products that partially fulfill the consumer's need can be purchased and used as substitutes for the new product.

Those products that are the least competitive to the new product are indirect competitors. Since these do not directly fulfill the same consumer need but merely vie for a share of the buyers' purchasing power, their price is not important.

Regardless of the type of competitors available, the price of any new product is very susceptible to competitive reaction. This is the one variable that is most easily duplicated. Since the competition can react so quickly, it is important to analyze the outcomes of various actions.

A useful technique for assessing the reaction of competitors to the price of the new product is Bayesian analysis. Through this approach, management can look at the various pricing alternatives and assess the effect on profits of possible competitive reactions. The technique requires that management assess the profits for each of the possible competitive reactions and then assign the probability

[9] This classification is developed in Barrie James, "A Contemporary Approach to New Product Pricing," in *Pricing Strategy*, ed. Bernard Taylor and Gordon Wills (Princeton, N.J.: Brandon/Systems Press, 1969), pp. 521-33.

that the competitors will react in this manner. Expected payoff can be determined from this by multiplying the profit with the probability of occurrence for each possible reaction. This technique can be better understood through the following example.

A company has just developed a new tire pump that weighs only four ounces.[10] The pump is designed for use on both automobile and bicycle tires and has a built-in pressure gauge to eliminate over and under inflation. The company wants to decide whether to price this new product at $8.95 or at $12.95. The firm has one major competitor who can effectively react to the new product and its price.[11] The new product manager determines that this competitor can take one of the following five possible reactions to the new product's price:

1. No response to price of the new product
2. New competitive product developed and priced higher
3. New competitive product developed and priced the same
4. New competitive product developed and priced lower
5. Decrease price of somewhat similar competitive product in market

The expected profits to each of these possible reactions have been determined based on various cost and demand estimates (see Table 11-2). The new-product manager also feels that there is a 30% chance that the competitive company will have no response to the new product if it has a price of $8.95; a 20% chance of this reaction if the new product has a price of $12.95. Table 11-2 indicates that there is a 40% chance that the competition will react by developing a new competitive product and pricing it higher regardless of whether the price of the new product is $8.95 or $12.95. All other competitive reactions have a probability of 10% except in the case where the new product is priced at $12.95. In this case, there is a 20% chance that competition will develop a new product with a similar price.

Table 11-2 also indicates the expected payoff for each competitive reaction. This was found by multiplying the profit by its respective probability. The expected payoff for no response to the

[10] This product is described in "A Wave of New Products for Work, Play, and Travel," *U. S. News and World Report* (November 29, 1976), pp. 73-76.

[11] Of course, this analysis can be easily expanded to more than two prices and one competitor. The methodology is the same, only expanded. With many computer software packages having a subroutine available, the number of options on both the prices to be analyzed as well as competitors is only limited by management's ability to assess profits and probable reactions.

Table 11-2. Bayesian Pricing Chart

	Profits of competitive reactions	Probability of reaction	Expected payoff
	A: $150,000	0.3	$45,000
	B: $90,000	0.4	$36,000
$8.95 Price	C: $110,000	0.1	$11,000
	D: $60,000	0.1	$6,000
	E: -$40,000	0.1	-$4,000
		Total payoff	$94,000
	A: $180,000	0.2	$36,000
	B: $110,000	0.4	$44,000
$12.95 Price	C: $80,000	0.2	$16,000
	D: $50,000	0.1	$5,000
	E: -$10,000	0.1	-$1,000
		Total payoff	$100,000

price of the new product, if the new product is priced at $8.95, is $45,000 ($150,000 × 0.3). Summing each of the five expected payoffs for each of the proposed prices yields the total payoff: $94,000 for a price of $8.95 and $100,000 payoff for a price of $12.95. Given that everything else is equal, the firm could elect to price the new product at $12.95 as this price yields the greatest total payoff. However, before setting the final price, the firm would have to take into account cost and demand considerations (discussed previously) and the relationship of other new product marketing decisions to the price.

NEW PRODUCT PRICE AND OTHER MARKETING DECISIONS

A carefully designed price for a new product is a virtual prerequisite for successful new product launching. Aside from being one of the many variables that determine the consumer's response to a new product, pricing decisions are interdependent on external forces and internal variables in the firm's marketing environment.

External forces, such as consumer demand, costs of other factors used in the marketing mix, domestic and foreign competition, government regulation of price differentials, labor and material costs, and sources of supply, affect the quantity of the new product produced and the price received. These forces establish constraints under which accurate pricing decisions must be made. Acting alone or in combination, any of these forces may necessitate that only certain prices or price levels be considered.

Similar interdependence exists between the price of a new product and internal variables. In establishing the price of a new product, a marketing manager must consider concurrently the product itself as well as its distribution and promotion. No decision regarding the price of the new product can be made without evaluating the impact on the other elements in the product's total marketing mix.

The price of a new product is influenced substantially by various aspects of the product and product policies. For example, the price greatly affects the quality of the new product and therefore its appeal. A high price relative to the cost of production enables quality features to be built in, which might differentiate the new product. A low price may mean that the impact of every quality feature must be carefully assessed in terms of its importance to the consumer and influence on cost. Similarly, the importance of a product in its end use also must be considered. For example, whether or not the new product plays only an incidental or major part of the cost and functioning of the final industrial product influences the degree of price flexibility. Another consideration is whether or not the private or national brand of the product will affect the price established. Finally, the relationship of the new product to the total product mix should be considered. Where interdependence exists, the price established for the new product affects all others in the line and therefore limits the flexibility in pricing.

The distribution of the new product affects the price. The channels selected, the types of middlemen desired, and the profit margins required by these middlemen influence the price set for the new product. In order to secure agressive middlemen and adequately compensate them for their services, the new product must be priced to allow an appropriate margin. In fact, the profit margin can be used as an incentive to secure an integrated marketing effort on the part of all distributors as well as to entice them to carry the product.

The amount and types of promotional methods used have a high degree of interdependence with the price of the new product. Whether the bulk of the promotional responsibility is placed upon the middlemen or on the manufacturer, the costs must be accounted for in the margin and consequently in the price. Since the price is related to the available promotion funds for the product, it is imperative to consider the promotional needs of the product when establishing its price.

Many consumer, intermediate customer, and industrial customer purchasing decisions are made under conditions of insufficient information regarding the available options as well as considerable uncertainty about the attributes of the new product. The price should consider the buyer's conception of value as it is possible to price a new product at such a low level that the value image of the product is lost. The initial price also establishes the base from which any price changes are viewed. The price of a new product influences not only the volume of the business transacted but the firm's profits.

SUMMARY

The price for the new product is one of the keys to successfully introducing it in the market. Establishing appropriate objectives and policies is necessary to implement a total new product-pricing approach. Objectives can generally be classified into three major categories: profit, sales, and other, such as image, product line, early cash recovery, and meeting competition. Whatever objectives are adopted, a sound pricing policy must be implemented to provide the guidelines for price establishment. Two general pricing policies—skimming and penetration—are useful depending on the specific market and product situation.

Three fundamental considerations in establishing the price for the new product are cost, demand, and competition. The cost of making and distributing the new product serves as the floor for the price. In all pricing decisions, the response of the market to the price is, of course, a basic issue. This demand for the new product can be tempered by the action of competitors whose possible reactions must be assessed.

Taking into account these three considerations, the price for the product must be established in view of the other marketing variables of the new product. This will allow a "total product" to be successfully introduced into the market.

SELECTED READINGS

Berlines, J. S. "Flexible Pricing and New Products in the USSR." *Soviet Studies* 27 (October 1975):524-44.

Braverman, Jerome. "A Decision Theoretic Approach to Pricing." *Decision Sciences* (January 1971):1-15.

Brenner, Vincent C. "Evaluation of Product Pricing Models." *Accounting for Managerial Decision Making*, ed. Don T. Decoster (Los Angeles: Wiley, 1974).

Darden, Bill R. "An Operational Approach to Product Pricing." *Journal of Marketing* 32 (April 1968):29-33.

Dean, J. "Pricing Policies for New Products." *Harvard Business Review*, vol. 54, no. 6 (November-December 1976):141-53.

Garbor, Andre, and Granger, Clive. "Price Consciousness of Consumers." *Applied Statistics* 10 (1961):170-88.

———, "The Price of New Products." *Scientific Business*, vol. 3, no. 10 (August 1965):141-50.

Gardner, David M. "An Experimental Investigation of the Price-Quality Relationship." *Journal of Retailing* (Fall 1970):25-41.

Hisrich, Robert D. "New Product Pricing: An Indication of Product Quality." Unpublished working paper, Graduate School of Management, Boston College.

James, Barrie. "A Contemporary Approach to New Product Pricing." *Pricing Strategy*, ed. Bernard Taylor and Gordon Wills. Princeton, N.J.: Brandon/Systems Press, 1969.

Lambert Zarrel V. "Product Perception: An Important Variable in Price Strategy." *Journal of Marketing* 34 (October 1970):68-71.

McConnell, Douglas J. "The Price-Quality Relationship in an Experimental Setting." *Journal of Marketing Research* 5 (August 1968):300-3.

Robinson, B., and Lakhani, C. "Dynamic Price Models for New Product Planning." *Management Science* 21 (June 1975):1113-22.

Seglin, Leonard. "How to Price New Products." *Chemical Engineering* (September 16, 1973):181-4.

Thomas, J., and Chhabria, P. "Bayesian Mode Is for New Product Pricing." *Decision Sciences* 6 (January 1975):51-64.

Woodside, Arch G., and Sing, J. T. "Retail Experiment in Pricing a New Product." *Journal of Retailing* 50 (Fall 1974):56-65.

Wotruba, T. R., and Nelson, R. H. "Evaluating Pricing Alternatives for a New Product: The Gas Light Case." *Akron Business and Economic Review* 4 (Summer 1973).

12

Distributing
the New Product

The development and launch of a new product often overlook the channel distribution decisions. It is assumed that channel systems are readily available to access target markets. However, with increased competition in new product development, new channel systems are often needed to differentiate the new product. A new channel system can provide the means to stimulate product growth when a product has apparently reached saturation in its product life cycle. L'Eggs pantyhose provides a good illustration of this strategy; it implements a compact display in supermarkets, a channel that has not yielded significant sales in the past.

Distribution decisions for the new product should be based on the firm's market segments and marketing objectives. The complexity of the channel strategy may be increased by the newness of the product. New products that are discontinuous or require high learning may also require unique channel strategies.

For example, in 1959 Mead Johnson and Co. introduced Metrecal, a liquid diet product that could be categorized as a high-learning product. Mead Johnson identified its market segments as those consumers who must diet for health reasons. The marketing objectives were to use their medical experience to market this new product and to use Mead Johnson's existing pharmaceutical distribution channels to reach the target segments and the product's objectives. Mead Johnson was able to dominate the market with this strategy until Pet Milk introduced Sego, a liquid diet product that was marketed through traditional food product channels. Pet Milk proceeded to capture 51% of the liquid food market compared with 46% for Mead Johnson.

Mead Johnson chose to market this high-learning product through those channels with which it had the most experience. This strategy was chosen to avoid the high risk of introducing a high-learning product via a channel with which the firm was not familiar. This decision resulted in eventual loss of market share due to competition and Mead Johnson's inability to adjust its marketing mix strategy.[1]

The process for channel strategy decisions is illustrated in Figure 12-1. For each new product introduced, management should carefully consider the elements in this process. Thorough evaluation is particularly important in those situations in which the product is new to the firm or is discontinuous with little or no established channel experience in the industry.

CHANNEL OBJECTIVES

The objectives of the distribution channels should specify the desired performance, the services needed, the control the firm wishes to retain, the financial support given to channel members, and any other operational objectives. These objectives are established based on a clear understanding of the market segments defined for the new product.

CHANNEL STRATEGY ANALYSIS

The required analysis to determine feasible channel alternatives is summarized in Table 12-1. Channel strategy analysis should consider the directness of the channel, selectivity of channel members, selection of middlemen, and the number of channels to be used.

Degree of Directness

Channel strategy formulation begins with a determination of the directness or length of the channel. This decision must be based on consideration of the environment, market conditions, target markets, product attributes, and middlemen requirements.

Market Factors   Target market objectives are important in determining the length of the distribution channel. First, management must consider the geographic density of the target market(s). If most of the end users are highly concentrated in one or a few

---

[1] For more information, see "The Rise of Instant Skinny," *Sales Management* (November 4, 1969), pp. 52-54; and "Tying Up a Market by Tying in Fashion," *Printer's Ink* 287 (May 8, 1964), pp. 39-41.

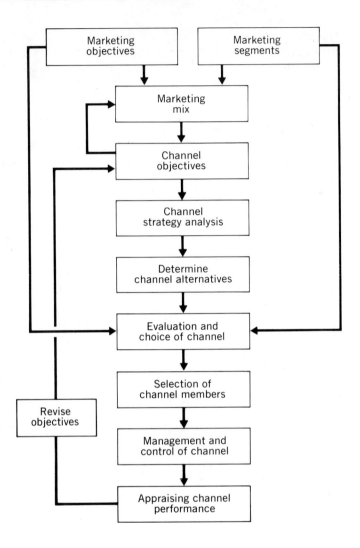

Figure 12-1. Channel of Distribution Decision Process

geographic areas, then the firm may use a more direct channel to reach them. The more dispersed the end users are, the more need there is to use middlemen, which would increase the cost of reaching these end users. Second, management must consider the number of potential end users for the new product. If there is an unlimited number of end users, such as there might be for a consumer packaged good, then management would consider middlemen necessary. If there are only a few end users, such as for a specialized industrial machine, then the manufacturer would consider a more direct channel of distribution.

Table 12-1. Channel Strategy Analysis

1.   Degree of directness depends on:

   a.   Market factors

   b.   Product factors

   c.   Middlemen factors

   d.   Company factors

2.   Degree of selectivity can range from:

   a.   Intensive

   b.   Selective

   c.   Exclusive

3.   Criteria to select middlemen:

   a.   Reputation

   b.   Services provided

   c.   Degree of cooperation

4.   Number of channels and their uses:

   a.   One channel: one target market, multiple target markets

   b.   Multiple channels: one target market, multiple target markets

   Some exceptions to using long channels are situations in which the market is geographically concentrated or dense and in which there is a large number of end users. Examples are firms such as Avon, Fuller Brush, Electrolux, and a number of encyclopedia companies. These manufacturers have elected to market their products through a direct, door-to-door distribution.

Product Attributes   The directness of the channel is affected by the nature of the new product. If the new product is perishable or a fad item, then the firm must use a more direct channel. This is necessary to avoid losses due to sudden shifts in consumer tastes (fad) or due to product spoilage. Bulky new products also require more direct routes to the end user because the costs of shipping and storage would be prohibitive. New products, such as jewelry, that appeal to very exclusive target markets have been traditionally marketed from the manufacturer directly to retail stores.

Middlemen Factors Different levels in the channel of distribution provide important services to the firm introducing the new product. Given channel objectives and target markets, management must carefully consider what each level in the channel could offer as value-added or cost benefits to the new product. If there are no benefits in using wholesalers, then they should not be considered when setting up the channel. Instead, more direct means would be more appropriate with the savings passed on to other channel members. Such savings can be used by the manufacturer to achieve more control over price or promotion or as incentive for more cooperation from middlemen.

Company Characteristics   The channel strategy is influenced by specific characteristics of the firm introducing the new product. Such factors as size, financial strength, previous channel experience, product mix, and marketing policy will affect the channel decision. Larger firms have more flexibility and power in obtaining cooperation from channel members. A new firm would be limited in its choice of channel members because it would lack financial strength, experience, and a wide product mix. Smaller firms must use high commissions to get channel members to store and deliver the new product. The larger firm with wider product lines and more experience would be able to provide its own storage and shipping and hence deal more directly with its end users.

Environmental Factors   When under depressed economic conditions, firms seek the least expensive means to move their products to the market. This usually results in shorter channels and fewer services. The firm introducing the new product should carefully analyze competitive techniques for distributing its products. This may be particularly important if the new product must be located in the same stores as competing products so that the consumer can compare the alternative products. Legal regulations also may affect channel directness.

Degree of Selectivity

Once the decision about the number of levels in the company's channels has been made, then management must decide how selective the distribution channel should be. This is generally a question of degree and is sometimes precluded by the nature of the product. When the strategy is to distribute to as many outlets as possible, the process is called intensive. Examples of intensively distributed products are cigarettes, aspirin, candy. The firm introducing a high-learning product would be foolish to consider intensive distribution until the product is firmly entrenched in the growth stage of its life cycle or has attained high awareness by consumers. For high-learning products, a more selective or even exclusive distribution policy is recommended because middlemen are hesitant to accept the new product until forced to do so by strong demand. Selective or exclusive distribution may be necessary when the firm is trying to develop or maintain an image of quality. The exclusive distribution strategy requires the selection of middlemen who have a reputation that conveys a quality image.[2]

Type of Middlemen

When considering the type of middlemen in the channel, management must place particular emphasis on the mix of services provided by each in view of the objectives in introducing the new product. The functions of a particular middleman must be coordinated with those of the manufacturer.

A small or young business would generally lack storage and transportation facilities and equipment or even marketing expertise. Middlemen provide a broad variety of services and will, in many instances, provide a fledgling company with much needed advice on how to market the new product.

The reputation of the middleman may be critical in achieving certain marketing objectives. For example, certain retail stores have a reputation for carrying quality products that may be desired for the new product. Some middlemen also have the knowledge or expertise to market the new product in a way that achieves the firm's marketing objectives. For example, Head skis selected specialty ski shops with personnel having professional knowledge of ski equipment. Cooperation from middlemen to market the new product in a consistent manner is important when trying to establish an image for the new product. Inconsistent efforts will slow the adoption process as well as give competition advantages.

Number of Channels

The decision of whether to have one- or multiple-channel patterns differs from selectivity, which affects the number of middlemen in each channel. An example of the use of multiple channels is a clothing manufacturer who markets directly to the end

[2] For more information on selectivity, see Edwin H. Lewis, *Marketing Channels: Structure and Strategy* (New York: McGraw-Hill, 1968), pp. 85-88.

user through a factory outlet store as well as distributing the products through retail clothing stores. This same clothing manufacturer also uses manufacturers' agents in certain sparsely populated areas, but at the same time it sells directly to large retail stores.

Many large firms use a multiple approach when they market the same product to different target markets. A calculator manufacturer distributes to large accounts in the industrial market using its own sales force; manufacturer's respresentatives are used for smaller accounts; and the same product is distributed to the household market through wholesalers. The decision of the number of channels to be used will depend on the objectives and target markets of the company.

CHANNEL ALTERNATIVES

The purpose of channel strategy is to select those channel alternatives that are best for the new product. Figure 12-2 shows some of the typical configurations of channel strategies. Several alternatives must be screened. This process should consider the following:[3]

1. *Financial investment needed.* Certain channel patterns require substantial financial commitment, such as promotional support for channel members, inventory, credit, transportation, and other activities. Those channel alternatives that place an unprofitable financial burden on the manufacturer should not be considered.

2. *Timing.* Some channel patterns may need a significant length of time for training and development before they can perform efficiently. Established channels would require less time but may, in the long run, provide little differentiation from the competition. Thus, compromises on timing and distinctiveness may be necessary.

3. *Strengths and weaknesses of manufacturer.* Those functions the manufacturer handles well should not be carried out by the channel members. Channel alternatives should be screened so that channel strengths complement the manufacturer's weaknesses and vice versa.

[3] For further discussion, see David W. Cravens, Gerald E. Hills, and Robert Woodruff, *Marketing Decision-Making: Concepts and Strategy* (Homewood, Ill.: Richard D. Irwin, 1976), pp. 539-45.

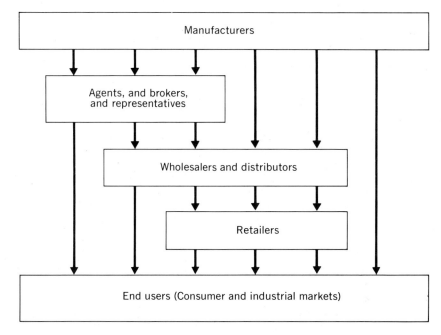

Figure 12-2. Alternative Distribution Channel Patterns

4.   *Bargaining power.*   The ability of the manufacturer
      to control channel members is an important con-
      sideration in the selection process. Channel mem-
      bers are typically most concerned with profit mar-
      gins and the new product's demand potential.
      Hence, high margins and strong support with
      advertising or other means of promotion can give
      the manufacturer a strong bargaining position with
      its channel system.

EVALUATION AND SELECTION OF CHANNEL MEMBERS

The decision on the distribution channel requires comparison
of the feasible alternatives based on a set of relevant criteria.
Table 12-2 illustrates a technique that management can use to
determine which configuration should be used. In this example, a
small corporation manufactured a new liquid grill cleaner for the
institutional market. This product has features which will revolu-
tionize grill cleaning: it is odorless, will operate on a hot grill, con-
verts grease to a dry ash and is inexpensive. Three alternative
channel strategies are being considered: Alternative 1 means distribution of this product through manufacturer's representatives, to

Table 12-2. Preference-Ordering Method for Evaluating Channel Alternatives

Factors in order of Importance	Minimum pass level	Channel alternatives		
		1	2	3
		Manufacturer Mfr.'s reps. Wholesalers Restaurants	Manufacturer Mfr.'s reps. Restaurants	Manufacturer Restaurants
1. Amount of investment needed to meet objectives	0.4	0.5 = P*	0.6 = P	0.3 = F
2. Profit	0.5	0.8 = P	0.8 = P	—
3. Reach of target market	0.4	0.8 = P	0.7 = P	—
4. Impact on future new product development	0.3	0.8 = P	0.5 = P	—
5. Flexibility to changing customer needs	0.4	0.4 = P	0.8 = P	—
Ranking		2nd	1st	3rd

*P = Pass, F = Fail

wholesalers, to restaurants. Alternative 2 sells the new product through manufacturer's representatives, then to the restaurant. Alternative 3 is direct sale from the manufacturer to the restaurant.

Each relevant factor or criterion for the channel decision is listed by order of importance. To the manufacturer, given its marketing objectives, these criteria must be determined by management based on their experience and judgment.

Alternative 3 failed to pass the most important criterion: the amount of investment needed to establish the channel. Alternatives 1 and 2 pass the minimum requirements for all five factors. Based strictly on the values assigned to each factor, alternative 2 would be chosen. However, since these two alternatives were so close to each other, management must consider other factors, especially since some judgmental error is inherent. Because of the constraint to keep price low and because wholesalers provide little cost benefit, it may be more advantageous to distribute the new product through manufacturer's representatives to the restaurants (alternative 2). All payments to the manufacturer's representatives for services will be in the form of commissions. Delivery of the product will be directly from the manufacturer, who will control production quality and keep distribution costs to a minimum. Considering all factors, alternative 2 would be selected.

It is also reasonable to consider multiple channels. For example, direct sales to large restaurant chains may be feasible in conjunction with alternative 2.

Other techniques are also available for evaluating alternative channel decisions.[4]

SELECTION OF CHANNEL MEMBERS

The last step in the design of the distribution channel is the selection of the channel members. If the firm has chosen to intensively distribute the new product, some effort should still be made to avoid selecting retailers or wholesalers who will damage the reputation of the manufacturer. Any negative outcomes from these middlemen could result in damage to the firm and new product.

Figure 12-3 is a sample list of some major criteria to be used by management to select channel members. It is also possible to

[4] Evaluation methods are described in Philip Kotler, *Marketing Decision Making: A Model Building Approach.* (New York: Holt, Rinehart and Winston, 1971), pp. 293-98; and Burton Marcus et al., *Modern Marketing* (New York: Random House, 1975), pp. 557-61.

Figure 12-3. Manufacturer's Rating Scale for Selection of Middlemen

1.   Contacts with customers in target market

Excellent   Poor
— — — — — — — —

2.   Reputation in target market

Excellent   Poor
— — — — — — — —

3.   Past performance with other new products

Excellent   Poor
— — — — — — — —

4.   Overall quality of services provided to manufacturer

Excellent   Poor
— — — — — — — —

5.   Compatibility of marketing mix strategy of middlemen
      with manufacturer

Excellent   Poor
— — — — — — — —

6.   Ability to maintain control of product with middlemen

Excellent   Poor
— — — — — — — —

7.   Probability of effective long-term working relationship

Excellent   Poor
— — — — — — — —

develop a technique, discussed earlier, where the criteria are listed
by order of importance with a minimum passing index for each.
The rating scale in Figure 12-3 may be administered as a questionnaire to the management or customers of the potential middlemen.
The complexity of the selection process will be based on how
critical the decision is for the company and how many middlemen
will be given the new product to sell.

There is an implicit assumption that the manufacturer can
choose whomever it wants to carry the new product. In many
instances, middlemen, particularly large retailers or distributors, are
reluctant to add new products, especially from an unknown firm.
Regardless of whether the new product is a consumer or industrial
product, the risk in handling new products from small or new firms
greatly reduces the number of willing middlemen. Only by provid-

ing them with incentives such as liberal credit or high margins will the firm entice the middlemen to accept a new product. Large corporations with a good reputation will have a much better chance of acceptance of any new product by middlemen. For example, if IBM introduced a new, high-risk product, it would probably have little difficulty in gaining acceptance from channel members, even if the establishment of a new channel system were required.

CHANNEL MANAGEMENT AND CONTROL

Once the channel systems have been designed and implemented, the responsibility for managing the channel must be assigned. This function includes providing operating policies and procedures, motivating channel members, and gathering and distributing control information.

Large manufacturers are usually able to assume leadership in the channel since they built it through previous success in their market. Generally, the leadership power results from the large manufacturer's financial strength, which enables it to maintain superior product research and development. In addition, it can purchase materials in large quantities, achieving economies of scale that afford high margins.

A small manufacturer may also have control of the channel of distribution, particularly when it has developed a good new product.[5] The small manufacturer with a desirable new product may be able to dictate how the new product should be sold. The only control mechanism available to the small firm is to withhold the product from middlemen if they refuse to accommodate the manufacturer's stipulations. In many instances, the small manufacturer must build this control as the new product gains acceptance by consumers. Strong consumer demand will permit the manufacturer to expand distribution and eventually increase its control of the channel system.

The larger the channel system, the further the manufacturer is from the end user of the new product. In such cases, it is important to develop effective communication and information flows in both directions to ensure satisfaction of the manufacturer's objectives.[6] In addition to communication with the middlemen in a long channel, it is also helpful to establish direct communication with the end user to satisfy complaints, requests for information, and other product-related questions.

[5] Robert W. Little, "The Marketing Channel: Who Should Lead This Extracorporate Organization?" *Journal of Marketing* 34 (January 1970), p. 34.
[6] Cravens, Hills, and Woodruff, *Marketing Decision-Making*, p. 557.

Channel management and control requires careful consideration of the necessary information to maintain channel efficiency,
incentives for middlemen, image development, servicing, and
guarantee of the new product.

APPRAISING CHANNEL PERFORMANCE

The appraisal of channel performance must be based on how
effectively the channel meets the manufacturer's objectives, which
were established in the first step of channel design. The most difficult aspect of the appraisal is quantifying the channel system's performance. Cost analysis, market share penetration, and consumer
satisfaction are a few measures that may be appropriate.

Cost analysis may be carried out by identifying sales and cost
data for individual channel members. Determining profit margins
and specific financial ratios will identify unprofitable accounts that
may either be eliminated or persuaded to modify their selling
effort.

If market share is used, it will be necessary to provide some
comparable historical data. Identifying such data will enable the
manufacturer to discern weaknesses and quickly remedy them. A
company may use competition to determine the overall attractiveness of its own products relative to the available alternatives. Such
questions as whether total industry sales are increasing or decreasing, whether the new product is having a negative effect on any
competitor's product, and whether market share has stabilized or
declined should be answered.

Surveys may also be conducted at various points in the channel system to determine customer satisfaction and/or complaints.
End-user surveys can determine specific problems with product
availability, service, retailer support, and other factors. In addition,
where larger channels are employed, surveys of retailers may be
conducted to determine the performance of wholesalers or manufacturer's agents. Survey data can be invaluable in identifying
specific problems that may negatively affect sales.

Channel appraisal may result in revisions, such as replacement
of intermediaries, change in objectives and channel strategy, or a
complete redesign of the channel system. Major changes may have
serious implications for the success of the new product and should
be given careful attention. Continuous monitoring and analysis of
the channel system can only aid the successful launching of the
new product.

SUMMARY

New product launches require careful analysis of all elements of the marketing mix, regardless of whether the product is continuous, dynamically continuous, or discontinuous. It is essential that a sound understanding of channel strategy be developed so that objectives can be achieved.

The channel system decision process must begin with identification of marketing objectives and target markets. Marketing mix decisions (including the channel system) must be made in this context. The firm's objectives and target markets provide the framework for the determination of the channel strategy.

After stating the channel objectives, a channel analysis should be conducted to identify channel system alternatives. This analysis includes consideration of degree of directness, selectivity, types of middlemen, and number of channels. Channel alternatives are then evaluated to determine which system or systems will best meet objectives.

The channel system requires careful management and control by the manufacturer. Leadership must be provided by establishing good information and communication flows in both directions. If performance of one or more channel members deteriorates, it is the responsibility of the manufacturer to take remedial action. Those intermediaries who perform poorly on such measures as cost analysis, market penetration, and consumer satisfaction may be eliminated or forced to improve performance.

The channel system decision process provides management with (a) an understanding of the purpose and structure of a channel system, (b) an approach for designing a new channel system if necessary, and (c) a framework for managing and appraising channel performance.

SELECTED READINGS

Bucklin, Louis P. *A Theory of Distribution Channel Structure.* Berkeley, Calif.: University of California Institute of Business and Economic Research, 1966.

Cravens, David W.; Hills, Gerald E.; and Woodruff, Robert B. *Marketing Decision Making: Concepts and Strategy.* Homewood, Ill.: Richard D. Irwin, 1976.

Kotler, Philip. *Marketing Decision Making: A Model Building Approach.* New York: Holt, Rinehart and Winston, 1971.

Lambert, Eugene W., Jr. "Financial Considerations in Choosing a Marketing Channel." *Business Topics* 14 (Winter 1966): 17-26.

Lewis, Edwin H. *Marketing Channels: Structure and Strategy.* New York: McGraw-Hill, 1968.

Little, Robert W. "The Marketing Channel: Who Should Lead This Extra-corporate Organization?" *Journal of Marketing* 34 (January 1970): 31-38.

Mallen, Bruce E. *The Marketing Channel: A Conceptual Viewpoint.* New York: Wiley, 1967.

McAnnon, Bert C., and Little, Robert W. "Marketing Channels: Analytical Systems and Approaches." *Science in Marketing,* ed. George Schwartz. New York: Wiley, 1965.

Stern, Louis W. *Distribution Channels: Behavioral Dimensions.* Boston: Houghton Mifflin, 1969.

_____ , and El-Ansary, Adel I. *Marketing Channels.* Englewood Cliffs, N.J.: Prentice-Hall, 1977.

13

Promoting
the New Product

Regardless of the type of new product or service to be marketed, effort must be expended in promoting it. The complexity of the promotion mix decision is a function of many variables, most important of which is the newness of the product. The truly unique or discontinuous product (see Chapter 1) requires that management carefully consider all possible, available means of communicating the product, funds available, company objectives, potential competition, market segments, distribution networks, and customer needs. The fact that the new product is unique presents problems to management in that there is little experience available to help make the promotional decisions.

Products that are dynamically continuous present less difficulty in promotion decision-making because substitutes and previous experience may be adapted to the new product. Me-too products or continuous innovations generally require the least additional effort in determining the promotion.

It is particularly important to recognize that the promotion mix will vary according to the stages in the product's life cycle. This chapter presents all aspects of developing the promotion mix for a new product relative to the internal and external variables that affect its design.

THE PROMOTIONAL BUDGET

One of the most important but difficult decisions is how much to spend on promoting the new product. Many managers are misinformed about the impact of the promotional dollar.

They believe that more money expended for promotion will bring more sales. However, promotion may reach a point of diminishing returns so that each additional dollar expended returns less than a dollar in sales.[1] It is also possible to spend less on promotion than is needed to achieve the optimum return. Both these dilemmas are difficult, if not impossible, to resolve. Nevertheless, every effort to minimize errors through careful analysis of all the variables inherent in the design of the promotional mix must be made.

Techniques are used by firms to determine the promotional budget are percentage of sales, funds available to spend, and copying competition.[2] These techniques are weak because they do not consider the nature of the market and the sensitivity of sales to the promotional budget. These weaknesses are enhanced when the product is discontinuous. For example, attempting to decide on a budget based on the percentage of sales assumes that sales can be accurately forecasted without any knowledge of how much is to be spent on promotion. If the new product is continuous (no new learning required), then the percentage-of-sales technique may be used since previous sales experience with similar or substitute products would be assumed to be valid for the new product. Markets for continuous products also tend to be more stable and predictable.

When the product is discontinuous or dynamically continuous, management should initially conduct market segmentation analysis (see Chapter 4) to determine the size of the potential market(s), competition, and the most effective promotion strategy to reach those segments.

Determining what is needed to reach the market segments is perhaps the most difficult aspect of setting the promotional budget. Table 13-1 shows a checklist that assists management in the preparation of the promotional strategy. Management should carefully determine what strategy is to be taken and how much is to be spent on each promotional mix element. For example, cents-off coupons that would reduce the total promotional costs may be mailed to consumers instead of free samples. Other similar decisions could also be made so that less expensive strategies could be substituted for more expensive ones in order to satisfy budget constraints. At the same time, budget allocation can also be more carefully determined since costs should be readily available for each item on the checklist. Most important is that the promo-

---

[1] Donald E. Sexton, Jr., "Overspending on Advertising," *Journal of Advertising Research* 11 (December 1971), pp. 19-24.

[2] James Engel, Hugh Wales, and Martin Warshaw, *Promotional Strategy*, (Homewood, Ill.: Richard D. Irwin, 1967), p. 115.

Table 13-1. Checklist for Promotional Strategy

Yes No (check)		Company allocation

Sales department

	Introduction of product to sales force	————
	Sales conventions	————
	Sales meetings	————
	Brochures and other mailings	————
	Sales force training or education	————
	Sales force incentives	————
	Contests	————
	Special quotas	————
	Revised compensation systems	————
	New sales force equipment	————
	Sample cases	————
	Miniature models	————
	Films	————
	Drawings, pictures, or paintings	————
	Printed matter	————

Dealer

	Dealer meetings	————
	Meetings with dealers' personnel	————
	Special deals	————
	Display material	————
	Counter displays	————
	Window displays	————
	Signs	————
	Printed material, i.e., folders, booklets, etc.	————
	Trade advertising	————
	Trade shows	————
	Films	————

Employees

	Employee magazines	————
	Posting advertisements	————
	Mailings	————
	Meetings	————

Consumers

	Media	————
	Newspapers	————
	Magazines	————
	Radio	————
	Television	————
	Direct mail	————
	Catalogs	————
	Outdoor advertising	————
	Car or bus cards	————
	Novelties	————
	Coupons	————
	Free samples	————
	Printed material	————
	Contests	————

tional budget be designed not by guessing but by applying available experience and scientific methodology.

NEW PRODUCT PUBLICITY

One of the most effective means to facilitate the introduction of a new product is to obtain free advertising either in a trade journal for an industrial product or in newspapers or magazines for a consumer product. A news release describing the company, its executives, and a description of the new product can provide much needed support in the initial phases of the product's life cycle.

Many trade magazines as well as consumer periodicals have new product sections. A news release usually contains the name of the company, a description of the product, and a phone number or address where a reader can obtain more information on the new product. Inquiries from news releases can, indirectly, be an important factor in marketing a new product, particularly in the design of the promotional mix. An innovative firm usually exploits opportunities for publicity as much as possible. Keeping the name of the firm before the consumer is the prime objective of advertising. It makes little difference how or what information source is used as long as the consumer sees it, reads it, and remembers it in future purchase decisions.

Rules for Issuing New Product News Releases

The general framework of the news release should include certain specific items regardless of the information source or the nature of the product. These items are:

1. The news release should be identified as such when mailed to the editor.

2. The release should begin with the new product's brand name.

3. List the features of the new product emphasizing the most important factors.

4. Condense the written news release to about 100-150 words to increase its chances of acceptance by the editor.

5. Include a high-quality glossy photograph of the product. In some instances, the firm may have to pay a

nominal fee to defray the cost of the printing of the photograph.

6. Issue separate releases for each model and size to maximize the exposure of the new product. It is also possible to issue separate releases for each major application of the new product.

It is important that the new product decision-makers maintain a list of potential sources for news releases. Inquiries from potential consumers based on reading news releases should also be carefully documented since these consumers are likely to represent the initial market segment in the product's introductory stage.

USING AN ADVERTISING AGENCY

The advertising agency can provide many important promotional services to the firm introducing a new product. Advertising agencies exist in various sizes with various functions and specialties. The largest agencies provide worldwide service in all possible promotional decision-making areas. Traditionally, the advertising agency has been perceived as an independent business organization composed of creative and business people who develop, prepare, and place advertising in advertising media for sellers seeking customers for their goods and services.[3] Today, advertising agencies perform many services related to the development of the promotional mix, such as market research, package designing, sales training, etc. For the small firm introducing a new product, these expanded services are necessary since it could not perform them economically on its own. The marketing experience of the advertising agency may also be used in the development of the market plan. Essentially, the agency follows the procedure given in Table 13-2 in the formulation of the promotional plan. Major services performed by the advertising agency are also identified in Table 13-2 at each stage in the planning process.

Evaluation of Agency Services

Whether the advertising agency is used exclusively for all promotional activities or whether it is used to complement the firm's

---

[3] Frederick R. Gamble, *What Advertising Agencies Are—What They Do and How They Do It*, 4th ed. (New York: American Association of Advertising Agencies, 1963), p. 4.

Table 13-2. Formulation of the Promotional Plan by the Advertising Agency

Competition	Analysis of client's product or service	Advantages and disadvantages
Location, seasonality, competition	Analysis of potential market segments	Market acceptance, industry conditions, economic conditions
Size, profitability	Analysis of characteristics of members of distribution channel	Competition, services, reputation
Reputation, influence, circulation	Analysis of available media that can best carry the message to all members of channel	Quality, location, costs
	Formulate definite plan and present to client	
Write, design, illustrate forms of message	Execution of promotion plan	Contracting for space, time, etc.
Monitor insertions, displays, etc.		Auditing, billing for services
Market research, analysis of sales by market segment	Feedback on promotional effectiveness	External services, i.e., Starch, A.C. Nielson, etc.

own advertising department, it is important to evaluate the services an agency can provide. Although the total services provided by any advertising agency will vary, the major items are:

1. Copywriting
2. Art techniques
3. Packaging design
4. Photography
5. Typography
6. Reproduction
7. Printing
8. Program planning
9. Public relations
10. Public speaking
11. Media analysis and selection
12. Market research
13. Space allocation
14. Trade shows
15. Sampling
16. Sales promotion
17. Others

The firm selecting the agency for a new product introduction should carefully determine which of these services are needed and whether some of them would be effectively completed within the firm's own advertising department. The advertising departments of most firms are weak in certain areas and would require the use of an advertising agency to fill the gaps. Duplication should be avoided to minimize cost and optimize the use of existing internal resources. It may be beneficial for the firm to evaluate the strengths and weaknesses of the advertising department on each of the services listed. If the agency is strong in the areas in which the advertising department is weak, then an ideal situation would exist for developing promotion strategy.

Selecting the Advertising Agency

Before choosing the advertising agency, management should thoroughly communicate their requirements including a description of the new product markets, budget restrictions, competition, other merchandising decisions, etc., to the firm's advertising department.

If possible, the agency chosen should have had some experience in promoting the type of product introduced. If the new product is dynamically continuous or continuous, it should be relatively easy to identify agencies that have had experience with similar products. Strengths demonstrated in campaigns for competitive products should provide enough information to judge the ability of any agency to handle the new product. However, if the new product is discontinuous, the choice of the agency will be more difficult, particularly since none of them would have had any previous experience. One means of judging or screening agencies at this point might be on the basis of the agency's ability to handle discontinuous new products in the past. Successful introductions of this type of new product may provide some insight into the agency's ability and its creativity in developing promotional campaigns for such products.

Once the initial screening has been completed, each agency should be invited to make a formal presentation to the marketing managers so that a final selection can be made. In order to help select the agency, a checklist is provided in Table 13-3. For each item in the checklist, management should evaluate the agency and its presentation by assigning some scale value—for example 1 to 7. Scoring each criterion on the checklist is subjective, but it will provide some basis for making the final selection. More than one of the marketing staff should be present at the formal presentation, and each should be given an opportunity to evaluate the agency on the items in Table 13-3.

The relationship between the agency and the company should be honest and open so that problems may be minimized and optimal results provided for the new product introduction.

PROMOTION AND THE PRODUCT LIFE CYCLE

In Chapter 1 the product life cycle concept was introduced to illustrate the relevance of varying marketing strategy over the life of a product. The changes in marketing strategy are not only a function of the product's life cycle but are also dependent, particularly in the introduction and growth stages, on whether the new product is continuous, dynamically continuous, or discontinuous. During the other stages, the new product's promotional strategy is no longer dependent on the newness of the product since product concept knowledge would have been achieved across the potential market.

Table 13-3. Checklist to Select Advertising Agency

Item	Value
1. Location of agency	————
2. Organizational structure of agency	————
3. Public relations department services	————
4. Research department and facilities	————
5. Creativity of agency staff	————
6. Education and professional qualifications of agency top management	————
7. Media department qualifications and experience	————
8. Account executives' (if identifiable) qualifications and experience	————
9. Interest and enthusiasm shown toward firm and new product	————
10. Copywriter qualifications and experience	————
11. Art director's qualifications and experience	————
12. Recommendations by other clients	————
13. Experience and success with new products	————
14. Ability of agency to work with company advertising department	————
15. Extra services provided	————
16. Accounting and billing procedures	————
17. Overall formal presentation	————

The Consumer Product

Figure13-1 illustrates the general promotion strategy that should be incorporated into each stage of the product life cycle. Some differences are noted for high- and low-learning (continuous to discontinuous) consumer products during the introduction and growth stages. Industrial products are discussed later. It is evident that the high-learning or dynamically continuous or discontinuous type products have longer introductory stages and hence are more likely to fail. Promotional strategy for these types of products must be carefully developed to avoid losses and ultimate failure. The biggest problem for the high-learning product is educating the consumer to the product's utility. Appeals must be based on the product concept rather than on the brand name until there is sufficient awareness among the potential users to warrant a more aggressive brand identification campaign.

As the product reaches the growth stage, it is likely that competition will enter the market and, in the case of the high-learning

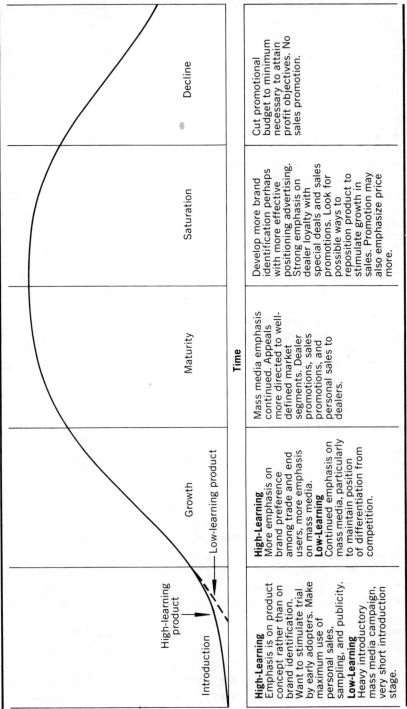

Figure 13-1. Promotional Strategy During Stages of Consumer Product Life Cycle (Adapted from Chester R. Wasson, *Dynamic Competitive Strategy and Product Life Cycles* [St. Charles, Ill.: Challenge Books, 1974], pp. 247-48.)

product, take advantage of that firm, now that the consumer is aware of the product and the needs it satisfies. The firm initiating the new product must be prepared for competitive introduction and should have its campaign in readiness for such changes in market conditions.

During the maturity stage, promotional strategy should appeal directly to important market segments. Special promotions and price deals may begin to be part of advertising copy. Emphasis on dealer promotions is necessary to ensure favorable treatment for shelf space, location, etc.

As the product moves into the saturation stage, the firm should begin to research ways to reposition the product or use promotion strategy to convey new uses or to reach new target markets. Special deals to channel members will be needed to maintain trade loyalty. If the firm is not able to stimulate growth in sales, a decision must be made about whether to continue marketing this product or to withdraw it. If management decides to continue, the promotion budget will be cut back. Efficiency should allow the firm to continue to earn some profits or contribute some revenue to fixed costs.

The Industrial Product

Industrial products also follow a life cycle pattern. The promotional strategy for an industrial product is also critical to the success of its introduction. For the industrial product, the emphasis during the introductory stage is on trade shows, publicity, and personal selling. If it is a high-learning product, in-house seminars, films, or other training devices may be necessary to educate users.

As the product moves into the growth stage and competition enters the market, the promotional strategy will be mostly personal selling to emphasize service to the user, particularly delivery and maintenance. The reputation of the innovative firm is also important to ensure its continued success despite competition.

In the maturity and saturation stages, the firm will continue to develop its loyalty among users. Just as in the consumer market, the firm will be seeking to expand sales through the development of new uses or new target markets. Figure 13-2 summarizes the promotion strategy for a typical new industrial product.

POSITIONING WITH PROMOTION

Many new products do not offer enough novelty to make switching by the consumer worthwhile. Consumers may try the

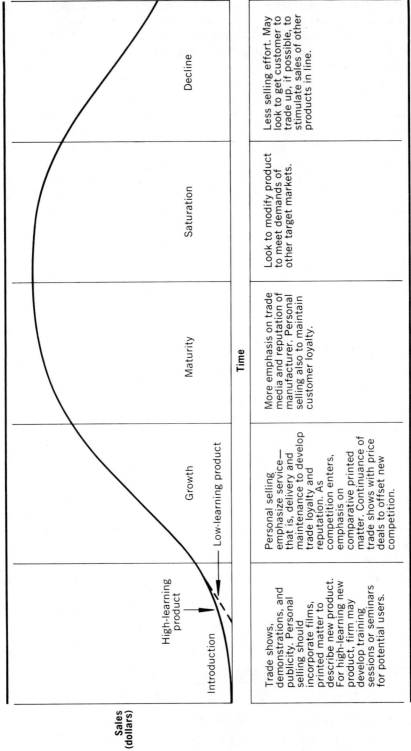

Figure 13-2. Promotion Strategy During Stages of Industrial Product Life Cycle (Adapted from Chester R. Wasson, *Dynamic Competitive Strategy and Product Life Cycles* [St. Charles, Ill.: Challenge Books, 1974], pp. 247-48.)

new product but will frequently switch back to the old one. The old product was probably very satisfactory, and the new product simply did not offer enough uniqueness to warrant switching. This is often the reason for product failures. Thus, new products should be positioned through promotional strategy to have novel attributes that are easily perceived by consumers.

Consumers often have difficulty remembering a particular product being sold but can recall everything else about the advertisement. One explanation for this phenomenon is that much advertising is burdened with creative and interesting formats that have nothing to do with the product. Marketers should ensure that the consumer learns the brand first. The brand name should be clearly stated or shown where appropriate to increase brand recognition.

High brand recognition may occur through either high media frequency or low media frequency but with high content efficiency. This last strategy entails making the new product the central element in all the advertising with careful thought about what is communicated. One good test of whether or not the advertising meets this objective is to substitute a different product for the one being advertised, still maintaining the same conceptual and visual elements. If this can be done, then the level of content efficiency is too low and new advertising copy should be developed.

The success of advertising a new product and obtaining high consumer recall also depends on how well the firm has defined its market segments, especially in relation to competition. The positioning of the new product using advertising has resulted in major success in highly competitive markets. A firm frequently has a wide range of positioning options for the new product compared to its competition.

Direct Comparative Advertising

It is possible to directly confront competition by comparing the new product with that of the leader in the market. This is done by placing the new product alongside the leading product in advertisements. At one time, this strategy was considered to be quite dangerous because the new product may only enhance the advantages of the more popular brand. Much of this fear was based on a Starch research study in 1969, which concluded that out of 1800 television commercials during prime time, an average of only 16% of the audience could recall the new product's brand name. Of this group, 8% credited the commercial to the

new product's competition.[4] In addition, similar research in 1970
and 1971 obtained similar findings, but with increased
misidentification.

More recent advertising strategy, however, seems to imply
that the direct confrontation approach can be successful. One
advertising agency executive indicated that when the new product is introduced in a category dominated by one or two well-
established competitors, the positioning strategy should be
head-on with the dominant brand.[5] Recent increase in the use of
comparison advertising seems to indicate that these fears have
diminished. Gillette, for example, positioned Earth Born directly
against Clairol's Herbal Essence, Johnson's Baby Shampoo, and
Head and Shoulders. In the industrial market, successful head-on
collisions have occurred with Xerox entering the computer field
and IBM's introduction of a copy machine. However, even with
this limited number of successes, the general consensus is to
use a variation of comparison advertising.

Reports from a study conducted by Ogilvy and Mather
revealed that comparative campaigns:

1.   Offer no advantage to the advertiser
2.   Do not increase brand identification
3.   Increase consumer awareness of competitors
4.   Decrease credibility of advertising claims
5.   Result in increased brand misidentification[6]

The products used in this survey were in the drug, health,
and beauty category.

The conclusions on comparative ads are not definitive.
Advertising for new products should be carefully designed and
developed, particularly if a strategy of comparative advertising is
undertaken.

Varying Direct Competitive Positioning

Most new products are introduced by varying the head-on
approach. In the 1960s Avis took a position as being number

[4] E. B. Weiss, "Advertising Must Revise Profit Concept Under Consumerism." *Advertising Age* (January 8, 1973), p. 38.

[5] Lawrence Wolf, "How to Make Your New Product Advertising Work
Harder," *Advertising Age* (October 21, 1974), p. 58.

[6] "Comparative Ads Ineffective: Ogilvy & Mather Study," *Advertising
Age* (October 13, 1975), p. 16.

two, but stated they would try harder to displace the dominant company. Coca-Cola introduced Tab by using the theme "Make Room for Number One." B. F. Goodrich launched a recent campaign to educate the consumer in the difference between Goodyear and Goodrich.

Greater variations have also been achieved by firms seeking to carve out a new market. Vick's Nyquil faced a very competitive market that was saturated with different brands of cold remedies. Instead of trying to introduce a new product to meet the competition head-on, Vick Chemical decided to position this new product by promoting it as a nighttime cold remedy only. The product is in liquid form, which also enabled the consumer to identify it easily and to recognize its purpose as a cold remedy to be taken before bed. More recently, Vick Chemical has introduced a daytime liquid cold remedy to compete directly with other products in this class.

A firm may find that the new product has not achieved the success anticipated, and it may be withdrawn from the market and repositioned using much advertising to enter a new market. Sealtest's Light 'n' Lively ice milk was initially positioned by using an advertising theme stating the product contained less fat and would be lower in calories. This diet image was successful for a short time until competition began to enter the market thereby reducing Light 'n' Lively's market share. Sealtest realized that the market for a diet ice milk was limited but could be expanded to compete with ice cream if consumers would believe that ice milk tasted good. After extensive research, Sealtest repositioned Light 'n' Lively with new bright packaging and flavors and a large advertising campaign that emphasized the good taste of the product. To enhance the creamy taste of ice milk, Sealtest also added milk solids. The results of the repositioning were very successful, and the product achieved a substantial increase in market share.

Industrial product advertising has generally lagged far behind consumer product advertising largely because many members of top management look upon advertising as a dispensible fringe contributor to sales. Thus, managements tend to minimize advertising. Quantitative data on the effectiveness of industrial advertising are generally limited to coupon returns, number of inquiries, and long-range volume trends. A study conducted on industrial advertising of 100 industrial firms in 408 trade papers and periodicals concluded that:

1. Sales increases followed advertising increases.
2. Sales increases prodded by increased advertising

were seldom experienced in full in the same
year.

3.   Curtailment of advertising decreased sales with
increasing momentum.

4.   A company must increase its advertising at least as
much as the overall industry to retain its market
share.

5.   Short-term advertising was generally ineffective.

6.   Advertising capacity should be increased during
business downswings to gain competitive
advantages.[7]

A small manufacturer of gas and fluid couplings had difficulty
marketing a new product that had an automatic shut-off feature
and greater adaptability than its competition. The product was
perceived by consumers to be the same as other products. A print
campaign was conducted to promote the product as different from
competition. Each ad contained copy on functional benefits and
quality by using two cartoon mice who explained the facts humor-
ously. The results were significant sales increases, 62% in the first
eight months.

RCA and General Electric had little success in attempting to
meet IBM head-on in the computer market. Both of these manufacturers were forced to dissolve or sell their computer interests
because their positioning strategy to match IBM was unsuccessful.
Yet Honeywell was successful in its bid to position itself as "the
other computer company."

The overall effect of a positioning strategy may be the critical
factor in determining the success of a new product. This strategy
must be based on research and market segmentation analysis to
ensure that the position sought does not belong to anyone else.

Push versus Pull Strategy

The decision to use a push or pull advertising strategy
depends on the acceptance of the product, particularly among
channel members. A push strategy would entail an advertising
campaign to support and aid sales at the retail level. When channel
members accept the new product, the promotional strategy should
be to inform the consumer through media, point-of-purchase displays, and coupons, the purpose being to increase turnover for the

---

[7] Special report, *Printer's Ink* (October 9, 1959).

retailer. Cooperative advertising may also be used to encourage media advertising on a local level. This practice is particularly evident in the food industry. Special promotional allowances may also be used to encourage channel acceptance (for example, buy 10 cases, get one free).

When the new product is unique or discontinuous, retailers may be reluctant to take the risk and use valuable shelf space for an untried product. This problem is one of the major causes of new product failures. If the retailer and other channel members cannot be induced to carry the product, then the probability of success is reduced significantly. In order to solve this problem, manufacturers have resorted to appealing directly to the consumer so that the consumer will pressure the retailer into carrying the product. This strategy can be very expensive since it is often necessary to use mass media during prime time to appeal to the largest audiences. Repetition and well-designed copy must be used to attract the consumer's attention as well as to make the consumer request the product.

Probably the most successful recent pull strategy was conducted by Pure 1 chicken. This product was faced with a saturated market as well as retailers who were reluctant to change suppliers or add a new brand of chicken. The only direction Pure 1 could take was to directly promote the product to the consumer with a unique advertising plan to facilitate retailer acceptance. Consumers were puzzled by the unique advertising copy and were curious enough to ask their retailers why they did not carry Pure 1. The word-of-mouth activity was effective since Pure 1 was able to take a solid position in the chicken market.

Matching Media with Target Markets

To ensure advertising success, the firm must use all available information on market segments (see Chapter 4). The profiles of target markets enable management to match the media's audience with the target market profiles. Generally, demographic data are readily available describing the audiences of various media. Nielsen product media ratings or target group indices are two sources that provide demographic characteristics for both products and media (print as well as television).

Profile-matching has been used by psychologists to compare characteristics of an individual represented by a set of test scores with those of another individual. The technique allows the researcher to compare the configurations of two sets of test scores, then combine them into a single index.[8]

In marketing, profile-matching has been used to determine whether the congruency between self-image (profile) scores and product or store image (profile) scores has any effect on purchase decisions. Results indicate that consumers are attracted to stores or products that reflect the image they have of themselves.[9] This same methodology has numerous applications in marketing, particularly in matching media audiences with target market profiles. The technique used for matching is a measure of distance between two profiles of demographic characteristics.[10] The goal is to determine which medium has the closest audience characteristics to the profile of market characteristics. The formula used is:

$$D_{12}^2 = \sum_{j=1}^{k} (x_{j1} - x_{j2})^2 \tag{1}$$

where

D_{12} = the distance between two sets of data, i.e., the market and media characteristics

j = any k number of demographic or other defined variables

x_{j1} = score of market variable j

x_{j2} = score of a medium's audience on variable j

Tables 13-4, 13-5, and 13-6 show the matching of five potential print media profiles with the profile of the 35mm camera market.[11] Thus, a firm introducing a new 35mm camera may have

[8] Lee J. Cronbach and Goldine C. Gleser, "Assessing Similarity Between Profiles," *Psychological Bulletin*, vol. 50, no. 6 (1963), pp. 456-73.

[9] See Ira J. Dolich, "A Study of Congruence Relationships Between Self-Images and Product Brands," *Journal of Marketing Research* 6 (February 1969), pp. 81-84; and Ira Dolich and Ned Shilling, "A Critical Evaluation of the Problem of Self-Concept in Store Image Studies," *Journal of Marketing* (January 1971), pp. 71-74.

[10] Jack Z. Sissors, "Matching Media with Markets," *Journal of Advertising Research* (October 1971), pp. 39-43; also see Ronald E. Green, "Numerical Taxonomy in Marketing Analysis," *Journal of Marketing Research* (February 1968), pp. 83-94.

[11] Target Group Index 1973, Axiom Market Research Bureau, Inc., vol. P-38, *Photography and Television*, pp. 152-67.

Table 13-4. Profiles for Occupation Status

Occupation	Professional, managerial		Clerical, sales		Craftsmen, foremen		Other employees		Total difference squared
	(%)	(Squared difference)	(%)	(Squared difference)	(%)	(Squared difference)	(%)	(Squared difference)	
Camera market profile	22		15		9		18		
Better Homes and Gardens	20	(4)	14	(1)	5	(16)	13	(26)	46
Esquire	30	(64)	14	(1)	11	(4)	14	(16)	85
Playboy	26	(16)	17	(4)	11	(4)	18	(0)	24
Time	32	(100)	13	(4)	4	(25)	11	(49)	178
Reader's Digest	22	(0)	14	(1)	6	(9)	13	(25)	35

Table 13-5. Profiles for Household Income

Income	$25,000+		$15,000-24,999		$10,000-14,999		$5,000-9,999		Less than $4,000		Total difference squared
	(%)	(Squared difference)	(%)	(Squared difference)	(%)	(Squared difference)	(%)	(Squared difference)	(%)	(Squared difference)	
Camera market profile	5		22		33		29		11		
Better Homes and Gardens	5	(0)	25	(9)	35	(4)	23	(36)	12	(1)	50
Esquire	7	(4)	31	(81)	32	(1)	22	(49)	8	(9)	144
Playboy	4	(1)	25	(9)	34	(1)	27	(4)	10	(1)	16
Time	10	(25)	32	(100)	30	(9)	21	(64)	7	(16)	214
Reader's Digest	5	(0)	23	(1)	33	(0)	27	(4)	12	(1)	6

Table 13-6. Profiles for Age Categories

Age	18-24		25-34		35-49		40-64		65+		Total difference squared
	(%)	(Squared difference)	(%)	(Squared difference)	(%)	(Squared difference)	(%)	(Squared difference)	(%)	(Squared difference)	
Camera market profile	20		25		30		19		6		
Better Homes and Gardens	14	(36)	21	(16)	29	(1)	25	(36)	11	(25)	114
Esquire	27	(49)	28	(9)	26	(16)	14	(25)	5	(1)	100
Playboy	38	(324)	35	(100)	17	(169)	8	(121)	2	(16)	730
Time	19	(1)	23	(4)	30	(0)	19	(0)	9	(9)	14
Reader's Digest	13	(49)	20	(25)	28	(4)	26	(49)	13	(49)	176

some difficulty in deciding which print medium to choose or how to allocate its print media budget. The problem here is simplified by selecting only five magazines and only three demographic variables. The process would also be appropriate in choosing specific television or radio programs based on similar matchings. For each magazine, distributions of the demographic variables occupation, income, and age are determined by secondary sources. In the 35mm camera market, distributions for these variables are identified and then matched in Tables 13-4, 13-5, and 13-6 by taking the squared difference in each category and summing to get the total squared difference for each magazine and demographic variable. In Table 13-5, which shows the distribution of occupation, *Playboy* magazine provides the best match for the 35mm market, indicated by the low total squared difference value of 24. Other magazines in Tables 13-5 and 13-6 provide the best match for household income and age in the 35mm camera market.

The total squared differences for each demographic variable are summarized in Table 13-7, which also ranks the print media, the lowest difference being the closest match. As indicated above, for occupation status, *Playboy* is the closest match to the 35mm camera profile. Income comparisons show *Reader's Digest* to be the best match, and *Time* magazine is the closest match for age. Summing the total differences for all three demographic variables indicates that *Better Homes and Gardens* would be the best match for the advertising of the new camera. However, there are some critical factors that should be discussed relative to this example. First, we have assumed that the three demographic variables are the most important in buying this product. Second, we do not know the relative weights of each demographic variable. If occupation and income were weighted the heaviest for the camera market, then *Playboy* and *Reader's Digest* would clearly be the top choices. Therefore, the firm should first carefully determine the relevant profile characteristics and also weight the variables based on its experience in this market.

The allocation of the budget for print media advertising can also use the information from profile matching. The top-ranked media would receive the highest proportion and subsequent media lesser amounts. Lower ranked media may be eliminated from consideration altogether.

The matching process may be used not only to compare magazine versus magazine and television program versus television program, but also for intermedia comparisons, such as magazine versus television program. As the number of variables as well as the media involved increase, the calculations will become difficult. Computer programs, however, may be easily developed to accommodate this simple algorithm.

Table 13-7. Sum of Squared Differences for Three Demographic Variables

Magazine	Total Differences Squared						Sum of squared differences	
	Occupation (Rank)		Income (Rank)		Age (Rank)		(Rank)	
Better Homes and Gardens	46	(3)	50	(3)	114	(3)	210	(1)
Esquire	85	(4)	144	(4)	100	(2)	329	(3)
Playboy	24	(1)	16	(2)	730	(5)	770	(5)
Time	178	(5)	214	(5)	14	(1)	406	(4)
Reader's Digest	35	(2)	6	(1)	176	(4)	217	(2)

SUMMARY

The decisions concerning promotion for the new product may be difficult and complex. The complexity of promotional mix decisions is dependent on the product's newness and management's experience. Where no internal expertise exists, the firm may choose to engage an advertising agency, which will aid in making promotional mix decisions ranging from setting the budget to the design of the ads.

When selecting an advertising agency, management must be aware of the important criteria in choosing the most capable agency. A checklist for selecting the agency can be used in the evaluation process.

This chapter has provided some insight into the significance of publicity in communicating the introduction of a new product. News releases are a means of gaining publicity for new products.

The product life cycle represents a valuable tool for studying and modifying the promotional mix strategy for the new product. The promotional mix strategy is also affected by the type of new product—that is, high learning versus low learning, particularly in the introduction and growth stages. The promotional strategies over the life cycles of both consumer products and industrial products are illustrated in this chapter.

Marketers must position a new product either close to, or dis-distinct from, competition in order to optimize its opportunities. Strategies for positioning a new product using promotion that may enhance the success of a new product introduction are:

1. Direct comparative advertising in which the new product is shown in ads beside competitive products and comparisons are made

2.   Varying the positioning by seeking a different approach than competition and thus avoiding direct comparisons

Two of the most difficult promotion decisions to make are the selection of media and subsequent allocation of the promotional budget. By matching media (both within the same medium and between two different media), the firm may optimize its allocation of the promotion budget. A distance formula may be used to match profiles of the market for a new product with media audiences.

SELECTED READINGS

Cronbach, Lee J., and Gleser, Goldine C. "Assessing Similarity Between Profiles." *Psychological Bulletin*, vol. 50, no. 6 (1953):456-73.

_____. "Comparative Ads Ineffective: O&M Study." *Advertising Age* (October 13, 1975):16.

Engel, James; Wales, Hugh; and Warshaw, Martin. *Promotional Strategy.* Homewood, Ill.: Irwin, 1967.

Frank, Ronald E., and Green, Paul E. "Numerical Taxonomy in Marketing Analysis." *Journal of Marketing Research* (February 1968):83-94.

Gamble, Frederic R. *What Advertising Agencies Are—What They Do and How They Do It,* 4th ed. New York: American Association of Advertising Agencies, 1963.

Morley, John, ed. *Launching a New Product.* London: Business Books, Ltd., 1968.

Sexton, Donald E., Jr. "Overspending in Advertising." *Journal of Advertising Research* 11 (December 1971):19-24.

"Special Report." *Printer's Ink* (October 9, 1959):25-31.

Target Group Index. New York: Axiom Market Research Bureau, 1975.

Wasson, Chester R. *Dynamic Competitive Strategy and Product Life Cycles.* St. Charles, Ill.: Challenge Books, 1974.

Weiss, E. B. "Advertising Must Revise Profit Concept Under Consumerism." *Advertising Age* (January 8, 1973):35-41.

Wheatley, John, ed. *Measuring Advertising Effectiveness: Selected Readings.* Homewood, Ill.: Irwin, 1969.

Wolf, Lawrence. "How to Make Your New Product Advertising Work Harder." *Advertising Age* (October 21, 1974):57-60.

Part Five

The New Product: Its Control and Outside Impact

14

Controlling
the New Product

The marketing program described in Chapters 10-13 is subject
to many controllable and uncontrollable variables. This chapter
discusses the importance of monitoring and managing these and
their effect on the new product during the stages of its life cycle.

NATURE OF CONTROL

Control is the means by which management assures achievement of the objectives of the marketing plan and takes the necessary steps to bring the actual results closer to the desired results.
Management must establish standards for comparing the actual
results of the marketing mix strategy with the planned results.
These performance standards are used to identify needed marketing strategy modifications. The control process must be active
throughout the product life cycle.

Control and the Product Life Cycle

The amount of control in each stage in the product life
cycle will differ for firms operating in different markets. Nevertheless, every firm must establish a system for monitoring market
characteristics to assure success in meeting market objectives.
Table 14-1 describes some of the elements considered critical
information in monitoring and controlling the new product.

In the early stages management must be particularly concerned with how well the product physically performs and

Table 14-1. Control During the Product Life Cycle

Stage of product life cycle	Probable control problems
Introduction	Emphasis should be on developing a system to identify product engineering problems and market segments.
Growth stage	Particular concern is given to the brand position, gaps in market coverage, new segments, and competition positioning.
Maturity	Repurchase rate, product improvement, market expansion, and new promotional techniques are the most critical concerns in this stage.
Saturation	Symptoms for product decline should be closely watched. Possible product improvements, new uses, new market segments should be evaluated.
Decline	Information needed to determine whether product should be withdrawn or dropped from product line.

whether the market segments are correctly identified. During the growth stage, concern must be given to competitive positioning and possible gaps in market coverage. The position of the new product and competitive brands will indicate how well the firm has achieved product differentiation.

As the product moves through the maturity and saturation stages, management must carefully monitor sales, profits, and costs. Efforts must be extended to find new uses, new users, or product modifications to stimulate sales. It is also during these later stages that a system must be designed to identify the critical turning point at which the product should be phased out. Product deletion is a critical decision and can be implemented at any stage in the product life cycle. Although costly, early product deletion may prevent more serious problems were the product to be retained.

The performance standards will change at each stage in the product life cycle because of changes in the competitive environment. A monitoring and control system is important regardless of whether the new product is a high-learning or a low-learning product.

THE CONTROL PROCESS

Figure 14-1 shows the process in establishing a control system for a new product. Each of the stages or control activities is interrelated and therefore must be coordinated when designing this system. Incorrect decisions at any stage may cause new product failure since these activities are so dependent on each other. For example, if errors were made in identifying the key marketing variables, such as not considering the growth rate of the industry, the company could assume that the new product was successful since product sales were increasing. However, this rate is less than that for the industry. A low rate of growth in product sales compared to industry sales may be indicative of poor product positioning.

Identifying the Marketing Activities To Be Controlled

Management must determine which marketing activities are most critical to achieving a successful product launch. Particular areas should be identified and then area managers should be asked for inputs about specific factors within their responsibility that they feel would significantly contribute to the success of the new product launch. Some of the most obvious areas to be controlled are sales, market share, profit contribution, marketing program costs, intensity of distribution, consumer awareness, and competitive activities. Each of these may be assigned priorities depending on the marketing objectives. The relevant variables may be more specifically defined by the area managers.

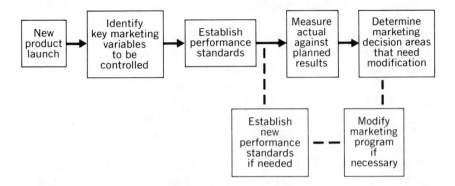

Figure 14-1. The Control Process for New Products

Establishing Performance Standards

Once the key performance areas have been determined, it is necessary to set standards. These standards should be in some measurable unit such as 10% market share at end of the first year after product launch.

For new products in the introduction stage, performance should be monitored in short intervals (monthly or quarterly) since this is such a critical stage. As the product moves on to another stage of the life cycle, the performance standards should change. If the new product is not meeting its standards, the problems must be diagnosed early so that the necessary modifications can be made at an early point in the life cycle.

Figure 14-2 illustrates how the control system operates. It provides all of the needed information for performance comparisons as well as written documentation of the suggested strategy modification. The measurement and strategy modification decisions are discussed below.

The performance standards in Figure 14-2 are established by the members of the management team responsible for the decision areas. It is expected that the new product will achieve a 10% market share by the end of the first year. At the end of the six months, the new product was expected to reach 5% market share. These estimates are based on market test data, experience of other similar products, market research data, or management's judgment.

Measurement of Expected versus Actual Results

The timing for measurement of expected and actual performance will vary depending on the newness of the product as well as management's knowledge of market conditions. In a high-risk market in which competition and consumer tastes are changing quickly, management may have to evaluate performance monthly. It is recommended even for low-risk new products that evaluations be considered on a quarterly basis.

In Figure 14-2 the actual results were less than expected for three of the objectives. Market share, intensity of distribution, and consumer awareness were below the standard established for the first six months. The lower-than-expected market share may be explained by the low distribution coverage as well as the low consumer awareness. In many instances the criteria for measurement and control are related so that a change in one area of the marketing plan may have a positive impact on all the interrelated marketing mix variables.

Figure 14-2. Monitoring New Product Launch

Objectives for first year	6 months			12 months		
	Expected	Actual	Corrective strategy	Expected	Actual	Corrective strategy
1. Achieve 10% market share	5%	3%	Increase advertising by 5%.	10%	8%	High awareness but low market share may indicate poor product performance. Consider possible product modification based on carefully designed research.
2. Achieve 25% intensity of distribution at retail	15%	12%	Provide better margins and incentives to distributors. Contact more wholesalers.	15%	15%	Product location in store may be a problem. Continue plan to develop better relationship with retailers.
3. Reach 50% awareness in target market	30%	25%	Modify advertising appeal to target market.	50%	60%	Advertising may need to express utility of product as well as awareness.
4. Achieve marketing costs of 50% of sales	60%	60%	Maintain close cost controls particularly with increases in advertising and higher margins to distributors.	50%	60%	Determine highest cost marketing items. Establish tighter cost controls and efficiencies with marketing expenses.

In measuring the performance, it will be necessary to identify sources of quantifiable information that will provide bases for comparison. Market share measurement requires some estimate of total industry sales. Secondary sources, such as trade data or government reports, would provide some data on industry sales. In order to determine the intensity of distribution, shipping invoices, salespeople's reports or wholesalers' records could be used. Consumer awareness may be more difficult to measure on a frequent basis. Even though this information can be derived from market research studies, the cost of such research may prohibit its occurrence more than once a year.

Marketing cost data should be readily available from accounting records. Each marketing cost item should be evaluated separately to determine the specific problems and the subsequent action.

Corrective Strategy

When actual performance deviates significantly from expected performance, corrective action is warranted. Figure 14-2 describes the corrective action at the six-month checkpoint and at the end of the first year. In order to correct the gaps in market share, management increased advertising by 5%. At the same time, it was determined that consumer awareness was below the desired standard so the advertising plan should be modified to appeal more directly to the target market(s).

The intensity of distribution (12%) may have contributed to the low market share. In order to increase the intensity of distribution, greater incentives may be used to spur distributors to obtain new retail accounts. Perhaps higher margins to the distributors will be passed on to the retailer, thus developing more interest in carrying the new product.

All corrective actions for items 1 through 3 in Figure 14-2 will have an impact on marketing costs. The corrective action should cause an increase in sales, which is disproportionate to the increase in marketing costs, so that all objectives are satisfied. With corrective action taken for the first three items, management must pay close attention to any changes in the ratio of marketing costs to sales.

Performance standards should not be rigid because the environment in which the firm operates is subject to change. Sudden changes in the environment, such as the energy crisis, would necessitate a change in performance standards. Thus, the purpose of the control system is not merely to measure and evaluate performance differences from the plan but also to accommodate environmental shifts by modifying the standards. For example, in Figure 14-2, the actual market share at the end of six months was 3%, significantly lower than the expected level of 5%. The corrective action may be the solution to closing the performance gap, but it is also conceivable, given information about the environment, that the standard is unreasonable and should be lowered.

At the end of the 12-month period, the actual performance improved somewhat but was still below standard for market share. In addition, marketing costs did not decrease to the desired 50% of sales. Surprisingly, consumer awareness had increased to 60%, which exceeded the expected level. Management felt that advertising may not have sufficiently expressed the utility or benefits of the product, which may have had a negative effect on sales. At the end of the first year, the major problems appear to be inefficiencies in distribution and advertising strategy resulting in high marketing costs and low yield in reaching the desired market. Other reasons or possible problem areas should also be explored so that other corrective action may be implemented. For example, salespeople may need more training or new marketing personnel may be needed to achieve marketing goals.

It is rare to find a situation in which a firm has been able to design an optimal marketing plan for its new product. Marketing management is a process of human activities and decisions that attempt to forecast and react to changes in the competitive environment. The control process exhibited in Figure 14-1 provides a mechanism to reduce error in judgment as well as to establish an adaptive system to ensure the success of the new product. The control process has significant responsibility in the new product management process.

PRODUCT ABANDONMENT: A CONTROL APPLICATION

All products eventually reach the point in their life cycle at which they should be eliminated from the product line. This decision is often a difficult one for many firms because the product has been a part of the company for such a long time that it has acquired some sentimental value. In addition, the impact of one elimination on other products in the product line must be considered. The relationship of the one product to others is often difficult to assess and complicates the elimination decision.

The product-abandonment decision is becoming more critical primarily because of the advent of the energy crisis in 1973 as well as the projection for continued shortages in the next ten years. In the past a firm would retain a product longer because there were sufficient raw materials and because the product may have been meeting minimum goal requirements. This option is not likely to exist in most industries today, and it should make the product-abandonment decision a more active element in marketing strategy. Most firms market more than one product; this requires a systematic approach to introducing or eliminating products. Too many weak products can result in the thinning of resources among all existing products, which can adversely affect potentially successful products. Resources appropriated to weak products should be diverted to work more efficiently for successful products, which could enhance the company's overall profit position.[1]

The resources absorbed by the weak product(s) may lead to delay in the development of profitable new products. Competitive strength may be reduced because of failure to provide an adequate system of controlling weak products.

Experience has shown that tremendous savings can result by eliminating marginal products. For example, Hunt Foods reduced its product line from over 30 to three products over an 11-year period, but still increased sales from $15 million to $120 million.[2] Another firm achieved similar success by eliminating 16 products with a total sales volume of $3.3 million, but increasing companywide sales by 5% and profits by 20 times.[3] However, these examples are limited to a few aggressive firms. Typically, companies only undertake a pruning of the product line when a crisis or near crisis occurs, such as drastic reductions in profits or sales. In fact, it is quite reasonable to conclude that new product planning and development activity far exceeds the managerial activity devoted to the product abandonment decision.[4] Management must give more attention to assessing the contributions of each member of the product line to the profitability of all its products, new and mature.

Despite the obvious need for the careful analysis of weak products, management's sentiments and rationalizing often cause retention of weak mature products. Philip Kotler cites the following factors that contribute to this abandonment aversion:

[1] For a good overview of the product abandonment decision, see Philip Kotler, "Phasing Out Weak Products," *Harvard Business Review* (March-April 1965), pp. 108-18.

[2] Ibid., p. 109.

[3] Ibid., p. 110.

[4] See James T. Rothe, "The Product Elimination Decision," *MSU Business Topics* (Autumn 1970), p. 45; and Richard T. Hise and Michael A. McGinnis, "Product Elimination: Practices, Policies and Ethics," *Business Horizons* (June 1975), pp. 25-32.

Sometimes it is expected—or hoped—that product sales will pick up in the course of time when the economic or market factors become more propitious.

Sometimes the fault is thought to lie in the marketing program, which the company plans to revitalize.

Even when the marketing program is thought to be competent, management may feel that the solution lies in product modification.

When none of these explanations exist, a weak product may nevertheless be retained in the mix because of the alleged contribution it makes to the sales of the company's other products.

If none of these functions are performed by the weak product, then the retention rationale may be that its sales volume covers more than just actual costs, and the company temporarily has no better way of keeping its fixed resources employed.[5]

Even though these seem to be logical reasons for retaining a weak product, they may be excuses for vested interests or sentimental interests. These rationales may be tenable in the short-run, but they will eventually fail to conceal the low profitability and contribution of the weak products. It is unfortunate that the inevitable is so often delayed since the company tends to incur significant costs by retaining weak products.

Techniques for Product Deletion

Several approaches have been suggested for the deletion or abandonment decision. Early publications were almost completely subjective and provided suggestions as to what factors needed to be evaluated periodically in conducting a product line analysis.[6] Some numerical assessments were made by assigning weights to each criterion, but these assignments were based on managerial judgment.

[5] Kotler, "Phasing Out Weak Products," *Harvard Business Review*, March-April 1965, p. 110. Copyright © 1965 by the President and Fellows of Harvard College; all rights reserved.

[6] See D'Orsey Hurst, "Criteria for Evaluating Existing Products and Product Lines," in *Analyzing and Improving Marketing Performances*, AMA Management Report No. 32 (New York: American Management Association, 1959), p. 91; and R. S. Alexander, "The Death and Burial of 'Sick' Products," *Journal of Marketing* (April 1964), p. 1.

The Kotler Control System   Philip Kotler's control system, illustrated in Figure 14-3, provides a significant contribution to the product deletion decision. The procedure is performed by a team of managers from various functional areas and is formal and systematic, ultimately yielding an index that indicates the product's weakness.[7]

The creation stage of the Kotler system consists of two steps. The first is the development of objectives and procedures for reviewing the product line. The second step involves meetings to define the factors that should be considered and the procedures to be used in the analysis. The format and procedures implemented by this management team may vary depending on the size of the company and the industry in which it operates.

The operational stage of the control system has six steps:

1.   The controller's office prepares a data sheet for every product. An example of this data sheet is shown in Figure 14-4.

2.   Identify which products should be further analyzed by considering such information as declining gross margin and declining sales relative to company and industry sales. A computer program can be written to scan these data to identify weak products.

3.   Develop comprehensive criteria to evaluate the weak products identified in step 2. These criteria are determined from meetings of the management team and are incorporated into a rating form illustrated in Figure 14-5. Each criterion is also assigned a weight by management. Members of the committee must then agree on a rating for each question.

4.   Calculate a product retention index that is based on the summation of the weights times the ratings for each criterion (see Figure 14-5).

5.   The committee reviews each product retention index. Those products with indices below the minimum established by the committee may be eliminated provided other justifications are also met. Marginal products must be carefully analyzed before a final decision is made.

6.   Management must establish a procedure for phasing out the product. Problems, such as replacement parts, sale of machinery and unfinished stock, and compensation for middlemen must be solved. Sched-

[7]Kotler, "Phasing Out Weak Products," p. 112.

Figure 14-3. The Kotler Control System

Creation stage

Appoint a product review committee

Hold meetings to set objectives and procedures related to product pruning

Operational stage

1. Controller's office fills out product data sheets

2. Computer program determines dubious products

3. Management team fills out rating forms for dubious products

4. Computer program determines product retention index for each dubious product

5. Management team reviews indices and decides on products to drop

6. Management team develops policies and plans for phasing out "dropped" products

SOURCE: Philip Kotler, "Phasing Out Weak Product," *Harvard Business Review* (March-April 1965), p. 110. Copyright © 1965 by the President and Fellows of Harvard College; all rights reserved.

ules for the phasing out procedure may be prepared by using critical path programs such as PERT.

The Kotler control process provides a systematic procedure for eliminating weak products. It does have some weaknesses of its own. For example, the management team responsible for determining criteria and weights also rates the criteria that may affect the committee's objectivity. Consensus may minimize this problem if committee members have equal power in the company.

Product Review and Evaluation Subsystem (PRESS)[8]   The PRESS model to delete weak products was developed by Hamelman and Mazze and consists of four integrated parts. PRESS I applies

[8] For a complete description of the model, see Paul W. Hamelman and Edward M. Mazze, "Improving Product Abandonment Decisions," *Journal of Marketing* 36 (April 1972), pp. 20-26.

Figure 14-4. Product Data Sheet

Product _____

Date _____

Criteria		Past years			Current years
		3	2	1	
Industry sales	($)				
Company sales	($)				
Physical volume					
Unit total cost	($)				
Unit variable cost	($)				
Price	($)				
Cyclical adjustment factor					
Overhead burden					

Comments:

SOURCE: Philip Kotler, "Phasing Out Weak Products," *Harvard Business Review* March-April 1965, p. 113. Copyright © 1965 by the President and Fellows of Harvard College; all rights reserved.

standard cost accounting and marketing performance data; PRESS II, III, and IV are concerned with price changes, sales trends, and product interaction.

PRESS I: Cost Analysis   This model is based on a variable cost accounting procedure, which includes standard cost, unit price, and volume for the most recent period. Only those costs that have specific contribution toward the production and sales of a product are included. Allocation of fixed costs is not included because of the difficulty in determining their impact on any one product and because they are sunk costs; therefore, they are not affected by the abandonment decision. A sample listing of costs for three hypothetical products is illustrated in Table 14-2.

In this model contribution margin is the primary criterion for comparing the several products in the line. However, it does not provide any information about the amount of resources required to attain that contribution. A more comprehensive meas- ure should include an adjustment for the use of resources to give a comparison of return on investment rather than earnings only.

Figure 14-5. Rating Form

Product no. _____

Date _____

Weight (W)	Criteria	Rating (R)	
1	What is the future market potential for this product?	.0 .2 .4 .6 .8 1.0 Low High	$W_1 R_1 =$
2	How much could be gained by product modification?	.0 .2 .4 .6 .8 1.0 Nothing A great deal	$W_2 R_2 =$
3	How much could be gained by marketing strategy modification?	.0 .2 .4 .6 .8 1.0 Nothing A great deal	$W_3 R_3 =$
4	How much useful executive time could be released by abandoning this product?	.0 .2 .4 .6 .8 1.0 A great deal Very little	$W_4 R_4 =$
5	How good are the firm's alternative opportunities?	.0 .2 .4 .6 .8 1.0 Very good Very poor	$W_5 R_5 =$
6	How much is the product contributing beyond its direct costs?	.0 .2 .4 .6 .8 1.0 Nothing A great deal	$W_6 R_6 =$
7	How much is the product contributing to the sale of the other products?	.0 .2 .4 .6 .8 1.0 Nothing A great deal	$W_7 R_7 =$

Product retention index[a]   _____

[a]All WR's are summed to obtain product retention index. The higher the index the greater the arguments for retaining the product.

Table 14-2. Standard Costs, Unit Price, and Volume Data

Product	Unit material costs	Unit labor costs	Unit variable overhead costs	Unit sales price	Unit quantity sold	Unit[a] variable S and A
A	4.00	3.00	1.80	22.00	1,500,000	2.00
B	1.50	1.00	.50	12.00	2,000,000	2.00
C	6.00	3.00	5.00	29.00	200,000	4.00

[a]Includes advertising, salespeople and other administrative and selling costs that can be attributed to each product.

All costs, where easily attributable to each product, should be included in this analysis.

Each product is compared in the PRESS I model by using a Selection Index Number (SIN). The formula for determining the SIN is:

$$\text{SIN}_i = \frac{\dfrac{CM_i}{\Sigma CM_i}}{\dfrac{FC_i}{\Sigma FC_i}} \cdot \frac{CM_i}{\Sigma CM_i} \tag{1}$$

where SIN_i = Selection Index Number for product i

CM_i = contribution margin for product i

FC_i = facilities costs for product i

ΣCM_i = summation of contribution margin for all products

ΣFC_i = summation of facilities costs of all products

Table 14-3 shows the SIN indices for products A, B, and C. It also includes the total contribution margin (unit contribution times units sold), product contribution margin as a percentage of the three products' contribution margins, cost of facilities used, and percentage of the firm's resources used to produce each product. The products are arranged by the order of their SIN value. The lower the SIN number, the more reason to consider the product for deletion. An SIN number lower than 1.00 is a definite sign that the product is marginal. Thus, product C is a candidate for deletion providing there are substitutes, no goodwill, or possible negative impact on other products in the line.

PRESS II: Price/Volume Relationships   PRESS II determines the effect of a price change on the marginal products identified by PRESS I. It is possible that a price increase of product C may increase marginal contribution with little reduction in total units sold. This situation would improve SIN and perhaps give new life to the marginal product. Again, all other factors mentioned above must be considered before final judgment is made on the deletion of product C.

Table 14-3. Rankings of Products

Product	Total contribution margin	% of total contribution margin	Costs of facilities used	% of costs of facilities used	SIN
A	16.8 M	52.8	400,000	47	59.32
B	14.0 M	44.1	300,000	35	55.57
C	1.0 M	3.1	150,000	18	.53
	31.8 M	100.0%	850,000		

One major problem with PRESS II is that sensitivity of demand to price increases cannot always be readily determined. Competitive actions may prevent the declining product from attaining a better position, thus limiting the probability for improving the failing product's marginal contribution.

PRESS III: Sales Trends   It is possible that product C in Table 14-3 is in the early stages of its life cycle and could conceivably become a good performer in the near future. The PRESS III subsystem forecasts future demand for marginal products by extrapolating from historical sales data using an exponentially weighted moving average.

Certain variables are assumed by PRESS III to remain constant. These are selling price, variable costs per unit, and selling and administrative costs. The projections that result from PRESS III can be used for a reiteration of the PRESS I model to determine whether the SIN has improved.

PRESS IV: Product Complementarity and Substitutability   It is likely that any product in a product line has some effect on the sales of other products in the line. The PRESS IV subprogram assesses the volume of sales of other products attributable to sales of the marginal product. This information may be provided by salespeople, product managers, and other members of management who are familiar with the product line. If the impact of the marginal product is considered minimal, then PRESS IV may be eliminated.

Since product C would be deleted without PRESS IV, where some substitution of one product for another occurs, the PRESS IV program calculates a factor called RESIN, which is the original SIN adjusted for tie-in sales associated with the marginal product. If the marginal product, product C, is deleted, it will be necessary to calculate new SIN for products A and B if there are any tie-in sales.

PRESS I provides valuable insight into the contribution of each product and gives management an index to evaluate marginal products. The major problem with the PRESS model exists in PRESS II, III, and IV where a great deal of subjective evaluation is applied. For example, PRESS II's assumptions regarding the estimation of the sensitivity of demand to price changes, and PRESS III's assumption of management's ability to forecast sales can result in weaknesses in the total PRESS program. PRESS IV requires careful analysis since it may be difficult to estimate the sales associated with any particular products. Nevertheless, the PRESS program is a valuable starting point for management to implement product deletions.

SUMMARY

Implementation of marketing mix strategy in a new product launch requires a monitoring system to determine the effectiveness of the program. In order to achieve optimal profitability, a control system for the new product during its launch and at subsequent points in the product's life cycle is necessary.

The control process consists of the following steps:

1. Identify key marketing variables to be monitored.
2. Establish performance standards.
3. Measure actual results against planned results.
4. Determine marketing mix modifications.
5. Modify marketing program.
6. Establish new performance standards, if necessary.
7. Repeat measure of actual and planned results at specified time intervals.

This chapter discussed how to design a control system and implement corrective marketing strategy.

One of the most difficult and complicated decisions faced by management is product abandonment. Two widely used methods for making the product abandonment decision are the Kotler system and Hamelman and Mazze's PRESS program. The Kotler system consists of six steps beginning with preparation of product data sheets. Then the system identifies marginal products based on declining gross margin or sales. It develops criteria for evaluating a product and calculates the product retention index. The indices are reviewed by management, which finally makes the decision to phase out the product. The Kotler process provides a systematic procedure for making the product-abandonment decision.

The product review and evaluation subsystem (PRESS) provides a computer analysis using standard cost accounting to determine the contribution of each product. PRESS I is the model that calculates the SIN to identify marginal products. PRESS II determines the effect of a price change on the demand and contribution margin of the marginal product(s). PRESS III forecasts the future demand for the marginal product to determine if the product may improve its SIN. PRESS IV determines the impact of sales on all products in the product line if the marginal product(s) is deleted. A new factor called RESIN, which is the original SIN adjusted for tie-in sales due to the marginal product, is calculated.

The major limitations of all processes for product-abandonment decisions are management's ability to identify and allocate costs to all products and to apply subjective criteria to the product's analysis.

Despite inherent weaknesses, it is mandatory that management implement a control process to monitor new products as well as products near the end of their life cycle. Insufficient control can result in inefficiencies, which can lead to low profits. Consistent new product failures or a continuation of low or negative profits is likely to force a firm into bankruptcy.

SELECTED READINGS

Brion, John M. *Corporate Marketing Planning.* New York: Wiley, 1967.

Cravens, David W.; Hills, Gerald E.; and Woodruff, Robert B. *Marketing Decision Making: Concepts and Strategy.* Homewood, Ill.: Richard D. Irwin, 1976.

Etzel, Michael J., and Ivancevich, John M. "Management by Objectives in Marketing: Philosophy, Process and Problems." *Journal of Marketing* 38 (October 1974): 47-55.

Fischer, Paul M., and Crissy, W. J. E. "New Approaches to Analyzing Marketing Profitability." *Journal of Marketing* 38 (April 1974): 43-48.

Kotler, Philip. *Marketing Management: Analysis, Planning and Control,* 3rd ed. Englewood Cliffs, N.J.: Prentice-Hall, 1976.

Simon, Sanford R. *Managing Marketing Profitability.* New York: American Marketing Association, 1969.

Talley, Walter J., Jr. *The Profitable Product: Its Planning, Launching and Management.* Englewood Cliffs, N.J.: Prentice-Hall, 1965.

Worthing, Parker. "Improving Product Deletion Decision Making." *MSU Business Topics* (Summer 1975): 29-38.

15

Social and Environmental Influences in New Product Development

A growing concern for the impact of social and environmental factors on new product development has emerged during the 1970s, evidenced by increased public awareness of social and environmental needs. Such concern will have a direct effect on product planners when decisions are made to add, modify, extend, or eliminate products from the product line. Failure to consider social and environmental factors invites government regulation, which will not only negatively affect new product introduction, but could also be detrimental to the reputation of existing products. Figure 15-1 shows the relationship between the three environmental elements which may affect new product development.

A number of specific forces stimulate concern for social and environmental factors. The major ones are:

1. As our society became more affluent, consumers also became more interested in social needs. In less-developed nations, greater concern is given to economic needs. However, with increased affluence, more emphasis will be placed on social marketing. A good example is the Arab nations, where wealth has been achieved from the increased world demand for petroleum. Initially, their only concern was to improve their profit position without any concern for the social impact of these decisions. Now these countries are beginning to recognize the need for careful evaluation of their position, less they destroy their environment. At present, these countries are

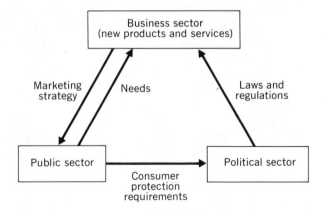

Figure 15-1. Social and Environmental Influences on New Product Development

spending millions of dollars to improve environmental conditions as well as developing plans which will ensure protection of that environment.

2. The young adults of our society demonstrated a strong interest in preserving the environment and protecting scarce resources. This concern has fostered new government regulations as well as greater public awareness of the potential problems that may be encountered should we ignore these factors.

3. Consumer organizations led by such individuals as Ralph Nader and Rachel Carson have heightened the general public's awareness of social and environmental problems.

4. Increased attention to the environmental and social problems by mass media has served an educational function to the general public.

5. Increased leisure time and social mobility have contributed to the broad public demand of industry to pay greater attention to social and environmental factors.

6. Events in the early 1970s, such as the Watergate scandal and the energy crisis, prompted consumers to urge greater attention to the welfare of society and the environment in which we live.[1]

[1] William Lazor and Eugene J. Kelley, *Social Marketing: Perspectives and Viewpoints* (Homewood, Ill.: Richard D. Irwin, 1973), p. 7.

Many of these factors contributed to new regulations and industry codes that must be accounted for in the new product development process. Agencies, such as the Food and Drug Administration, Environmental Protection Agency, and the Office of Consumer Affairs, can enforce regulations, which if not adhered to by firms, could result in financial losses and possible deterioration of their competitive positions.

In 1962 President John F. Kennedy issued his Consumer's Bill of Rights message. It proposed the nation be more concerned with four basic rights of consumers:

1. Right to safety
2. Right to be informed
3. Right to choose
4. Right to be heard

This message had far-reaching effects on new product development as well as on the management of existing products. Since Kennedy's message, a strong commitment has been made by the federal government to ensure these rights. New legislation was passed to protect these rights and to establish consumer agencies, which ensure that the laws are upheld.

This chapter presents the major regulations and external forces that influence the development of new products. Neglect or ignorance of these forces may contribute to new product failures. Consideration of these factors may be used to a firm's advantage if its new products are marketed so that they satisfy these external demands more effectively than existing, competing products.

PRODUCT DEVELOPMENT AND THE MARKETING CONCEPT

The traditional market concept requires the firm engaged in new product development to first consider customer needs and wants designing the product.[2] New social pressures have altered the meaning of the marketing concept so that protection may be imposed on the consumer to an undesirable extent. Protection provided by seat belts, automobile bumpers, removal of lead in gasoline, removal of phosphates from detergents, and packaging restrictions are examples of changes imposed by the government because

[2] Philip Kotler, *Marketing Management: Analysis, Planning and Control*, 3rd ed. (Englewood Cliffs, N.J.: Prentice-Hall, 1976), p. 15.

of public pressures, but the average consumer may not feel that such protection is desirable. Thus, public pressures in some instances induce nonessential product changes that result in additional production costs and consequently a higher price to the consumer.[3]   Consumer protection presents a difficult decision for many consumers, especially those who have been impoverished by inflation and unemployment. For example, product trace-and-recall programs enforced by consumer protection groups result in increased costs to the firm, which, in turn, are passed on to the consumer through higher prices. Other examples exist in which economic, social, and environmental factors are in conflict. Some of the recently passed legislation on emission standards for automobiles has had an adverse effect on fuel economy, yet reduction of gasoline consumption and good air quality are both important goals of consumer protection groups.

Problems with the marketing concept do not imply that firms should revise their thinking about consumer needs in the planning and development of new products. On the contrary, consumer preferences must continue to be the primary concern. What firms must *not* do is to rely on preconceived concepts (either their own or those of public policy groups) of what is best for the consumer. Only when a firm emphasizes consumer preferences will it be able to introduce new products successfully.

In addition to the pressures to modify products, companies are also asked to provide more information so that customers are better informed as to the available alternatives. However, requirements regarding product labeling and unit pricing meant to provide more information at the point of purchase have been paid only minimal attention or have confused consumers.[4]   It appears that more thought should be given to decisions to provide increased consumer protection or more information so as to avoid any additional unnecessary cost to the consumer.

Raw materials and energy shortages has recently led to the public demand for products deemed necessary rather than luxury ones.[5]   If shortages become more severe, the government, with consumer protection organizations' support, may apply pressure to firms to curtail production of products and packaging that are deemed nonessential. This rationing, if forecasted early by firms using these materials, will force the development of substitutes or some other solution. The company that can anticipate such events

---

[3] Douglas L. MacLachlan, "Editor's Comments," *Journal of Contemporary Business* (Winter 1975), p. ii.

[4] Kert B. Monroe and Peter J. LaPlaca, "What Are the Benefits of Unit Pricing," *Journal of Marketing* (July 1972), p. 22.

[5] Maclachlan, "Editor's Comments," p. iii.

will gain a competitive advantage by modifications of product and packaging strategy. Companies that lag in this forecasting are likely to suffer serious declines in market share.

A few firms have already established environmental study groups whose responsibility is to analyze changes in the environment and their effect on new product development as well as their influence on the existing marketing strategy. Unfortunately, many firms do not concern themselves with these external variables until a crisis occurs that forces them to make costly disruptive decisions.[6]

ADVANTAGES OF ENVIRONMENTAL AND SOCIAL EVALUATION

The inclusion of social and environmental factors in evaluating new product alternatives will result in a product line that will gain wider consumer acceptance. It may also result in less objection by nonusers because there are no ill effects on the natural and social environment.[7] One recent study supports this contention. It was found that new products that seem to alleviate environmental problems have greater probability of being accepted.[8]

Concern with social and environmental factors has recently become a requirement of government agencies that provide funds in the form of contracts, grants, or loans to firms engaged in new product development. For example, the Environmental Protection Agency will withhold funds from violators of water or air pollution standards. These funds may be withheld even after a contract, grant, or loan has been made. The company in violation would be required to rectify its problem before funds would be released. Equipment for pollution reduction can be very costly. In most cases, careful scrutiny of the pollution problem from the start would have saved the firm the cost of adding pollution reducing equipment later. Recognition of undesirable effects on the enviornment caused by a new product manufacturing process should lead to immediate elimination or modification to avoid significant later investment due to major changes in design. Firms must not evaluate a new product idea purely on economic terms without consideration for environmental and social factors.

[6] George Fisk, "Impact of Social Sanctions on Product Strategy," *Journal of Contemporary Business* (Winter 1975), p. 2.

[7] Dale L. Varble, "Social and Environmental Considerations in New Product Development," *Journal of Marketing* (October 1972), p. 14.

[8] Harold H. Kassarjian, "Incorporating Ecology into Marketing Strategy: The Case of Air Pollution," *Journal of Marketing* (July 1971), p. 61.

DISADVANTAGES OF
ENVIRONMENTAL AND SOCIAL EVALUATION

Evaluation of environmental and social factors in new product decisions results in the following disadvantages to the firm:

1. The costs incurred in product development will substantially increase especially as the scope of the evaluation process increases.

2. Timing of new product introductions will be affected because this evaluation must be included as part of the development process.

3. Ideas for new products will have to be more carefully screened due to increased costs, thus possibly eliminating products that are otherwise potentially successful.

On the surface, these disadvantages seem quite severe. However, failing to conduct an environmental and social evaluation could result in far greater costs if the new product fails because it does not meet social and environmental requirements.

PRODUCT SAFETY

The Consumer Product Safety Act was signed into law by President Richard M. Nixon on October 28, 1972.[9] This law went into effect on December 26, 1972 creating an independent, five-member Consumer Product Safety Commission. The commission retains the power to prescribe safety standards for nearly all consumer products except where regulation already exists. The act contains some important implications for the new-product development process. It may also have significant effects on the existing product line if any of the offerings are subject to these regulations.

The concern for safety in consumer products has existed for many years, but early standards were vague. Injuries attributed to unsafe products are believed to number 20 million per year; 100,000 persons are permanently disabled and 30,000 others lose their lives. The annual cost of these injuries exceeds $5.5 billion

[9] Consumer Product Safety Act of 1972, Publication L. No. 92 (October 28, 1972) 41 U.S.L.W. 57 (October 31, 1972).

and is increasing at an alarming rate.[10] It is argued that many
injuries could have been prevented if manufacturers had been more
conscious of product safety. Regardless of where the fault lies,
firms must realize that the government and consumer protection
groups intend to press the product safety issue in order to alleviate
the large number of injuries. This realization must be manifested
at an early stage during the product development process in order
to prevent costly modifications or complete withdrawal of a new
product. Modification will require lead time for redesigning the
new product, which could place the firm in an unfavorable market
position.

At the present time, more than 10,000 products are subject
to the legal powers of the Consumer Product Safety Commission.
Its prerogative is designed to include consumer products defined as
"any article, or component part thereof produced or distributed
(i) for sale to a consumer for use in or around a permanent or
temporary household or residence, a school, in recreation or
otherwise, or (ii) for the personal use, consumption or enjoyment
of a consumer in or around a permanent or temporary household
or residence, a school, in recreation or otherwise. . . ."[11] This
definition is broad and could conceivably affect hundreds of
thousands of retailers, distributors, and manufacturers who will be
policed to assure compliance with these product safety regulations.
It is possible that the range of consumer products could be further
expanded to include even more products.

Product Safety Standards and Procedures

Consumer Product Safety Standards are the means by which
the objectives of the act are attained. These standards "consist of
(1) requirements as to performance, composition, contents, design,
construction, finish, or packaging, or (2) requirements that a consumer product be marked with or accompanied by clear and
adequate warnings . . . or (3) any combination of (1) and (2)."[12]
According to the specifications of the Consumer Protection Act, the
development of standards begins with a majority agreement by the
five commissioners that a product poses "an unreasonable risk of
injury" thus necessitating some criteria for safety. The commission
then publishes a notice in the Federal Register and the press inviting
any person or group to submit an existing standard or an offer to

---

[10] U.S., Congress, Senate, Commission on Commerce, Hearings on
National Commission on Product Safety, 91st Cong., 2d sess., 1970, p. 37.

[11] Public Law 92-573, 92nd Congress, S. 3419, October 27, 1972 p. 2.

[12] 15 U.S.C. 2052 (a)(1) 1972.

develop a mandatory standard. This offer is extended by the commission to ensure representative public participation in the development of these standards. The act allows any trade association, consumer organization, professional society, testing laboratory, university or college department, wholesaler, retailer, federal, state, or local government agency, ad hoc association, or any company or person to submit an offer to develop a proposed consumer product safety standard.

Once the commission evaluates any responses, it can then proceed in one of three ways: (a) publish an existing standard as a proposed mandatory standard, (b) accept one or more offers to develop a standard, or (c) proceed independently to develop a standard. These standards fulfill the main objective of the Consumer Product Safety Act: reduce unreasonable risks of injury associated with the use of consumer products.

Substantial Hazards and the Commission

During the first year of operation, the Consumer Product Safety Commission received about 130 defect notifications involving some 14 million product units.[13] These complaints included such products as baby cribs, soft drink bottles, bicycles, swimming pools, minibikes, snowmobiles, power lawn mowers, sliding doors, and artificial turf. The most unusual notification involved the artificial turf. The Professional Football Players' Association, which submitted the notification, feels it causes twisted ankles, torn ligaments, skin burns, and other ailments that reduce the average career span of its members. The National Football Players' Association wants the commission to ban its installation in new football fields until federal safety standards are established.

The five-member commission has a great deal of responsibility and power to resolve what it considers to be substantial hazards under section 15 of the act. Some people feel that the authority of the commission is too extensive because it can determine the fate of many new or existing products. The commission feels that this power must be used with discretion so that not necessarily all risk will be eliminated, but to eliminate what it considers to be unreasonable risk.

Despite its intent to remain inconspicuous, the first regulatory action the commission made resulted in much controversy. This ruling stated that mattresses must be made of material that does not catch fire from cigarettes, and during a six-month transition

[13] U.S. Consumer Product Safety Commission, *Fact Sheet,* no. 32 (Washington, D.C.: August, 1974), p. 1.

before new requirements take effect, the mattresses must be labeled flammable.[14] Both consumer groups and the mattress industry took the commission to court. The consumer groups want the commission to require that all mattresses meet federal safety requirements immediately. The industry claims the ruling is unfair because of the high cost of switching materials and because it feels that it has been given the total burden of resolving a problem caused by negligent cigarette smokers. The reaction of the mattress industry is likely to be duplicated by many others that are forced to bear the responsibility for careless consumers. This problem is a particularly difficult one, and the commission is determined to weigh each action carefully, especially in those instances in which consumers can voluntarily avoid or reduce the risk.

Regardless of how extensive the powers of the commission, success depends significantly on cooperation from business. Business has the responsibility of reporting to the commission any product defect that could be a substantial risk to consumers. Business includes, specifically, manufacturers, importers, distributors, and retailers who market any product that comes under the jurisdiction of the commission. Failure to report a defect or furnish required information could result in civil and criminal penalties.

Notification to the commission must be made within 24 hours of discovery of the violation and must be certified by the chief executive officer of the notifying company or by some other designated person. This initial notification must include the following information:

1. Identification of the product
2. Name and address of the manufacturer, if known
3. Nature and extent of the defect
4. Name and address of the person informing the commission[15]

Manufacturers, importers, distributors, or retailers are requested to apprise the commission of the corrective action that will be taken regarding the defect and whether buyers have been notified and will be given a refund, a replacement, or the defective product will be repaired.

The section-15 group is responsible for determining whether or not a product defect may pose a substantial risk of injury. This

[14] "New Product Safety Agency Aims to Cut Household Accidents, But Battles Are in Offing," *Wall Street Journal* (July 11, 1973), p. 34.
[15] U.S. Consumer Product Safety Commission, *Fact Sheet*, p. 1.

group contacts the party making the notification to gather details about the product and any associated injuries. The risk of injury, if found to be substantial, results in a "pre-15(b) letter" to the manufacturer, distributor, or retailer indicating the commission's knowledge of the situation. This letter requests that the firm provide an estimate of the number of products involved and any corrective action that may have been taken. If the commission and the firm concur that no substantial hazard exists, no further action is taken.[16]

Section 15 of the Consumer Product Safety Act is an important section because it enables the commission to ensure that the public is quickly notified of product hazards and that industry must repair, replace, or repurchase those defective products. Section 15 places the responsibility on manufacturers, importers, distributors, and retailers to monitor the safety of their products.

Although the commission has established itself as an important element in product safety, its members feel that the agency needs better tools to accomplish its responsibilities. Some of the areas needing improvement are:

1. The power to independently file civil and criminal cases against violators rather than working through the Justice Department, which in many instances, has declined to pursue referred cases

2. Authority to seize products judged to pose substantial hazards

3. Elimination of the present system of public participation in setting standards so that the commission may avoid delay and confusion, especially because it usually rewrites the standards anyway

Firms involved in the development of new products must pay close attention to the requirements of the Consumer Product Safety Act. The act is meant to offer firms in the new development process incentives to introduce safe products so as to avoid federal intervention.

NEW PRODUCTS AND WARRANTY POLICY

A warranty is an affirmation by the seller of the quality or performance of the goods. Express warranties make such an affirmation in writing, ranging from simple statements about

[16] Ibid., p. 2.

product attributes or product performance—that is, satisfaction guaranteed—to the complex documents limiting the legal responsibilities of manufacturers of such products as appliances and automobiles. It is also implied by the Uniform Commercial Code that each product is fit for the purpose for which it is sold.

Typically, warranties have not been applied to frequently purchased products, such as packaged goods. The reason is that there is very little public pressure for a written guarantee because even when the product does not meet expectations, a complaint is unlikely. In case of complaint, the producer will most often replace, refund, and/or apologize to the consumer.

A recent audit of more than 500 branded supermarket products found that less than 15% of these products carried written warranties. Of the manufacturers of cosmetics, soaps, and detergents studied, 45% offered some type of warranty with most offering a warranty on only a portion of their product line. Most of the express warranties offered the consumer "satisfaction."[17]

Manufacturers may conclude from the above study that there is very little interest among industry members to provide express warranties. Thus, the reaction may be to avoid warranties on frequently purchased products. However, manufacturers, particularly those introducing new products, may find that an express product warranty will provide the following advantages:

1. It can encourage legitimate complaints that can improve product introduction.
2. It may reduce the perceived risk of purchasing a new product.
3. It provides product differentiation, which is most critical in situations in which a firm is attempting to introduce a new product in a highly competitive market.

New Warranty Disclosure Laws

The regulations regarding written warranties have recently changed resulting in more stringent requirements for those firms providing written warranties. The new regulations implement the Magnuson-Moss Warranty Act, which went into effect July 4, 1975. The Federal Trade Commission (FTC) will enforce these

[17]C. L. Kendall and Frederick A. Russ, "Warranty and Complaint Policies: An Opportunity for Marketing Management," *Journal of Marketing* (April 1975), p. 37.

regulations and has also been given the responsibility by Congress to finalize rules for those sections of the law that need more specific wording.

The warranty law does not make product warranties mandatory, but it does require that all written warranties disclose their terms in simple language. To enforce this requirement, the FTC has issued disclosure regulations, which apply to those consumer products costing the consumer more than $15. These regulations, which became effective January 1, 1977, are described in Table 15-1.

The last statement in Table 15-1 is one of the most revealing for firms introducing new products. The implication is that consumers will make comparisons of competitive products and will select the one that provides the best warranty. Firms marketing products subject to these new disclosure laws will be able to differentiate their product offerings. The warranty, if not at least equivalent to the competition's, may result in an unfavorable

Table 15-1. New Warranty Disclosure Regulations (Effective January 1, 1977)

Clear description and identification of products, parts of components covered by, and when necessary for clarification, not covered by the warranty.

Statement of what the manufacturer or store (warrantor) will do in the event of a defect of the product, including a description of what items or services the warrantor will pay for; and when necessary for clarification, which items will not be paid for.

Identity of the person to whom the written warranty is extended must be provided (for example in the warranty extended to second owners of the product).

Duration of the warranty must be stated, particularly whether the term commences at the purchase date or when the company receives the owner registration card.

Step-by-step explanation of what the consumer should do to get repair or replacement. This should include such information as (a) the name of the warrantor, (b) the address of the warrantor, (c) name, title, and address of the department responsible for warranty obligations, and (d) a telephone number that consumers can use without charge to get warranty information.

Information must be provided about any settlement mechanism to resolve warranty complaints.

All consumers must be given an opportunity to read and compare warranties at the time of sale. This can be done by either displaying the warranty near the product, maintaining a binder for different competing products, or a sign containing the warranty text.

consumer reaction. It is conceivable that a firm attempting to introduce a new product in a highly competitive market may be able to enhance its early adoption by providing a more comprehensive warranty.

Figure 15-2 is an example of an express warranty for a portable radio. It is obvious that this warranty does not explicitly give much of the information required in the new warranty disclosure laws, effective January 1, 1977.

Figure 15-2. Sample Express Warranty for Consumer Durable

XYZ 90 Day Service Warranty

The XYZ Corporation guarantees this AM/FM Portable Radio to be free of defective workmanship and material for a 90-day period from date of purchase.

Your AM/FM Portable Radio has been thoroughly tested, inspected and adjusted and is warranted against all manufacturing defects for 90 days from the date of purchase. Any part that is defective or that develops defects under normal use, will be replaced or repaired without cost, except for a handling and postage charge of $2.50, which must be enclosed when you return your AM/FM Portable Radio for service together with your dealer's sales slip indicating your date of purchase.

XYZ Corporation assumes no responsibility for service or replacement parts, should it be determined upon examination that the AM/FM Portable Radio system has been tampered with, subjected to abuse or mishandling, or used with unauthorized accessories. This Warranty shall be applicable only to your XYZ AM/FM Portable Radio system and shall not cover any accessory equipment used in conjunction therewith.

In order to validate this Warranty, the attached Registration Card must be properly filled out and received by XYZ Corporation within 14 days from date of purchase of this unit.

Warranties and the Industrial Product

Many industrial products do not have express warranties. However, most purchases of industrial products are made either as a competitive bid or under some type of written contract. These written contracts will state clearly the requirements and/or responsibility of the seller with regard to any defects in the product. For example, a firm buying coffee beans for processing into various blends of coffee requires the raw materials to meet certain quality standards. Thus, the warranty is actually implied as part of the written contract.

There are a number of instances, particularly in equipment industries, in which a guarantee or warranty is an explicit part of the standard terms rather than implied. Figure 15-3 depicts a portion of a standard contract used by a large equipment manufacturer. As can be seen by the bold print on the bottom of this section, the firm makes no express warranties other than what is explicitly stated in the paragraph. In effect, this warranty provides little protection for the buyer other than for defective workmanship or material.

A study of the purchase process of small computers indicated that the most critical criterion for the lease or purchase of a new small computer is the support provided by the seller, especially that it guarantee and stand by its new product.[18] This finding seems to indicate that in the equipment market, an industrial firm introducing a new product can differentiate its new product by providing an express warranty that offers the buyer greater protection. It is possible that the growing concern for protection of the buyer and the increasing intensity of competition may necessitate a change in the use of express warranties by industrial firms.

OTHER LEGAL REQUIREMENTS FOR NEW PRODUCTS

In addition to the major laws and governing agencies mentioned, there are many other regulations that firms must consider before introducing a new product. Laws relating to labeling, packaging, advertising, pricing, etc., may affect any new product and should be carefully surveyed to ensure that the firm has complied with all requirements.

PATENTS

A patent is a grant given by the government that provides an inventor protection for 17 years from others who may seek to make, use, or sell the invention. By law, "any person who invents or discovers any new and useful process, machine, manufacture or composition of matter, or any new and useful components thereof may obtain a patent" subject to the conditions and requirements of the law.[19]

To be patentable, an invention must be new as defined in the statute; that is, it must not have been used for more than one year prior to the date of application, no other person can have known

[18] Michael P. Peters and M. Venkatesan, "Exploration of Variables Inherent in Adopting an Industrial Product," *Journal of Marketing Research* 10 (August 1973), pp. 312-15.

[19] *United States Code Annotated, Title 35, Patents* (Brooklyn, N.Y.: Edward Thompson Co.) section 101, p. 172.

Figure 15-3. Standard Terms and Conditions of Sale

1.   *Guarantee.* The Company warrants all equipment manufactured by it or bearing its name plate to be free from defects in workmanship and material, under normal use and service, as follows: (a) Equipment not installed by the Company which is returned transportation prepaid to the Company's originating factory within 12 months after date of shipment and is found by the Company's inspection to be defective in workmanship or material will be repaired or replaced, at the Company's option, free of charge and return-shipped lowest cost transportation prepaid. (b) Equipment installed by the Company, or under the direct supervision of the Company, which within 12 months after date of installation is found by the Company's inspection to be defective in workmanship or material will be repaired or replaced, at the Company's option, free of charge. If inspection by the Company does not disclose any defect in workmanship or material the Company's regular published rates will be charged as they apply. Items such as Thermocouples, Electrodes, Glassware, Chart Paper and similar items subject to wear or burnout through usage, shall not be deemed to be defective by reason of wear or burnout through usage. Equipment not manufactured by the Company or bearing its name plate is guaranteed in accordance with the published guarantee of the manufacturer. WITH EXCEPTION OF THE 12 MONTH WARRANTY, SET FORTH ABOVE, THE COMPANY MAKES NO EXPRESS WARRANTIES, NO WARRANTY OF MERCHANTABILITY AND NO WARRANTIES WHICH EXTEND BEYOND THE DESCRIPTION ON THE FACE HEREOF. In no event will the Company be liable for indirect, special or consequential damages of any nature whatsoever.

2.   *Patents.* The Company agrees that it will at its own expense defend any suit that may be instituted against the Purchaser for alleged infringement of United States patents relating to products of Company manufacture furnished the Purchaser hereunder, provided such alleged infringement shall consist only in the use of such product by itself and not as a part of any combination of other devices and/or parts, and provided the Purchaser gives the Company immediate notice in writing of any such alleged infringement and of the institution of any such suit and permits the Company, through its counsel, to answer the charge of infringement and to defend such suit, and provided the Purchaser gives all needed information, assistance and authority to enable the Company to do so, and thereupon in case of a final award of damages in any such suit the Company will pay such award, but shall not be responsible for any settlement made without its written consent.

3.   *Delivery.* Delivery of equipment not agreed on the face hereof to be installed by or under supervision of the Company shall be F.O.B. at the Company factory, warehouse or office selected by the Company. Delivery of equipment agreed on the face hereof to be installed by or under supervision of the Company shall be C.I.F. at the site of installation.

        The Company shall not be liable for any delay in the production, delivery, supervision or installation of any of the equipment covered hereby if such delay shall be due to one or more of the following causes: fire, strike, lockout, dispute with workmen, flood, accident, delay in transportation, shortage of fuel, inability to obtain material, war, embargo, demand or requirement of the United States or any government or war activity, or any other cause whatsoever beyond the reasonable control of the Company. In event of any such delay, the date or dates for performance hereunder by the Company shall be extended for a period equal to the time lost by reason of the delay.

4. *Damage or Loss.* In the case of equipment not to be installed by or under supervision of the Company, the Company shall not be liable for damage to or loss of equipment after delivery of such equipment to the point of shipment. In the case of equipment to be installed by or under supervision of the Company, the Company shall not be liable for damage or loss after delivery by the carrier to the site of installation; if thereafter pending installation or completion of installation or full performance by the Company, any such equipment is damaged or destroyed by any cause whatsoever, other than by the fault of the Company, the Purchaser agrees promptly to pay or reimburse to the Company, in addition to or apart from any and all other sums due or to become due hereunder, an amount equal to the damage or loss so occasioned.

5. *Claims for Shortages.* Each shipment shall be examined by the Purchaser immediately upon his receipt thereof, and any claim for shortage or any other cause must be reported to the Company promptly after such receipt.

6. *Taxes.* With regard to sales of equipment not installed by the Company, the amount of all present and future taxes and governmental charges upon the production, shipment, sale, installation or use of the equipment covered hereby shall be added to the price and paid by the Purchaser. With regard to contracts for the installation of equipment by the Company, the amount of all present or future taxes and governmental charges upon labor or the production, shipment, sale, installation or use of the equipment covered hereby are not included in the price and, unless otherwise stated in the proposal, shall be added to the proposal price and paid by the Purchaser.

---

about or used the invention, and it cannot have been described in a printed publication in the United States or a foreign country prior to the application for the patent.

Application for a Patent

The application for a patent and the procedure for obtaining it requires knowledge of patent laws and practices and thus necessitates the services of a patent attorney or patent agent.[20] The inventor may prepare the application and file it with the Patent Office without the services of an attorney or agent, but such an application would likely result in a patent that does not adequately

[20] For general information, see U.S. Department of Commerce, *Patents*, revised ed. (June 1974).

protect the particular invention. The Patent Office recognizes
patent attorneys and agents and admits them to a special register
that allows these individuals to render patent services to inventors.
Qualifications for admission to this register must be demonstrated
by a special examination.

The formal application, once filed and accepted by the Patent
Office, is followed by a patent search to determine whether or not
the invention is indeed new. During the period between filing the
application and issuance of the patent, the firm may mark the product "patent pending." This has no legal effect other than to indicate the existence of a formal application for a patent. Once the
patent is granted, the firm is required to mark all products with
"Patent" followed by the number of the patent. If this is not
done, the firm may not be able to recover damages from
infringement.

Figure 15-4 illustrates the patent application oath for a single
inventor; it is short and reasonably simple. The critical aspect of
the patent is the written document that comprises the product
specification. This document generally requires the services of an
attorney.

Patent Infringement

Infringement of a patent allows the person or firm holding the
patent to sue for redress in a federal court. The patentee may also
seek an injunction from the court to prevent the continuation of
the infringement. Damages may be awarded by the court if it
finds that infringement has occurred.

The major concern with most court cases is the cost of any
suit for damages. Many smaller firms fear patent infringement
and feel that if a larger firm attempted to copy their new product,
there would be little they could do because attorney's fees and
court costs—if they lost the suit—could force them out of business.
This risk has perhaps resulted in many infringements that never
reached the courts. On the other hand, larger firms are concerned
with the continued pressure placed on them by the government
through antitrust laws, and in many instances they would rather
not involve themselves in a court case that might affect the competitive structure of the market in such a way that they may be
considered a monopoly.

Patent Costs

The costs involved in the application and issuance of a
patent generally range between $200 and $300. However, the cost

Figure 15-4. Sample of Patent Oath

To the Commissioner of Patents:

   Your petitioner, _____, a citizen of the United States and a resident of _____, state of _____, whose post office address is _____, prays that letters patent may be granted to him for the improvement in _____, set forth in the following specification and he hereby appoints _____, of _____ (Registration No. _____), his attorney (or agent) to prosecute this application and to transact all business in the Patent Office connected therewith. (If no power of attorney is to be included in the application, omit the appointment of the attorney.)

   [The specification, which includes the description of the invention and the claims, is written here.]

_____, the above-named petitioner, being sworn (or affirmed), deposes and says that he is a citizen of the United States and resident of _____, state of _____, that he verily believes himself to be the original, first and sole inventor of the improvement in _____ described and claimed in the foregoing specification; that he does not know and does not believe that the same was ever known or used before his invention thereof, or patented or described in any printed publication in any country before his invention thereof, or more than one year prior to this application, or in public use or on sale in the United States more than one year prior to this application; that said invention has not been patented in any country foreign to the United States on an application filed by him or his legal representatives or assigns more than twelve months prior to this application; and that no application for patent on said invention has been filed by him or his representatives or assigns in any country foreign to the United States, except as follows: _____.

_____

(Inventor's full signature)

State of _____
County of _____
ss:

   Sworn to and subscribed before me this _____ day of _____, 19___

_____

(Signature of Notary of Officer)

[seal]

_____

(Official Character)

of a patent attorney will, on the average, increase the overall cost of the patent to $2000-$3000. Of course, more complicated patents cost much more. Thus, the cost for a well-written patent that gives maximum protection is not prohibitive and would, in most cases, be a valuable investment.

SUMMARY

The development, planning, and marketing of new products are greatly affected by social and environment factors. Firms generally have little control of these factors, so they must educate themselves and understand what these forces are and how they may be used to advantage in new product introduction.

The United States has become more conscious of consumer rights than ever before. Recognition of consumer and government pressure during the development process could save a firm substantial sums of money. Confrontation and modification of a new product after commercialization will not only affect costs but could affect the reputation of the firm.

To develop an appreciation for all the existing regulations that could affect a new product would require a text of its own. This chapter discussed some of the more recent and perhaps more important regulations and how they affect new products. In particular, laws relating to product safety and warranty disclosure were discussed. In addition, some discussion was provided on the procedure for filing a patent and the inherent advantages and disadvantages of a patent.

SELECTED READINGS

Busch, Paul. "A Review and Critical Evaluation of the Consumer Product Safety Commission: Marketing Management Implications." *Journal of Marketing* 40 (October 1976): 41-49.

"Consumer Product Safety Act Seen Affecting Business Actions." *Commerce Today* (June 9, 1975): 7-8.

Corley, Robert N., and Black, Robert L. *The Legal Environment of Business,* 3rd ed. New York: McGraw-Hill, 1973.

Feldman, Lawrence P. "New Legislation and the Prospects for Real Warranty Reform." *Journal of Marketing* 40 (July 1976): 41-47.

Ferrell, O. C., and LaGarce, Raymond, eds. *Public Policy Issues in Marketing.* Lexington, Mass.: D.C. Heath, 1975.

Kendall, C. L., and Russ, Frederick A. "Warranty and Complaint Policies: An Opportunity for Marketing Management." *Journal of Marketing* 39 (April 1975): 36-43.

National Science Foundation. *Public Policy and Product Information.* Washington, D.C.: U.S. Government Printing Office, 1975.

"Product Advertising and Consumer Safety." *Advertising Age* (July 1, 1974): 47-50.

U.S. Department of Commerce. *Patents.* Washington, D.C.: U.S. Government Printing Office, 1974.

Name Index

Aaker, David A., 75
Abrams, George J., 25
Ahl, David H., 210
Ames, B. Charles, 38
Arndt, John, 191
Assmus, Gert, 74, 76
Ayal Igal, 76

Bailey, Earl L., 231
Banting, Peter M., 231
Barnard, J., 175
Barrett, F. D., 77
Barrie, James, 262, 267
Bass, Frank M., 111, 187
Baty, E. B., 77
Baver, Judith, 232
Bell, William E., 190
Bellas, C. J., 77
Benge, E. J., 101
Bengston, Roger, 129
Berby, Edwin M., 125
Berlines, J. S., 266
Black, Robert L., 346
Braden, J. H. C., 218
Braverman, Jerome, 266
Brenner, H., 129
Brenner, Vincent C., 266
Breton, E. J., 77
Brien, Richard H., 231
Brion, John M., 327
Britt, Steuart Henderson, 175
Brozen, Yale, 189
Bucklin, Louis P., 281
Budd, Alan P., 226
Buell, Victor P., 39
Burton, John, 58
Busch, Paul, 346
Buzzell, Robert D., 13, 14

Cadbury, N. D., 127
Cardozo, Richard N., 192
Carter, C. F., 189
Chhabria, P., 267
Chambers, J. C., 218
Charles, A., 69
Churchill, Gilbert A., 191
Clarke, Darral G., 204, 218
Clarke, T. J., 129
Claycamp, Henry J., 73, 128, 129
Cochran, Betty, 13, 14
Cochran, William G., 93, 119
Cole, Victor L., 125
Coleman, James, 190
Coleman, Richard P., 176
Constandse, William J., 43
Cook, Victor J., 245
Cooper, Robert G., 25
Corley, Robert N., 346
Coskun, A., 77
Cox, Keith K., 58, 122
Cravens, David W., 274, 279, 281, 327
Crawford, C. Merle, 101
Crissy, W. J. E., 327
Cronbach, Lee J., 301, 305

Dague, M. F., 218
Dalrymple, Douglas J., 45
Darden, Bill R., 261, 266
Davidson, J. Hugh, 25
Day, Ralph, 129
Dean, J., 267
Dhalla, N. K., 218
Dobbs, W.,
Dodds, W., 218
Dolich, Ira J., 301

Donnely, James H., 63, 66
Dunlavey, D. C., 101
Dutka, S., 127

Ehrenberg, A. S. C., 127
El-Ansary, Adel I., 282
Ellington, C. E., 77
Engel, James, 284, 305
Enis, Ben M., 122
Enzie, W. H., 245
Eskin, Gerald J., 73, 77
Etzel, Michael J., 327
Evans, Franklin B., 165
Evans, Gordon H., 36

Faris, Charles W., 192
Feldman, Lawrence P., 346
Ferrell, O. C., 346
Finn, R. H., 231
Fischer, Paul M., 327
Fisk, George, 332
Forman, Howard I., 102
Fourt, Louis A., 73
Fox, H. W., 102
Frank, Ronald E., 127, 176, 183, 190, 305
Frankel, L., 127
Freimer, M., 102, 128

Gabor, Ander, 267
Gamble, Frederick R., 287, 305
Gamble, Theodore R., 245
Gardner, David M., 267
Gedimen, Louis, 82
Gemmill, Gary R., 39
Gleser, Goldine C., 301, 305
Globe, S., 102

Gold, Jack, 124, 125
Goslin, Lewis N., 102
Gottlieb, Maurice J., 176
Graham, Saxon, 186
Granger, Clive, 267
Grayson, Robert A., 42, 45, 77
Green, Paul E., 129, 239, 305
Green, Ronald E., 301
Groome, Harry C., 124
Guss, Leonard M., 245

Haas, Raymond M., 46, 102
Haire, M., 186
Haley, Russell J., 166, 176
Halstrom F. N., 102
Hamelman, Paul W., 319
Hamilton, H. Ronald, 102
Hanan, Mark, 164
Hancock, Robert S., 176
Hanse, Morris H., 93
Harris, J. S., 77
Harris, Remus, 118
Hartley, Robert F., 25
Haug, Arne F., 160
Heidingsfield, Myron S., 176
Hendrickson, Carl H., 124
Hicks, Charles R., 136, 147
Higginbotham, James B., 58
Hill, James M., 46
Hill, Richard M., 40
Hills, Gerald E., 274, 279, 281, 327
Hilton, Peter, 53
Hisrich, Robert D., 160, 267
Hlavacek, James D., 40, 46
Holloway, Robert J., 176
Holt, Knut, 102
Hopkins, David S., 232
Hurst, D'Orsey, 317
Hurwitz, William N., 93

Immermann, Milton, 245
Ivahnenke, Alexandre, 216
Ivancevich, John M., 63, 66, 327

Jackson, Thomas W., 102
Johnson, S. C., 9, 10
Jolson, M. A., 232
Jones, C., 9, 10

Kassarjian, Harold H., 332
Katona, George, 176
Katz, Eliha, 190
Kendall, C. L., 346
Kendall, M. G., 93
Kennedy, James N., 190
King, Charles V., 190
King, Robert L., 102
Konson, A., 218
Kotler, Philip, 20, 158, 223,

277, 281, 316, 317, 318, 319, 320, 327, 330
Kovac, F. J., 218
Kroeger, A. R., 87, 124
Kuehn, Alfred A., 127, 165

LaGarce, Raymond, 346
Lakhani, C., 77, 267
Lambert, Eugene W., J., 281
Lambert, Zarrel V., 267
Lanitis, T., 77
Lanzillotti, R. F., 251
LaPlaca, Peter J., 331
Lawrence, Paul R., 46
Lazo, Hector, 13
Leavitt, Theodore, 5
Lerner, David B., 69, 127
Levy, G. W., 102
Levy, Sidney J., 20
Lewis, Edwin H., 273, 282
Liddy, Lucien E., 73, 128, 129
Lintner, John, 226
Lipstein, Benjamin, 129
Little, B., 102
Little, Robert W., 279, 282
Litzenberger, Robert H., 226
Lorsch, Jay W., 46, 102
Luck, David J., 25, 39
Lynn, Robert A., 248

MacLachlan, Douglas L., 331
Madow, William G., 93
Mallen, Bruce E., 282
Mansfield, Edwin, 189
Martin, J. C., 102
Massy, William F., 72, 183, 190
Mathews, H. Lee, 160
Mazze, Edward M., 319
McAnnon, Bert C., 282
McCarthy, E. Jerome, 169
McConnell, Douglas J., 267
McMurry, Robert N., 245
Menzel, Herbert, 190
Mitchell, Jerome N., 245
Monroe, Kert B., 331
Montgomery, David B., 70, 72, 75
Moranian, T., 77
Morley, John, 245, 305
Morrison, Donald G., 72
Mossman, Frank H., 129
Mount, John F., 160
Myers, James H., 160

Naples, Michael J., 75
Nelson, R. H., 267
Nickels, W. G., 232
Nourse, Robert E. M., 13, 14

O'Meara, John T., Jr., 78, 129
Osborn, Alex F., 59

Osgood, C. E., 239
Oxenfeldt, Alfred R., 249
Ozanne, Urban B., 191

Painter, John J., 165
Parsons, Leonard J., 45, 77
Pessemier, E., 77
Peters, Michael P., 160, 192, 341
Peterson, Russell W., 30
Phelps, D. Maynard, 46
Platten, Jack, 90
Popielarz, Donald T., 191

Raymond, Shirley, 90
Reinmuth, J. E., 218
Reitter, Robert N., 97, 130
Reynolds, William H., 176, 245
Richman, Barry M., 78, 130
Robertson, Thomas, 8, 177, 189, 190
Robinson, B., 77, 267
Robinson, Patrick J., 192
Rogers, Everett M., 177, 182, 187, 188
Root, H. P., 77
Rosenstein, Alvin J., 58
Ross, Randolph E., 231
Rothberg, Robert R., 46
Rothe, James T., 316
Rowan, Bayard F., 232
Rubinstein, Mark E., 226
Russ, Frederick A., 346

Scheuing, Eberhard E., 245
Schlaifer, Robert, 111
Schneider, J., 102
Schwartz, C. M., 102
Seglin, Leonard, 267
Sexton, Donald E., Jr., 284, 305
Shapiro, Ernest L., 246
Shoemaker, R., 218
Shutte, Thomas J., 245, 246
Simon, L. S., 102, 128
Simon, Sanford R., 327
Sing, J. T., 267
Sissors, Jack Z., 301
Slocum, John W., Jr., 160
Smith, B. B., 93
Smith, Samuel, V., 231
Spitz, A. Edward, 26
Springate, J. R., 102
Spurlock, Jack M., 102
Staelin, R., 218
Stafford, James E., 231
Stanfield, David J., 187
Stanton, Roger R., 160
Stein, Philip W., 35
Steiner, Gary A., 165

Stern, Louis W., 282
Suci, G. J., 239

Talley, Walter J., 327
Tannenbaum, P. H., 239
Tauber, Edward M., 62, 77, 216, 218
Taylor, James D., 232
Thomas, J., 267
Thompson, G., 13, 14
Toll, Ray, 77
Tucker, W. T., 165
Tull, Donald S., 130, 239
Tuttle, Donald I., 226
Twedt, D. Warren, 176

Urban, Glen L., 70, 71, 77

Van Horne, James C., 224
Varble, Dale L., 332
Venkatesan, M., 192
Virkkala, V., 102

Wales, Hugh, 284, 305
Walker, K. R., 232
Warshaw, Martin, 284, 305
Wasson, Chester, 6, 26, 305
Webster, Frederic E., Jr., 192
Weinberg, Charles B., 75
Weiss, E. B., 125, 297, 305
Westfall, Ralph, 165, 176
Wheatley, John, 305
Wheelwright, Steven C., 204, 205, 218
White, Darral G., 205
Whiting, Charles S., 59

Wileman, David L., 39
Wind, Yoram, 192
Wineck, Charles, 165
Wolf, Lawrence, 297, 305
Woodlock, Joseph W., 73
Woodruff, Robert B., 279, 281, 327
Woodside, Arch G., 267
Worrell, Malcolm L., Jr., 129
Worthing, Parker, 327
Wotruba, T. R., 267

Yankelovich, Daniel, 166, 176
Young, Robert W., 237, 246
Yuspeh, S., 218

Zarecor, William D., 46, 102
Zwicky, Fritz, 77

Subject Index

Abandonment, product,
   315-325
Acceptance of new product,
   153-218
Adopter categories, 181
Adopters, early, characteristics of, 188
Adoption of new products,
   177-194
Adoption process
   defined, 183
   stages in, 183-185
Advertising
   cooperative, 300
   direct comparative, 295-296
   matching with target mar-
      kets, 299-302
   push versus pull strategy,
      298-299
   varying direct competitive
      positioning, 297-299
Advertising agency
   evaluating services of,
      287-289
   promotional plan, formula-
      tion of, 288
   selecting a, 289-290
      checklist to use in, 291
   services provided by, 289
   using an, 287-290
Age categories, profiles for,
   302
Anoloz, failure of, 15
Attribute listing
   generating product ideas
      by, 58-59
   major drawback of, 59

Automobiles, marketing
   trends and, 18
Average rate of return, use in
   evaluating new product
   mix proposals, 225-226
Avis, positioning of in advertising, 297-298
Ayer new product model, 73

Bank services, market grids
   for, 171-174
Bargaining power, distribution channels and, 275
Bayes' theorem, 114-115
Bayesian approach, 111
Bayesian pricing chart, 264
B. F. Goodrich, advertising
   strategy for, 298
Black and Decker, new products from, 4
Blanket branding, 235-236
Bonus system, new product
   forecast and, 209
Brainstorming
   generating product ideas
      using, 60
   reverse, generating product
      ideas using, 60
   rules for, 60
Brand(s)
   individual, 236-237
      trade name and, 237-238
   multi-, strategy, 236-237
Brand name
   company image and, 234
   image of, scaling example,
      240

implying meaning without
   advertising or external
   information, 233
importance of, 234-238
industrial products, 233
price comparisons and, 234
product line expansion and,
   235
Brand name research tech-
   niques, 238-240
   motivational research,
      239-240
   rank order, 238-239
   scaling, 239
Branding
   blanket, 235-236
   family, 235-236
Branding the new product,
   233-246
Branding policies, 235
Branding strategies, 235
   mixed, 237
Break-even analysis, 256-258
Break-even chart, 257
Brown-Forman Distillers, 15
Budget, promotional, 283-286
Business analysis, product
   development and, 22
Buyer's expectations, forecasting using, 206-207,
      209-210
By-products of production,
   new product ideas from,
      56

Campbell, dry soups, failure
   of, 14-15

Cash flow
  marketing mix and, 224
  pricing and, 252
Cash recovery, early, pricing
  and, 250, 251
Census of Business, use of,
  83-84
Census of Manufacturers, use
  of, 83
Census of Retail Trade, use
  of, 84
Channels of distribution; *see*
  Distribution channels
Chesebrough-Pona, new
  product development by,
  5
Cluster sampling; *see*
  Sampling
Coffee, instant, early marketing problems of, 185-186
Commercialization, product
  development and, 22
Communication, product diffusion and, 179
Company characteristics, distribution channels and,
  272
Company image
  brand names and, 234
  pricing and, 250, 251
Comparison tests, 89
Competition
  effects of, on new products, 18
  new product idea evaluation and, 79
  pricing and, 250, 251,
  261-264
  product failure and, 14-15
  as source of new product
  ideas, 53-54
  test-marketing effect of,
  123
Competition reaction, product failure and, 14
Competitive positioning,
  varying direct, 296-298
Complementarity, product,
  325
Computer
  small, factors relating to
  adoption of, 192
  test-marketing use of, 127
Computer manufacturers,
  new products by, 7
Concept testing techniques,
  22
Confidence level, 214-215
Consumer considerations,
  pricing and, 261

Consumer goods, factors
  affecting adoption of,
  189-191
Consumer lists, source of, 91
Consumer panel
  new product evaluation
  using, 88-89
  questioning techniques,
  89-101
Consumer perception of new
  product, 185-188
Consumer preference, effects
  of, on new products, 17
Consumer product, promo-
  tion of, 291, 292, 293
Consumer Product Safety
  Commission, function of,
  334-337
Consumer Product Safety Act
  of 1972, 333
Consumer Protection Act,
  specifications of, 334-335
Consumer's Bill of Rights
  message, 320
Consumers, basic rights of,
  330
Control
  marketing activities and,
  312
  nature of, 309-310
  new product, 309-327
  product life cycle and,
  309-310
Control process, 311-315
Control system, Kotler, product deletion and, 318-319
Corfam, market failure of, 14
Cost analysis, product deletion and, 320-323
Cost estimating, 254-255
Costs
  classification of, 254
  product failure and, 14
  unit price, and volume data,
  322
Cricket lighters, success of, 17
Customers, as source of new
  product ideas, 53

Decision mapping via optimum GO-NO networks;
  see DEMON
Delphi method, forecasting
  using, 206-207, 210
Demand
  elasticity of, 256
  operational approach to,
  260-261
Demand estimation of new
  products, 153-218

Demand and market con-
  siderations, 255-261
Demarketing, effects of,
  20-21
Demographic market con-
  siderations, 159
Demographic segmentation
  variables, 161-162
Demographic variable, advertising and, 303-304
DEMON, test-marketing and,
  127-128
DEMON product model,
  69, 71
  decision networks for new
  product evaluation in the,
  70
"Depth of repeat" forecasting
  model, 72-73
Development process, environments effect on, 17-21
Diet foods, marketing trends
  and, 18
Diffusion
  defined, 178
  elements of, 178-181
  time dimension and,
  179-181
Diffusion curve, cumulative,
  182
Diffusion of new products,
  177-194
Diffusion process, 178-183
  communication and, 179
  innovation, 178-179
  social system and, 179
Diffusion research, historical
  perspective of, 177-178
Discontinuance, defined, 184
Displays
  effect of, on sales, 143-146
  point-of-purchase, sales
  and, 135-139
Distribution, door-to-door,
  271
Distribution channels
  alternative patterns,
  274-275
  alternatives, preference-
  ordering method for
  evaluating, 276
  appraising performance of,
  280
  bargaining power's effect
  of, 274
  company characteristics
  and, 272
  control of, 279-280
  decision process in, 270
  degree of directness, 269-272

factors determining choice of, 274-275
financial investment effect on, 274
large manufacturer, 279
management of, 279-280
manufacturer's strengths and weaknesses effect on, 274
market factors, 269-271
members of
    evaluation of, 275, 277
    selection of, 275, 277-279
middlemen in, 273
    selection of, 278
middlemen factors in, 272
number of, 273-274
objectives, 269
product attributes effect on, 271
small manufacturer, 279
as source of new product ideas, 54
strategy analysis of, 269-274
timing effect on, 274
Distribution decisions, position in marketing mix, 222
Diversification, 10, 11, 12

Earth Born shampoo, success of, 17
Eastman Kodak Company, new products from, 4
Economic activity, test-marketing effect of, 123
Economic factors, packaging design and, 243
Economics, adoption of a new product and, 189
Employee suggestions, new product ideas developed from, 56-57
Energy crisis
    consumer impact, 20
    and production, 4-5
Environment, effect on development process, 17-21
Environmental evaluation
    advantages of, 332
    disadvantages of, 333
Environmental factors, packaging design and, 243
Environmental influences
    on marketing concept, 330-332
    new product development and, 327-347

Evaluation; see New product evaluation

Factorial design in test marketing, 146-152
    Family branding, 235-236
Fast food franchises, marketing trends and, 18
Federal government, as source of new product ideas, 54
Federal Trade Commission, function of, 338-339
Financial criteria, marketing mix and, 223
Financial structure, new product idea evaluation and company's 79-80
Focus group interviews, 58
Focus groups, generating product ideas in, 57-58
Forced relationships, generating product ideas by, 59
Ford Edsel, failure of, 14
Ford Mustang, success of, 16
Forecasting
    "depth of repeat," 72-73
    problems in, 217
Forecasting methods, 204-216
    acceptance and use of alternative, 205
    buyer's expectations, 206-207, 210
    comparison of, 206-207
    correlation of, 210-215
    Delphi, 206-207, 210
    jury of executive opinion, 205, 206-207
    regression analysis of, 210-215
    sales force composite, 205-209
    specialized techniques, 215-216
Forecasting new product sales, 195-218
    factors affecting, 195-196
Frost, failure of, 15
FTC, function of, 338-339

General Electric, marketing failure in computers, 299
General Foods, 16
Geographic market considerations, 159
Geographic segmentation variables, 162-164
Gillette, head-on advertising used by, 297

Gillette Dry Look hair spray, success of, 17
Government-Owned Inventories Available for License, as source of new product ideas, 54
Government regulations, as source of new product ideas, 55

Hewlett-Packard Company, new products from, 4
Honeywell, advertising position of, 299

IBM, competitor's advertising failure, 299
Idea generation, product development and, 21
Image, new product idea evaluation and company's, 80
Impeachment
    randomized design for test marketing, 134
    test marketing of, 199-120
Income
    household, profiles for, 302
    personal, social changes owing to increased, 18-20
Income projections, family, 19
Industrial goods, adoption of, 191-193
Industrial products
    promotion of, 293, 294
    warranties and, 340-341
Innovation
    characteristics of, 185-188
    product diffusion and, 178-179
Innovativeness, correlates of, 188-193
Input/output method of product assessment, 83, 84
Input/output table, United States, 86
Investment
    financial, distribution channel and, 274
    initial, recovery of, 224
    return on, market mix and, 224

Jury of executive opinion, forecasting using, 205, 206-207

Kotler control system, product deletion decision and, 318-319

Latin square design, test marketing using, 141, 142
Launching a new product, monitoring, 313
Legal requirements, new product idea evaluation and, 80
L'Eggs pantyhose
  distribution of, 268
  packaging of, 7
Leisure activities, marketing trends and, 18
Lestoil, competitions effect on sales of, 125-126
Life cycle, product; see also Product life cycle
  control and, 309-310
  promotion and, 290-294
Lifecard, market test results of, 211-215
Light 'n' Lively, advertising repositioning used in selling, 298

Magnuson-Moss Warranty Act, 338
Management
  role in marketing new products, 27-28
  as source of new product ideas, 56
Market(s)
  distribution channels and, 269-271
  new, 10
  strengthened, 10
  target, matching media with, 299-302
Market analysis, inadequate new product failure and, 15
  product failure and, 13
Market approach, undifferentiated, 155, 156
Market evaluation checklist, use of, 82
Market extension, 10
Market grid
  bank for industrial market, 172-174
  commercial bank, 171
  for industrial market, 171
Market grid concept, 169-175
Market maturity, new products and, 5
Market myopia, 5-6
Market opportunity, new product idea evaluation and, 78-79
Market-oriented approach for new products, 157

Market saturation, new products and, 5
Market segmentation
  bases for, 158-175
  benefits of, 156-157
  breakdown groups in, 159
  conditions for, 157-158
  defined, 156
  for new products, 155-176
  by type of market, 168
  undifferentiated approach, 155, 156
  variable, 161-169
  variable selection, 160
  variables in, 159
Market selection, marketgridding in new product, 169-175
Market shares for a new product, 112
Market size determination, 198-203
Market structure, test marketing effect of, 123
Market test; see Test market
Market test sample, designing, 92
Market trends prevailing in the United States, 18
Marketing
  adoption of a new product and, 189
  deemphasis of, 20-21
  environmental influences, 330-332
  packaging design and, 241
  pricing and, 264-266
  research and development, interface with, 44
  social influences, 330-332
Marketing activities, identifying those to be controlled, 311
Marketing effort, inadequate, product failure and, 14
Marketing mix
  designing, 222
  elements of, 3-4
  use in selection of test market, 118
Marketing mix decisions, integrating, 221-223
Marketing mix/profit relationship, establishing, 223
Marketing mix strategy, implementation of, 326
Marketing models
  mathematical, 66, 67
  descriptive, 67
  normative, 67

types of, 63, 66-67
  verbal, 66
Marketing new products
  company organization, large versus small, 29
  organizing for, 27-46
  top management's role in, 27-28
Marketing performance
  corrective strategy for, 314-315
  standards, establishing, 312
Marketing plan, importance of, 16-17
Marketing program, for new products, 219-305
Marketing stages, pretest, 80-90
Marketing strategies, sound, 17
Marketing system, new product idea evaluation and, 79
Markov chain analysis, 126
Maxim coffee, success of, 16
Media, matching with target markets, 299-301
Metrecal, marketing problem with, 268-269
Middlemen
  cooperation with, 273
  selection of, manufacturer's rate scale for, 278
  types of, distribution channels and, 273
Middlemen factors, distribution channels and, 272
Model; see New product model
Monadic test, 89-90
Monitoring new product launch, 313
Motivational research techniques, brand name determination using, 239-240
Multibrand strategy, 236-237
Multistage sampling, see Sampling

Natural foods, marketing trends and, 18
Nescafe, 6
New product(s)
  acceptance of, 153-218
  adoption of, 177-194
  assessing need for, 83
  basis and organization, 1-46
  classification of, 8-12
  consumer's viewpoint, 8-9
  examples of, 11
  firm's viewpoint, 9, 12

classifying
   based on product objec-
      tives, 10
   continuum for, 9
control of, 309-327
costs; see Costs
defining, 6-8
demand estimation of,
   153-218
diffusion of, 177-194
increasing sales volume by
   adding, 7
marketing; see Marketing
   new products
packaging and, 6-7
past and future, 3-26
pricing, 247-267; see also
   Pricing
publicity, 286-287
real, 7-8
test marketing; see Test
   marketing
testing; see Testing new
   products
New product committee
   advantages of, 32
   marketing organization
      using, 31-33
   weaknesses of, 32
New product department
   functions of, 31
   market organization struc-
      ture using, 30
   relationship to other
      departments, 31
New product development
   alternative organizations
      for, 29-41
   environmental influences
      in, 328-347
   planning to commercializa-
      tion, problems in, 43-44
   product manager organiza-
      tion, 33-40
   product managers role in,
      34-38
   social influences in,
      328-347
   venture team organization,
      40-41
New product distribution,
   268-282; see also Distribution channels
New product early warning
   system model; see NEWS
New product evaluation
   concept stage, 87-88
   idea stage, 82-87
   product development stage,
      88-90

sampling methodology for,
   103-107
New product executives,
   value of, 42
New product failure
   examples of, 14-15
   leading cause of, 188
   reasons for, 13-14
New product ideas
   evaluating, 78-102
   evaluation criteria, 78-80
   methods for generating,
      57-61
   obtainment and evaluation,
      47-152
   screening, 57
   sources of, 53-57
New product information system, establishing, 229,231
New product introduction
   network, 230
New product launch, moni-
   toring, 313
New product mix
   evaluating investment in,
      224-225
   planning, 221-232
New product models, 69-74
   development, 67-69
   limitations of, 74-75
   primary steps in develop-
      ing, 67
   uses of, 74-75
New product research, questionnaire design for,
   98-101
New product sales and profit
   determination, 200, 201,
   202
New product successes, examples of, 15-17
NEWPROD product model, 74
NEWS product model, 73
News releases, rules for
   issuing, 286-287

Occupation status, profiles
   for, 301
Official Gazette, as source of
   new product ideas, 54
Ogilvy and Mather study, 296
Old products, new image for, 7
Organization, traditional,
   product manager and, 36
Organization structure,
   choosing, 42
Organizational alternatives,
   executive support of, 42
Oyster stew, frozen, 6

Package
   effective, attributes of, 244
   promotional advantage of,
      244
Packaging
   design considerations,
      241-243
   economic factors, 243
   environmental factors,
      243
   marketing considerations,
      241
   product protection, 241,
      243
   sales effect of, 152
   test marketing effect of, 124
Packaging the new product,
   6-7, 233, 246
Pantyhose, new marketing
   strategy for, 7
Patent(s), 341-346
   application for, 343-344
   cost of, 344, 345
   infringement of, 344
Patent oath, sample of, 345
Patent Office file, new product ideas in, 54
Payback method, use in
   evaluating new product
   mix proposals, 224-225
Performance, corrective strategy for, 314-315
Performance standards,
   establishing, 312
PERT, new product introduction using, 228-229, 230
PIS, 229, 231
Planned obsolescence, 17
Point-of-purchase displays,
   sales and, 135-139
Point-of-purchase information, packaging and, 244
Polaroid Corporation, instant
   photography, 16
Population, determination of,
   90-91
Population sampling, 91-97;
   see also Sampling
Positioning of new product,
   promotion determining,
   293-302
Predicting sales; see Forecast-
   ing new product sales
PRESS I, cost analysis, 320-323
PRESS II, price/volume rela-
   tionships, 323-325
PRESS III, sales trends, 325
PRESS IV, product comple-
   mentarity and substitutability, 325

Price, initial asking, 261
Price comparisons, brand
  name effect on, 234
Price determination model,
  258-260
Price/demand relationship,
  258
Price elasticity, 255-256
Price objectives
  company, 247-251
  company image and, 250,
  251
  competition and, 250, 251
  passive, 250, 251
  potential, 249
  product line comforming,
  250, 251
  profit-oriented, 248-249
  sales-oriented, 249-250
Price/quality relationship, 261
Price/sale/quality relationship, 258
Price/volume relationships,
  PRESS II, 323-325
Pricing
  break-even analysis,
  256-258
  break-even chart, 257
  competitive considerations,
  261-264
  consumer considerations,
  261
  cost considerations,
  253-255
  marketing decisions and,
  264-266
  policy formulation,
  251-253
  target rate of return, 250
Pricing chart, Bayesian, 264
Pricing decisions, position in
  marketing mix, 222
Pricing the new product,
  247-267
Pricing policy, skimming,
  252-253
Probability assignments for a
  new product, 112
Problem inventory analysis,
  generating product ideas
  using, 61, 62
Procter and Gamble
  brand manager organiza-
  tion, 33, 34
  product manager, interfacing of, 35
Product(s); see also New
  product(s) and Old
  products
  high-learning, 269

improvement, 10, 11, 12
industrial, warranties and,
  340-341
new uses for, 10
ranking of, 324
rating of, form for, 321
unsafe, injuries from,
  333-334
Product abandonment, con-
  trol application, 315-325
Product data sheet, 320
Product decisions and features, position in marketing mix, 222
Product defects, product
  failure and, 13
Product deletion, 317-325
Product development
  length of time for,
  examples of, 52
  process, 21-24
  sales and profits during,
  24-25
  as stage in new product
  evaluation, 88-90
  stages in, 81
Product life cycle
  consumer, promotional
  strategy during stages of,
  292
  control and, 309-310
  industrial, promotional
  strategy during stages of,
  294
  major stages of, 3, 4
  promotion and, 290-294
Product line, pricing in, 250,
  251
Product line expansion, brand
  name effect on success of,
  235
Product line extension, 10,
  11, 12
Product manager
  consumer, duties of, 38
  contribution from other
  departments, 37
  development of, 33-34
  duties of, 37
  industrial, duties of, 38
  main objective of, 221
  role conflict and the, 38-40
  role of, in developing new
  products, 34-38
  traditional organization
  and, 36
Product planning and development process, 49-52
  stages of, 50-51
Product protection, packag-

ing design considerations,
  241, 243
Product reformulation, 10
Product-related market con-
  siderations, 160
Product-related segmentation
  variables, 166-169
Product replacement, 10, 11
Product review and evalua-
  tion subsystem; see PRESS
Product safety, 333-334
  standards and procedures,
  334
Product segmentation; see
  Market segmentation
Product compatibility, new
  product idea evaluation
  and, 80
Profile-matching, use in
  advertising, 299-302
Profit determination, 200,
  201, 202
Profit-oriented price objectives, 248-249
Profitability index, product
  mix and, 227-228
Profits, sales and, during
  product development and
  life cycle, 24, 25
Profits for a new product, 112
Program evaluation review
  technique; see PERT
Promoting the new product,
  283-305
Promotion; see also
  Advertising
  of consumer product, 291,
  294
  of industrial products,
  294, 295
  packaging and, 244
  positioning with, 294-303
  product life cycle and,
  290-294
Promotion decision, position
  in marketing mix, 222
Promotional budget, 283-286
Promotional strategy, checklist for, 285
Prototype development,
  product development
  and 22
Psychological market considerations, 159
Psychological segmentation
  variables, 164-166
Publicity, new product,
  286-287
Pure 1 chicken, pull advertising strategy used by, 300

Push versus pull strategy in advertising, 298-299

Quality, price and, 258, 261
Questionnaire design for new products, 98-101
Questioning techniques, 98, 99
dichotomous questions, 98, 99
open-ended, 100, 101
preference, 98, 99
ranking, 98, 100
rating, 98, 100

Random sampling; see Sampling
Randomized block design, test marketing using, 136-137
Rank order, brand name determination using, 238-239
Rating form, for possible product deletion, 321
RCA, marketing failure in computers, 299
Red Kettle dry soups, failure of, 14-15
Regression analysis in sales forecasting, 210-215
Remerchandising, 10, 11
Research, development/marketing interface and, 44
Research design, factors in, 90-99
Research and development, as source of new product ideas, 55
Results, expected versus actual, measurement of, 312-314
Reverse brainstorming, generating product ideas using, 60
"Roll-out method" of new product introduction, 128
Rural sociology, adoption of a new product and, 188

Safety, product, 333-334
standards and procedures, 334
Safety standards and procedures, 334-334
Sale, standard terms and conditions of, 342-343
Sales
favorable factors affecting, 195-196

forecasting
lagging indicators, 197
leading indicators, 197
marketing size determination and, 198-203
new product, 195-218
simultaneous (coincident) indicators, 197
series indicators for, 196-198
unfavorable factors affecting, 196
Sales determination, 200, 201, 202
Sales force, as source of new product ideas, 56
Sales force composite, forecasting using, 205-209
Sales measurement in test marketing, 125
Sales-oriented price objectives, 249-250
Sales and profits during product development and life cycle, 24, 25
Sales trends, PRESS III, 325
Sales volume, expanding by adding new products, 7
Sample(s); see also Test market and Test marketing
judgment, 92
size determination of, 117-121
Sample population, selection of, 91-97
Sample size
determination of, 117-121
mean of, 103
standard deviation of, 103
Sample survey, projection from, 93-94
Sampling; see also Test market and Test marketing
cluster, 95-97
in new product research, 96
multistage, 97
nonprobability, 92
probability, 92
random, 103
simple random, 93
stratified, 94-95
comparison with other sampling methods, 107
in new product research, 95
standard deviation of, 105-106
Sampling methodology for new product evaluation, 103-107

Scaling, brand name determination using, 239
Screening, product development and, 21
Screening criteria, qualitative, 61, 63, 64, 65
Segmentation; see Market segmentation
Sego, marketing success of, 268-269
Selection index number, 323
Shortages, outcome of, 20-21
SIC code method of product assessment, 83
SIN, 323
Social change, effects of, on new products, 18-20
Social evaluation
advantages of, 332
disadvantages of, 333
Social influences
on marketing concept, 330-332
new product development and, 327-347
Social system, product diffusion and, 179
Specifications of profits with interaction under trial and error response; see SPRINTER
SPECS product model, 73-74
SPRINTER product model, 71-72
SPRINTER MOD I, 71
SPRINTER MOD II, 71-72
SPRINTER MOD III, 72
Standard industrial classification system of product assessment, 83
Standard terms and conditions of sale, 342-343
STEAM product model, 72
Strategic planning, evaluation, and control model; see SPECS
Stratified sampling; see Sampling
Substitutability, product, 325
Sunbeam electric skillet, copying of, 125
Systematic sampling; see Sampling

Tab, advertising strategy for, 298
Technological advances, social change and, 18
Telephone industry, research and development in, 55

Test experiment, design of,
    121-123
Test market
  checklist for selection of,
    118
  computer used in, 127
  conditional probability of
    outcomes of, 114
  determination of need to,
    111-116
    Bayesian approach, 111
  joint probabilities and revi-
    sion of prior probabilities,
    115
  selection of, 117
  setting up, product develop-
    ment and, 22
  size determination of,
    117-121
Test market experiment,
    design of, 121-123
Test market model, practical-
    ity of, 127
Test marketing, 88, 109-152;
    see also Sample(s) and
    Sampling
  alternatives to, 126-128
  analysis of variance table,
    132
  ANOVA table, 132
  competition having effect
    on, 126
  costs of, 124
  experimental design in,
    131-152
  factorial design, 146-152
  factors affecting, 123-124

factors used in evaluating
    need for, 109
  inaccuracy of, 124
  Latin square design and,
    141, 142
  nature of, 108-111
  new products, experimental
    model for, 122
  primary objectives of, 108
  problems in, 124-126
  randomized block design,
    136
  randomized design, com-
    pletely, 131-132
  relationship and composi-
    tion of, 110
  remedies for, 126-128
  risk, inherent in, 109
  "roll-out method," 128
  sales measurement in, 125
  time for, 125-126
  types of experimental
    designs used in, 123
Test sample, market, design-
    ing, 92
Testing, concept, techniques,
    22
Testing new products, early
    stage, 80-90
Tests
  monadic, 89-90
  paired comparison, 89
Time dimension, product dif-
    fusion and, 179-181
Timing
  distribution channel and, 274
  product failure and, 14

Toni home permanents, 6
Toy manufacturers, new
    products from, 4-5
Trac II, success of, 17
Trade journal advertising, 286
Trade name and individual
    brands, 237-238

Venture team, characteristics
    of, 40
Venture team concept
  advantages of, 40-41
  disadvantages of, 41
Venture team organization,
    example of, 41
Vick's Nyquil, Advertising
    strategy used in market-
    ing, 298

Warranties, industrial prod-
    ucts and, 340-341
Warranty, sample express, for
    consumer durable, 340
Warranty disclosure regula-
    tions, 338-340
Warranty policy, function of,
    337-338
Whiskey, dry, failure of, 15
Women
  changing role of, 20
  working, new product mar-
    marketing and, 20

Xerox, head-on advertising
    used by, 297

Zonkers, 6